TANK WARFARE
1939-1945

How many men can you fit on a tank? There are at least 18 and two crew members visible on this Sherman heading toward Ghuta on Okinawa in April 1945. The men are from 29th Marines.

TANK WARFARE
1939-1945

SIMON & JONATHAN FORTY

Pen & Sword
MILITARY

First published in Great Britain in 2020 by
PEN & SWORD MILITARY
an imprint of
Pen & Sword Books Ltd,
47 Church Street,
Barnsley,
South Yorkshire.
S70 2AS

A CIP record for this book is available from the British Library.

ISBN 978 1 52676 762 2

The right of Simon and Jonathan Forty to be identified as Authors of this Work has been asserted by him in accordance with the Copyright, Designs and Patents Act 1988.

Printed and bound in India by Replika Press Pvt. Ltd.

Pen & Sword Books Ltd incorporates the Imprints of Pen & Sword Aviation, Pen & Sword Maritime,
Pen & Sword Military, Wharncliffe Local History, Pen & Sword Select, Pen & Sword Military Classics and Leo Cooper.

For a complete list of Pen & Sword titles please contact
Pen & Sword Books Limited
47 Church Street, Barnsley, South Yorkshire, S70 2AS, England
E-mail: enquiries@pen-and-sword.co.uk
Website: www.pen-and-sword.co.uk

Acknowledgements

The text includes a number of directly quoted or edited excerpts from a number of works which are identified in the text and covered in the Bibliography. Most of these documents came via the brilliant online resources of the Ike Skelton Combined Arms Research Library (CARL) Digital Library. Other important assistance was provided by a number of online sites, in particular: http://www.6thcorpscombatengineers.com/fieldmanuals.html, which provides access to many US Army Field Manuals; http://the.shadock.free.fr/ – indispensable information on Shermans; http://www.theshermantank.com – this site also provides access to US Army Field and Technical Manuals and much more with its related info on ammunition, radios, etc etc; https://www.vmars.org.uk for information of military radios; https://www.eucmh.be – an excellent site with masses of primary and secondary source material; and www.tankdestroyer.net – another wonderful website filled with information on the US tank destroyer arm.

The photographs came from a number of sources including the US National Archives and Records Administration, in College Park, MD, the US Naval History and Heritage Command (for US Navy and USMC photos), the Library and Archives of Canada, Battlefield Historian and the collection of our late father, George Forty. Thanks to Leo Marriott and Martin Warren for their valuable contributions. There are a number from the US Army Technical and Field Manuals (particularly FM17-12, TM9-731b, TM9-754 and FM30-40) and *Tactical and Technical Trends* (particularly 16, 40, 118). Other photographs came from online sources. We'd also like to acknowledge: Peter Anderson p99; Greene Media (Mark Franklin) pp7, 137BL&BR, 163; Tanis pp20, 25B, 34; Bundesarchiv pp25T, 38, 45T, 61, 169, 176BR, 204; RSignals Museum p77; Lt Alexander M. Stirton/Canada. Dept. of National Defence/Library and Archives Canada/PA-153181 p155TR; https://ww2db.com p62; worldwarphotos pp58, 121; and WikiCommons – p118 (Unknown - СОКМ НВФ-1421/4 ФОТОГРАФИЯ. ВЕЛИКАЯ ОТЕЧЕСТВЕННАЯ ВОЙНА. Сахалинский областной краеведческий музей/), p102T (Dōmei Tsushin) p122 (Erin Magee-DFAT (13252789195)), p125 (Megapixie), p141B, p118B (Autopilot) InfoAge museum at Camp Evans Historic District in Wall, NJ, p200 (Library of Congress).

Contents

Abbreviations and Glossary

Note: Abbreviations relating to ammunition are explained on page 136.

AA Antiaircraft.

AAMG Antiaircraft machine gun.

Abteilung German unit roughly equivalent to a battalion.

AFV Armored fighting vehicle.

AP Armour-piercing.

APC Armored personnel carrier.

APCBC/APDS see page 136.

Armored/armoured US/British (including Canadian/Polish) versions. US units are spelled as they were without a u – eg US 7th Armored Division.

ARK Armoured bridge carrier.

ARV Armoured recovery vehicle.

ATk antitank.

Ausf *Ausführung* = model in German.

AVLB Armoured vehicle-launched bridge.

AVRE Armoured vehicle Royal Engineers.

BCC *Bataillon de chars de combat* = tank battalion in French.

Befehlswagen/panzer Command tank.

Bergepanzer ARV.

blindée Armoured in French.

BT *Bystrokhodnyy Tank* = fast tank in Russian.

calibre (cal) The diameter of the bore of a gun barrel. Also used as a unit of length of a gun barrel. For example a 10in/20cal gun would have a barrel 200 inches long (10 × 20). This is specified in millimetres, centimetres, or inches depending on the historical period and national preference.

Cav Recon Sqn (Mecz) Cavalry Reconnaissance Squadron (Mechanized).

CCA/B/R Combat Command A/B/Recon

CDL Canal defence light.

char Tank in French.

CMG Cavalry-mechanised group

DD Duplex Drive – DD Shermans were swimming tanks.

DLI Durham Light Infantry.

DLM *Division Légère Mécanique* = Light Mechanised Division (French).

FA Field artillery.

Funkpanzer Radio (tank).

Funkgerät Radio set.

Funksprecher Radio/telephone.

GMC Gun motor carriage.

HB eg M2HB – heavy barrel, usually air-cooled and did not require a water jacket around the barrel for cooling.

HE High explosive.

HMC Howitzer motor carriage.

HVSS Horizontal volute spring suspension: this type of suspension involved springing the road wheels on a bogie against each other with a horizontally oriented volute spring.

IS eg IS-3 – Iosif Stalin, a Russian heavy tank series named after 'The Boss', Joseph Stalin.

k *klein* = small.

KE Kinetic energy.

Kwk *Kampfwagenkanone* = tank gun.

l *leicht* = light.

le FH *leichte Feldhaubitze* = light field howitzer

LCT Landing craft tank.

LST Landing ship tank.

LVT(A) Landing vehicle tracked (armoured).

m *mittlere* = middle (as in weight).

Mk Mark, eg Churchill Mk VIII.

(O)QF (Ordnance) quick firing. A gun that does not use separate loading ammunition; i.e., the propellant case and projectile are a single unit.

Pak *Panzerabwehrkanone* = antitank gun in German.

Panzer Armoured in German.

Panzerbüchse Antitank rifle in German.

PzB *Panzerbüchse*.

PzBefw *Panzerbefehlswagen* = Command tank.

PzKpfw *Panzerkampfwagen* = tank in German.

PzSp *Panzerspähwagen* = armoured car.

Recce/Recon Reconnaissance (British/American).

Regt regiment.

RTR Royal Tank Regiment.

s *schwer* = Heavy, so *sPzAbt* = *schwere Panzerabteilung* = heavy tank battalion.

Schürzen = Side skirts = stand-off armour to protect against bazookas.

SdKfz = *Sonderkraftwagen* = Special purpose vehicle, the German designation system for armoured, often but not always tracked or halftracked vehicles. Examples: SdKfz 2 was the Kettenkrad, SdKfz 10 a halftrack prime mover and SdKfz 181 the Tiger I.

Semovente Self-propelled in Italian.

sIG *schwere Infanteriegeschütz* = Heavy infantry gun.

SP self-propelled.

SPW *Spähpanzerwagen* = Light armoured cars.

sPzAbt see s above.

StuG *Sturmgeschütz* = assault gun.

StuH *Sturmhaubitze* = assault howitzer.

StuK *Sturmkanone* = assault gun.

Tak *Tankabwehrkanone* = antitank gun.

TD Tank destroyer – towed (antitank guns) or tracked (such as the M10 or M18).

TF Task force.

VVSS Vertical volute spring suspension: this suspension involved mounting the road wheels to a bogie in pairs on arms and pivoting them against a vertically mounted volute spring, which was protected from damage by the bogie frame.

W As in M4A1(76)W. Wet ammunition stowage meant that main gun ammunition was stored in double-walled boxes, between which was a mixture of water, antifreeze, and an anticorrosive agent. When penetrated, the water delayed or eliminated the ammunition fire, giving crews time to escape. The ammunition storage location was also moved—from the tanks' sponsons to under the turret.

Zimmerit Paste painted on German tanks to provide a surface that prohibited the application of anti-magnetic mines or sticky bombs.

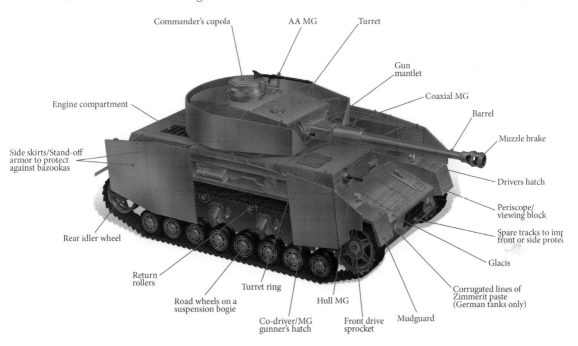

World War I tanks suffered frequent mechanical breakdowns, and often outran the infantry, but they destroyed the dominance of the machine gun and enabled the attack to go forward. The tank was a game changer and all the armies of the world had to do was work out how to use it.

Introduction

The armoured and mechanised gun platform we call the tank is the modern incarnation of the ancient axioms of combat – firepower, protection and mobility; its development path links back to the armoured punch of heavy cavalry: cataphracts, medieval knights and Heavy Brigade dragoons. A seismic change came with the increased technical knowledge and capacity for the industrialisation of warfare that occurred in Europe in the 19th and 20th centuries. The catalyst was the Industrial Revolution that led to a surge in the development and use of new armaments, particularly the machine gun. Horsepower began to replace horses, armour plate enclosed a group of fighters rather than an individual and guns increased their range, their accuracy and their rate of fire. As with all real fighting, experience was learnt hard and paid for in blood in the American Civil War, the Franco-Prussian War and the Russo-Japanese War.

The tank was born out of desperation, an attempt to break the horrific attritional trench warfare of World War I. It combined the latest agricultural machinery (commercial caterpillar-track tractors powered by internal combustion engines) with armour plate and weapon systems, its potential was hinted at rather than achieved in its first appearances, since in this experimental phase there were so many unknowns and no manuals. Design flaws, mechanical failures, inexperienced crews and the lack of communications and a clear tactical doctrine – all contributed to its underperformance. So it is with any new technology requiring a new paradigm, coalescing on the boundary between the possible and the realistically achievable.

The British and French developed different vehicles simultaneously, with Britain using them first (15 September 1916). Rushed into combat and riddled with faults and limitations, they were not the hoped for war-winning weapon but had a spectacular visual and psychological impact on the static battlefield. With a single central committee coordinating design, the British built trench-crossing rhomboidal tanks with their weapons carried in side sponsons – 'males' armed with two 6pdrs and three .303in Lewis machine guns, 'females' with five Lewis guns. The more heavily armoured 1917 Mark IV was the most produced and was used more successfully in large concentrations. Aside from these heavy tanks, late in the war the British also introduced a lighter armoured vehicle: the Whippet, armed with four .303in Hotchkiss machine guns, whichenjoyed some success in fast, mobile assaults and in exploiting breakthroughs.

The French had a less integrated approach, leaving development to individual arms manufacturers. Their two heavy tank designs of the war, the Schneider CA1 and the St Chamond, were commercial rivals – neither of which could be considered successful. Both were simple armoured boxes that overhung their tracks front and back, with their fronts beaked. The beak contained the 75mm main gun in the case of St Chamond, while the Schneider's was in a right-hand side sponson. Both were cumbersome with inferior mobility and a tendency to get stuck, and both were underpowered. The French light tank, the Renault FT-17, was a different matter. Now considered the first modern tank, since almost all others have followed the basic precepts of its design, its weapon was mounted in the first rotating turret atop a body containing the engine at the back, the driver at the front and the tracks on the sides. Produced in two versions – a male armed with a Puteaux SA18 37mm short-barrelled main gun and a female with a 7.92mm Hotchkiss machine gun – it had a two-man crew and was best used in concentrated numbers to overwhelm enemy positions. Despite inevitable flaws the FT-17 was the most successful and most produced tank of the war, with over 3,700 built. Postwar variants sold to over 20 countries worldwide.

Germany, in defensive mode, remained unconvinced about the tank, producing only 20 of a single design in 1918. The A7V Sturmpanzerwagen was an unstable, underpowered, overheating, moveable metal fort with a crew of 18, armed with a 57mm main gun in the nose and six 7.9mm machine guns distributed about its lumbering frame. Instead, the Germans sometimes used captured Allied tanks and also developed their antitank capability. Tanks drew all fire automatically, but aside from the astute use of bunched grenades, mortars, artillery and a tungsten-cored round, their first specific design was a giant beefed-up bolt-action rifle, the Mauser 1918 T-Gewehr, firing a 13mm bullet of hardened steel that could (at the correct range and perpendicular angle) penetrate the thin armour plate of the time – hence the increasing thickness in armour of Allied tanks. They also began developing antitank mines and a specifically antitank gun, the 3.7cm Tankabwehrkanone.

Tanks were first used spread out in penny packets supporting infantry; they began to be used in concentration as they became more available. By the time of the Allied 100 Days Offensive and the 8 August 1918 Battle of Amiens, the armour, infantry, artillery and airpower of the Allies were beginning to be coordinated successfully and tanks played an important part in deciding the outcome, their continuing combat vulnerability revealed by their casualty rate: over 70% were destroyed in just four days.

By the war's end some 6,000 Allied tanks of various models had been produced. The war left the conservative English and French high commands viewing the tank almost exclusively as an infantry support weapon. The British Tank Corps was reduced from 25 battalions to just five one year later, while the Americans abolished theirs completely and subjugated their tanks to infantry control. Things were little better in France,

Above: Heinz Guderian, who would go on to become a prime user of tank forces, commanding XIX Army Corps in the campaigns against Poland, France and the Soviet Union and *Generalinspekteur des Panzertruppen* (Inspector of Armoured Troops) was one of the leading German interwar armour theorists, working under the father of the German *Panzerwaffe* – armoured force – General Oswald Lutz who ran the German Panzer Troop Command from 1935. Lutz made Guderian write *Achtung Panzer!* in 1937, distilling the theories of modern warfare. In it he emphasised, 'Speed makes possible the maximum degree of surprise because it overcomes delay in concentrating forces at chosen points. Speed neutralizes the enemy defense by limiting the possibilities of fire from his antitank weapons.' A US Army FT-17 shows its paces.

Below: The first French tank was the Char Schneider CA which had a short 75mm howitzer. Less mobile than the British tanks because of its short tracks and overhanging body it also suffered from mechanical unreliability mainly down to its innovative but underdeveloped transmission system.

While the Americans did not enter the war until late and were stubborn enough to emulate many of the Allies' mistakes rather than learn from them, nevertheless they were able to experience tank warfare from its start in 1917. One man on whom it made an impression was George S Patton, Jr (A), who was in charge of the US 1st Provisional Tank Brigade (redesignated the 304th Tank Brigade on November 6, 1918).

where their tank arm was retained, but only to support the all-powerful infantry, whilst even the cavalry re-emerged, despite its now proven battlefield vulnerability, in many countries that should have known better. In France, there was little interwar theorising. Heavy-handed control from the very top ensured that no officer could discuss military subjects without express approval from on high. Indeed, it's surprising but true that the first French armoured division was only established on 16 December 1939 – a full two and a half months after the invasion of Poland.

However, the strategic thinking wasn't all backward-thinking. The technology of the time continued its fast advance, with increased civilian use of cars, further development of engines, transmission and suspension systems, and continuously improvement to aircraft and aero-engines. Mobile armoured warfare was still a new concept and attracted radical, maverick theorists – such as J.F.C. Fuller and B.H. Liddell Hart in England, and Mikhail Tukhachevsky in Russia – who could make the mental leap and envisage what it could be like if the technology worked properly.

The interwar period became a ferment of new ideas and experimental designs. Tanks and armoured vehicles of every conceivable size and shape were built and tested, from one-man tankettes to multi-turreted land battleships, using combinations of wheels and tracks. In Britain and France development was led by the geographical requirements of their colonial empires with the emphasis on fast light tanks for reconnaissance and to fight natives, cruisers to take on cavalry roles and slow heavy tanks to support infantry: thus the basic division of light, medium and heavy tanks remained. The British, with a string of red herrings such as the multi-turreted Vickers A1E1 Independent, never developed a viable heavy tank and plumped for cruisers and

The British establishment was slow to pick up on the theories of armoured warfare and while Fuller and Liddell Hart gained a following, they didn't alter the view that tanks should be primarily used for infantry support.

mediums. The most produced was the Vickers Medium Mk II with a fully rotating turret mounting a 3pdr gun firing high explosive and antitank shells, and a coaxial machine gun.

In 1927 the British Experimental Mechanized Force was formed, to test the theory of motorised mobility for tanks and supporting arms, and began to develop the first mobile tactics. After a few years it was renamed the Armoured Force, then in 1933 established as the first permanent Tank Brigade under the command of another unique armour specialist and theorist (whose ideas Guderian followed), the Royal Tank Corps officer Percy Hobart. In 1935 the Tank Brigade was sent to Egypt to combine with other elements into the Mobile Force. It later was named the Mobile Division, then the Armoured Division, and finally 7th Armoured Division – Britain's longest serving armoured division. It formed the basis for the spectacular successes against the Italians in North Africa in 1941, vindicating its formation and Hobart's original ideas.

The French didn't have an independent tank corps, the cavalry and infantry arms still dominated, but they led the way in design with a wide range of tanks assigned to one or the other, including light, medium, heavy and cavalry. Unlike the British, their heavy type, the Char 2c (the largest operational tank ever built), wasn't a red herring but rather a useless white elephant (they wasted more money on it). Again Renault came up with the most-produced light tank, the R35, mounting the very short-barrelled Puteaux SA18 37mm main gun with a coaxial Reibel machine gun. The mediums of note

Both sides in the Spanish Civil War were assisted by friendly external powers. A lot is made of the German's Condor Legion and their 'rehearsal' for World War II; however, don't forget the Russians were there, too. These are T-26s parading in Seville.

were the Char B1 and Somua S35, both well armoured and well armed with a 47mm SA35 main gun. The critical design flaw of all these armoured vehicles was their one-man turret which forced the commander to load and fire the main weapon (after having rotated the turret into position himself), command the driver and also handle radio communications when they were eventually fitted. A smaller turret enabled thicker armour but was a recipe for trouble when up against a three-man turret crew of commander, gunner and loader.

Although the US Army had shut down its tank arm, civilian automotive and heavy plant in the USA continued to develop and spread faster than anywhere else in the world. The innovative but irascible engineer and inventor J. Walter Christie designed racing cars, fire engines, tractors, an amphibious light tank and then in 1928 a revolutionary prototype tank chassis, the distinctively slope-armoured M1928, fitted with his new vertical coil suspension system that gave fast cross-country performance. Although this was not taken up by the US government it was bought by the Russians and the British, both of whom incorporated it in their own designs.

The British used it in their fast but under-armoured and mechanically unreliable A13 Cruisers. The Russians, in their BT and T tanks, came up with something more substantial, using the Christie suspension. They had already bought or stolen and copied various British and French designs and from 1929 built up the numerically largest armoured force of mainly unexceptional tanks. It did not help their armoured development when Stalin carried out his savage Great Purge in 1936–38, removing many of those who had been advocating the theories of Fuller and Liddell Hart.

The Russian BT series was lightly armoured, quite well armed for the time and with Christie's suspension had excellent mobility. It was produced from 1932 to 1941 in many variants, with different turrets and guns, as well as later flamethrower, rocket-launcher, command and amphibious versions and saw action in Spain, Finland and Asia. Following this bout of real combat testing the Soviets recognised the need for a heavier AFV and from 1939 began developing the T-34 – one of the outstanding tanks of the war – which showed that Russian tank technology was no longer derivative but had come of age.

Czechoslovakia had a skilled and flourishing arms industry making good quality equipment, its tanks influenced by originals purchased from France and Britain but which they improved and modified. After having been 'absorbed' by the Third Reich, the Germans commandeered much of their output for themselves or their Axis allies and continued production of the rugged and reliable LT vz 35 and LT vz 38, which became the PzKpfw 35(t) and PzKpfw 38(t). These were critical tanks for the forthcoming German campaigns of 1939–40. They then recycled the chassis into the Marder and Hetzer tank destroyers and the Grille series of infantry-support SP howitzers.

Under the terms of the Treaty of Versailles Germany was not allowed to produce tanks of any kind, but in 1926 it began an unofficial project, tested with Russian collusion, that was the progenitor of the early 1930s tank programme. PzKpfw I was an experimental training tank designed before the experience of the Spanish Civil War, yet it became the first mass-produced tank of the Wehrmacht and saw combat in various theatres early in World War II. Thinly armoured and armed with only two 7.92mm MG34 machine guns, it was used for scouting and supporting infantry but soon proved vulnerable to antitank guns or other tanks, highlighting the need for thicker armour and a bigger main gun. As the PzKpfw II, III and IV came on stream, the PzKpfw I resumed its original training role and

The Czech LT vz 38 – known by the Germans as the PzKpfw 38(t) (t for Tschechoslowakei/ Czechoslovakia) – used a suspension system that looks like that invented by Christie but in fact each pair of road wheels is mated to a central spring and arm.

One of the many Nazi parades showing off their armed forces, in this case PzKpfw I. Note the band and the distinctive black uniforms and oversized beret. The British Royal Tank Corps adopted the black beret in 1918 and since then it has become standard tanker headgear around the world.

its chassis became the basis of various tank destroyers and assault guns as well as a *Befehlswagen* (command tank).

The PzKpfw II was the most numerous German tank at the start of the war, most versions armed with a 2cm Kwk 30 L/55 autocannon and a 7.92mm MG34 coaxial machine gun. As with the PzKpfw I it had been designed before combat testing in Spain identified the weakness of its armour and armament, but it would play an important part in the early campaigns in Poland and France. When replaced by later tanks its sturdy chassis was then used to mount various SP guns such as the Marder and the Wespe.

At this time worldwide armoured developments and theories had been closely followed by a certain Freikorps officer, a linguist, who now had a tremendous impact of the future of tank warfare. Taking the wartime tactic of deep penetration by storm-troopers at a critical focal point of the front (the *Schwerpunkt*), Heinz Guderian began envisaging an expanded armoured force which not only contained tanks but a mix of all fighting arms and services, to form a completely motorised all-arms primary strike force. In chosen terrain and with the requisite aerial support, this mobile armoured fist could punch a hole through the enemy's front line and cause chaos in his rear areas, destroy command and control centres, and surround and cut off large portions of enemy troops, while moving fast to maintain surprise and keep the initiative. In the reverse of the accepted (British and French) approach, the infantry and artillery were to accompany and support the armour. Most importantly all vehicles would have radio communication to be able to operate seamlessly in unison, in conjunction with airpower. German tank crews would have a dedicated radio operator and the organisation of divisional signals troops would enable a commander to direct the division from any unit, allowing critical forward control.

In 1933 Hitler came to power. Positively gleeful with Guderian and his ideas, in 1935 he created the first three armoured divisions of the *Panzerwaffe* (lit: armoured arm of service). Guderian, commanding the second, was given free rein and in 1936 produced his seminal book *Achtung – Panzer!* in which he expounded the ideas – many of them developed by his boss, Oswald Lutz and Ludwig Ritter von Eimannsberger, the latter in his book *The Tank Warfare* (1934) – that would become the basis of the German *Blitzkrieg* – lightning war. He was also instrumental in the creation of the PzKpfw III and IV – the next generation of German tanks that would become the backbone of the Panzerwaffe after its initial phase. The convenience of the Spanish Civil War for a brief road-testing of some German equipment and ideas confirmed the potential. However, it also showed that tanks fighting against other tanks and against antitank guns would now be a major factor and that future tanks would need to be more heavily armoured and carry larger guns.

On the eve of World War II in actual numbers the Panzerwaffe was still small and its tanks relatively undergunned, as would be discovered a little later on the Eastern Front. The vast majority of the German army (over 80%) was unarmoured and unmotorised, relying on railways for rapid movement and on horse-drawn transport to move cross-country. Bearing this in mind, the forthcoming impact of the Panzerwaffe was extraordinary. It was the burgeoning completeness of the mechanised all-arms vision and organisation that was ahead of its time when compared to other armies. The British had experimented, but its tank forces and motorised infantry brigades generally operated independently of each other. The tanks were undergunned, mostly underarmoured, too slow and often mechanically unreliable. The French had firepower and protection in their Char B1 and Somua, but they too were slow and unreliable. More importantly, their command structure left no tactical initiative to crews in front-line combat. The Germans, on the other hand, stressed initiative and decision-making at low command levels and this would pay dividends as countries geared up for the second round of global hostilities – one that would finally witness the manifestation of the true potential of the tank.

Crew of a German PzKpfw IV tank

[Tactical and Technical Trends 12, 19 November 1942.]

The duties of the five crew members of the PzKpfw IV tank – commander, gunner, loader, driver, and radio operator/hull machine gunner – are generally similar to those performed by the crews of US Army medium M3 and M4 tanks and show what became the norm for World War II.

(1) Tank Commander: An officer or senior NCO, he is responsible for the vehicle and the crew. He indicates targets to the gunner, gives fire orders, and observes the effect. He keeps a constant watch for the enemy, serves the zone for which he is responsible, and watches for any orders from the commander's vehicle. In action, he gives his orders by intercom to the driver and radio operator, and by speaking tube and touch signals to the gunner and loader. He receives orders by radio or flag, and reports to his commander by radio, signal pistol or flag.

(2) Gunner: He is the assistant tank commander. He fires the turret gun, the turret machine gun, or the submachine gun as ordered by the tank commander. He assists the tank commander in observation.

(3) Loader: He loads and maintains the turret armament under the orders of the gunner. He is also responsible for care of ammunition, and when the cupola is closed, gives any necessary flag signals. He replaces the radio operator if the latter becomes a casualty.

(4) Driver: Operates the vehicle under the orders of the tank commander or by radio from the commander's vehicle. He assists in observation, reporting through the intercom the presence of the enemy or of obstacles in the path He watches the gasoline consumption and is responsible to the tank commander for the care and maintenance of the vehicle.

(5) Radio Operator: He operates the radio under the orders of the tank commander. In action, and when not actually transmitting, he always keeps the radio set to receive. He operates the intercom and takes down any useful messages he may intercept. He fires the bow MG. If the loader becomes a casualty, the radio operator takes over his duties.

Signal photo showing tank commander at his station in a PzKpfw IV.

Crew of US M4 tank

[FM 17-7, 15 September 1944]

The medium tank crew is composed of five members:

(1) Tank commander: A lieutenant or sergeant, in the turret, standing on the floor, or sitting or standing on his turret seat.

(2) Gunner: He sits on the gunner's seat, on the right of the gun.

(3) Bow Gunner: He's also the assistant driver and radio operator in tanks equipped with SCR-506). He's the BOG and can be found in the bow gunner's seat.

(4) Tank driver: He sits in the driver's seat on the left front.

(5) Cannoneer: He's the loader and assistant gunner and tends voice radio. He stands in the turret, or sits on the cannoneer's seat at the left of the gun.

a. The speed, firepower, armor protection, and crushing power of the tank must be used to the utmost. To secure the maximum effectiveness, the tank commander must control his crew and the crew must have the maximum of coordination and cooperation.

b. The tank commander controls the direction of movement by orders to the driver and controls the fire by orders to the gunners. The tank commander should not have to give long, detailed orders. His orders must be brief.

c. The tank commander directs the driver to drive in a certain direction or on a certain point. From time to time he tells him to vary the direction as necessary. The driver makes changes of directionto avoid irregularities in the ground, to take advantage of good terrain, and to avoid antitank gun fire. He must not make a sudden change of direction or stop without notifying the tank commander and gunner. Such action will interfere with the aim of the gunners.

d. The tank commander designates targets to the gunners and controls the fire of the guns by specifying the type of ammunition and by adjusting fire.

A late war shot of 25th Tank Bn, 14th Armored Division, ready to roll.

The Germans made good use of their life-expired armoured vehicles, often adding field guns to provide SP artillery. The PzKpfw I provided the chassis for the Panzerjäger I and, as here, the Sturmpanzer I Bison armed with a 15cm gun and mobile enough to support the Panzer divisions.

1 Blitzkrieg

Following the 1938 annexation of Austria and the Sudetenland and the March 1939 occupation of the rest of Czechoslovakia, on 1 September 1939 two German army groups, spearheaded by two Panzer corps, swept across the Polish frontier. Their aim: to encircle and destroy the Polish army in a gigantic pincer movement. Unleashed on the Poles was the new tactical system currently being perfected by Guderian (although not called Blitzkrieg at the time). As *Chef der Schnellen Truppen* (Chief of Fast Troops) he had been responsible for the recruiting, training and tactics of all the Wehrmacht's motorised and armoured units with the exception of the infantry's tracked assault guns. As planned, the objective was to pierce the enemy's front on two flanks, then encircle and destroy all or part of his forces in a huge cauldron battle (*Kesselschlacht*) of annihilation.

Its main elements were surprise, speed of manoeuvre and constant retention of the initiative. To achieve this required that all commanders used their own initiative to achieve the stated objective. Reconnaissance elements led, accompanied by artillery forward observers who could call quickly for fire support. Having located the main enemy positions, the recce would bypass, pressing on quickly to maintain the attack's momentum. They were in constant radio communication with the force commander who controlled the speed of advance, deciding whether the whole force should bypass enemy positions or engage them. The centre of gravity (*Schwerpunkt*) of the assault was clearly where the commander, who was well forward, decided was the best point to attack. He then concentrated overwhelming force to punch a hole through the enemy lines, immediately followed by other fresh units that would pass through and press forward, avoiding main enemy positions, to create havoc in their rear. Following up would be motorised infantry and artillery, who would mop up and ensure the gap was permanent by bristling its shoulders with heavy weapons.

Such operations demanded teamwork, good communications and as much surprise as possible. There would be no more predictable build-ups, long artillery barrages or plodding set-piece attacks that gave the enemy time to prepare. Instead, the overwhelmingly powerful attacking force would hit without warning, smashing through on a narrow front. It was accompanied by a simultaneous 'shock and awe' display of devastating air power attacking enemy concentrations, transport hubs and cities in a deliberate attempt to create confusion, disruption and terror.

It was entirely successful. Guderian commanded the XIX Army Corps and in the battles won two bars to his 1914 Iron Cross followed by the Knight's Cross. For the Polish campaign PzKpfw Is and IIs dominated, with a few of the new IIIs and IVs available for combat testing. With the benefit of hindsight it can be said this was a proto-Blitzkrieg, for although the Panzers spearheaded the attack they were neither given nor took complete freedom of movement, instead being used to isolate pockets of enemy troops for the infantry and artillery to destroy.

A few months later came the invasion of France (*Fall Gelb*). Having feinted first into the Low Countries drawing away some of the best British and French units, the Germans erupted into action, the operation hinging on a critical crossing of the River Meuse. Lacking artillery, they used overwhelming airpower to carpet and dive-bomb throughout the battle, shattering the French command and control structure, isolating individual units and stunning them into submission. Uniquely for this operation Guderian met and discussed the plan with the Luftwaffe so that the air arm would be used as he envisaged – as a rolling artillery barrage breaching defensive lines to enable his armour to penetrate; then delaying the intervention of any approaching enemy reserves so that the breakthrough could be consolidated. The Luftwaffe, with air superiority and close forward-operating bases, launched its largest single continuous air attack of the war.

What developed was a highly mobile all-arms affair that the German high command didn't quite understand. Even as events in the west unfolded, they repeatedly reined their armour in, worried it would be outflanked. The Panzers demonstrated their tactical superiority and Guderian and Rommel regularly disobeyed orders to keep the attack moving and it was they that created the real Blitzkrieg in the process – Guderian with his knowledge and experience and Rommel with his instinct and intuition.

In fact, the Panzers did not have it all their own way. The very first tank-on-tank battle of World War II occurred at Hannut in central Belgium between the German 3rd and 4th Panzer Divisions and two French armoured divisions (2nd and 3rd DLM) armed with Somua S35 and Hotchkiss H35 tanks in which large numbers of PzKpfw Is and IIs were destroyed. The Germans soon learnt to avoid frontal attacks and specific tank-on-tank engagements, either bypassing enemy armour, attacking from the flanks or by luring it onto the divisional antitank guns. The tanks were also held shy of Dunkirk itself as Hitler was rightly worried about armour fighting in built-up areas and had been reassured by a jealous Hermann Göring that the Luftwaffe would be able to handle it.

The disorganised and demoralised French who remained, their armour spread out to support the infantry, were no match for the concentrated German assault, whilst the British Expeditionary Force struggled to escape over the Channel. There were bright moments, the most notable the Arras counterattack by the 4th and 7th Royal Tank Regiments. It certainly scared Rommel who thought he'd been attacked by five divisions and helped hold up the Panzers, allowing the BEF to head for Dunkirk and – as it turned out — rescue. But it was too little, too late. After a spirited if costly defence 336,000 British, French, and Belgian troops managed to escape. Having reached the English Channel, Panzergruppe Guderian was created and next thrust deep into central France. By 18 June, Paris was taken and on 24 June France surrendered. The Panzerwaffe had performed a miracle of momentum that had completely overwhelmed the Allies. It was a triumph of organisation and training, for their armour was in truth rather feeble.

Their almost 2,400 tanks consisted mainly of 1,400 PzKpfw Is and IIs, and the converted Czech PzKpfw 35(t)s and 38(t)s. The PzKpfw 35(t) was armed with 37mm Skoda A3 short-barrelled main gun, the PzKpfw 38(t) with a longer 37mm Skoda A7 and both had two 7.92mm machine guns. The few new IIIs and IVs available (349 and 278 respectively) were problematic and already almost undergunned, their saving grace being their larger turret rings that enabled future upgunning. Despite teething problems the PzKpfw III was a compact, sturdy chassis that would serve the Germans well. It was intended as a tank killer, with 15mm armour, but its 3.7cm Kwk 36 L/45 gun struggled against the frontal armour of the heaviest Allied tanks. The heavier, thicker armoured (30mm) PzKpfw IV was an infantry-support tank with a five-man crew, armed with a short-barrelled 75mm gun, which fired low-velocity rounds with poor armour penetration, and high-explosive rounds deadly to exposed infantry and gun crews. For these early campaigns this equipment sufficed — because of the way the Panzerwaffe was organised and the way it communicated. Aside from its armour each Panzer division also contained a brigade of motorised infantry and an artillery regiment, plus reconnaissance, antitank, air defence, engineer and signals battalions. The Allies, though they had a large number of tanks, had no equivalent formations at that time. However, as well as antitank guns, the tanks the Germans feared were the British Matilda IIs, so it was fortunate for them that the British only had 16 available. They were slow but tough with 78mm of frontal armour, a crew of four and their 2pdr guns could pierce 37mm of 60-degree sloped armour at 500 yards.

The French had a some useful tanks whose thick armour was resistant to most German guns. The Char B1bis had up to 47mm and was armed with a hull-mounted 75mm SA35 howitzer, a 47mm SA35 turret gun and two 7.5mm Reibel MGs. The faster medium Somua S35 was probably their best, with up to 47mm of frontal armour as well, a 47mm SA35 gun and a 7.5 mm Reibel MG. The Hotchkiss H35/39 had up to 40mm, armed with a short-barrelled 37mm SA18 gun and 7.5mm MG. All these tanks had one-man turrets and were for the most part spread out supporting infantry. On top of this, the French had more artillery. However, except for small temporary tactical victories they achieved little. With the emphasis on speed, flank attacks, encirclements and swift deciding battles the Germans soon overcame them. The French tanks lacked radios, their troops weren't as well trained, the Germans had mobile SP artillery, better anti-aircraft guns (the soon-to-be-famous 88mm) and more aircraft: the Luftwaffe proved a significant component of the all-arms battlefield.

Concepts of armoured warfare

'The most important facet of German tactics remained the mission directive, allowing subordinates the maximum freedom to accomplish their assigned task. That freedom of action provided tactical superiority over the more schematic and textbook approach employed by the French and English.' (Generalfeldmarschall Günther von Kluge)

France capitulated and immediately after the armistice the French General Staff looked closely at the events of the German 46-day campaign in the west. The American War Department published *Special Series No 2 The German Armoured Army* based on their report because, as the introduction explains, 'The clarity and incisiveness of this document are evidences of its coming from a staff that has learned this lesson, though at tragic cost.' Edited extracts over the following pages 24–36 outline its salient features:

At the end of the first World War two German generals, Eimannsberger and Guderian, devoted themselves to developing the theory of the tank. They had been much impressed by the shock, even the panic, that the sudden introduction of the tank had caused among the German troops, but they were convinced also that the Allies had used the new instrument timidly and sparingly. They saw united in the tank the three main elements of decision in a modern battle: (1) surprise, (2) powerful and instantaneous fire, and (3) breadth, flexibility, and relative invulnerability of movement. They saw that the arm could be employed with much greater effectiveness than the Allies had imagined.

a. Speed and the radius of action must be utilized to the utmost
'The attack by tanks,' wrote Guderian in 1936, 'must be conducted with maximum acceleration in order to exploit the advantage of surprise, to penetrate deep into enemy lines, to prevent reserves from intervening, and to extend the tactical success into a strategic victory. Speed, therefore, is what is to be exacted above anything else from the armoured weapon.'

b. Tanks will impose their rhythm on the modern battle
Infantry and artillery link their action as closely as possible to that of the tanks. The German standard regulations state the new law: 'In the zone of action of the tanks, the action of other arms is to be based on that of the tanks.' Armour became, on the ground, the essential arm of combat and no longer figured, as it had in the French conception, merely as support for infantry and artillery.

c. The combined action of the air and armoured forces will govern the battle
The decisive factor is no longer the infantry-artillery team, because the air units,

Rommel's 7th Panzer Division regroups after crossing the Somme. At left, PzKpfw 38(t)s; at right, a PzKpfw IV. Rommel's division became known as the *Gespensterdivision* (Ghost Division) because of its bold advance out of the Meuse bridgehead cutting off the Allied troops in Belgium.

The Germans made considerable use of captured equipment – and those countries it subjugated were exploited: workers, industries and cultural items were all ruthlessly taken for use by the Reich. This is one of over 3,000 Renault UE tankettes captured during the fall of France. It had a nifty tracked trailer and was used to pull antitank guns such as the Pak 36.

Guderian: 'Speed makes possible the maximum degree of surprise because it overcomes delay in concentrating forces at chosen points. Speed neutralizes the enemy defense by limiting the possibilities of fire from his antitank weapons.' (**Above** PzKpfw Is.)

Guderian: 'The armoured division is the basic combat unit. It receives from the corps commander the direction in which it is to exert its effort; its zone of action must necessarily be limited except when the defense is weak, in which case it can push forward toward the ultimate objective of the entire groupment.' **Above** A *kleiner Panzerbefehlswagen* (small command tank built on a PzKpfw I chassis) during the May 1940 campaign.

being better qualified to furnish immediate, brutal, and accurate support for the mobile and rapid tanks, will henceforth constitute the 'attack artillery'. Guderian identified in 1936:

• Infantry, artillery, and engineers need to be motorised and partially armoured. They will adjust their new tactical program and employment to their new speed.
• An important role will be played by the engineers, who will be trained to cross gaps rapidly and to oppose enemy tanks by the rapid construction antitank obstacles.
• To protect armour against counterattack by its most dangerous enemies – tanks and aircraft – the Panzer division will need numerous antitank and antiaircraft weapons.

As soon as the breakthrough is effected, exploit it immediately with the armoured forces acting in close liaison with the air and the combat forces. Assign them objectives in depth that will coincide as far as possible with the sensitive points – important crossroads, regulating stations, and depots of every kind, and insist on speed.

Do not slow down the armoured forces by requiring them to widen the breach. This role is reserved for the infantry of the normal divisions following after the assault of the fast-moving units. Armour greatly diminishes the vulnerability of the exploitation forces initially confined in a narrow breach.

Do not require the armoured units to maintain approximate alignment with other fast-moving units advancing to the right or left; on the contrary, demand that they push forward, seeking the point of least resistance without wasting time at the defensive areas.

Do not lose sight of the fact that this arm – an expensive one, an arm of quality rather than of quantity, an arm subjected to an extreme attrition of man and matériel – cannot do everything. It must be constantly relieved by normal infantry divisions. The close union between the armoured units and these following armies must be emphasized. They are two echelons of one force and not two separate and independent armies.

General characteristics of the action of the armoured army in battle
a. The Officers
Commanding officers of armoured or motorised units were chosen for their strong personalities. The obligation for them to grasp the situation rapidly in order to exercise effective command requires that they move to the front. Most of the time they are in the midst of the battle. As a rule, the citations awarded to commanding generals of armoured divisions mention the personal part they played in the front lines. These high-ranking officers also used airplanes, preferably the Fieseler Storch.

The desire to leave freedom of action and initiative with the various commanders is illustrated in the orders issued at the end or at the beginning of the day. They are always short, clear, and easily read. They do not pretend to regulate every minor detail.

In the course of operations, battle orders adjust the initial missions of subordinate units to the unforeseeable development of events. Rapidity of reaction is dependent on the presence of the commanding officer at the front.

Non-combat vehicles are kept to the absolute minimum for rapid movement. The staff is divided into two sections. One assists the commanding general close to the battle line and handles tactical decisions. It includes all the officers charged with conducting the operations. The administrative staff, whose duties include handling questions of matériel, personnel and morale, operate in the rear section.

b. Importance of signal communications

Immediate effective action is possible because of the development of signal communications. The Germans had simple and practical sets in all arms, and personnel were trained in all methods of communication.

In the motorised arm, every armoured vehicle had a radio set. The commanding general of a division communicates by radio with both his subordinates and with the air forces. In the lower echelons, every commanding officer issues his orders by radio, reports problems to higher commanders, and receives their instructions by the same means.

c. Judicious offensive spirit

At every level, the action is resolutely offensive, if not actually bold. The determination to push forward at all costs gives the commanding officer valuable contact information and enables him to grasp the situation accurately.

German regulations attach great importance to reconnaissance. The enemy cannot be overcome unless one first acquires exact data as to his methods of combat, his available means, his units, and the weak points of his defence. Cultivation of the offensive spirit does not mean that the commander should neglect the ordinary exercise of prudence. Should the tanks encounter an obstacle, they do not necessarily try to force their way through but search elsewhere for an opening; when they discover it, they plunge forward without worrying about the resistance remaining in their rear, and without endeavouring to maintain a rigid alignment with adjacent units. If the attack encounters a continuous line or an obstacle liable to render the advance impossible or hazardous, other means (such as bombardment aviation) are brought into play.

d. Combined action of the motorised arm with the aerial arm

The armoured-mechanised arm does not fight alone. In every phase of action, tanks act in close liaison with aviation:

(1) Reconnaissance aviation informs tank units as to their axis of march.

(2) Observation aviation enable commanders to follow the development of the battle.

Matilda *Glanton* of 7th Royal Tank Regiment was part of 'Frankforce' that attacked the Germans at Arras. The 6th and 8th Battalions DLI supported by the 4th and 7th RTR – just 74 tanks – attacked the German flank. Using 88s as antitank guns Rommel held the attack but not before they had scared the Germans who, shortly after, stopped to consolidate their forces.

The PzKpfw I may have been puny compared to tanks later in the war, but in 1939 it was still a front-line armoured vehicle with all the destructive capabilities of a tank. What it lacked in firepower (it was armed with only machine guns) it made up for in robustness.

(3) Pursuit aviation protects the troops against enemy bombers or intercepts fighters liable to attack dive bombers.

(4) Dive bombers, or Stukas, became the principal auxiliaries of tanks.

Artillery can provide armour a more permanent support than aviation; less dependent on the hour of the day or the seasons, and supplying a greater volume of explosives. However, the rapidity of the advance frequently isolated it from its artillery, even though the artillery was fast-moving and maneuverable. In such cases, the action of the Stukas proved to be the determining factor in almost every instance, whether acting to a preset plan or on a radio request from the armoured units.

e. Defensive precautions Flak and Pak

The Germans had not just studied the attack. Commanders of large units were always careful to protect against hostile air attacks. They emplace Flak in the very midst of their armoured brigade and a complete battalion of AA artillery is organized for use against tanks and assigned to an armoured division.

The antitank guns of the tank-destroyer (*Panzerjäger*) battalions are pushed boldly forward, close to the tanks, or even ahead of them when the riflemen attack in first echelon. However bold may be the action of the German motorised arm, the command never fails to deploy and put into action the defensive means capable of insuring its protection.

Combat of the armoured division

a. Attack

Quick and brutal action; maximum use of surprise; the adversary must not be allowed time to recover from his surprise and to react. Maneuver must always be inspired by the desire to disconcert the enemy command through its very boldness and rapidity but it must not degenerate into a disorderly onrush. Armoured weapons (light or heavy), infantry, artillery, engineers, signal communications, not to mention the air forces—all these arms contribute to the common aim: overcoming the adversary by an irresistible assault, followed by complete destruction.

b. Tactics

Speed is the primary factor that determines the tactics of the armoured division.

(1) Should the terrain be open, and the enemy have a discontinuous front:

(a) The armoured brigade will rush forward in first echelon.

(b) Its reconnaissance group will keep it informed as to the possible points of penetration.

(c) Frequently motorcyclists are sufficient to keep the armoured elements informed.

(d) At other times, heavy armoured cars, followed by motorcyclists, are themselves kept informed and on the alert by the radio of the light-armoured cars.

The German Panzers were inconvenienced by the demolition of the bridges over the River Meuse, but at Sedan and elsewhere they were able to improvise quickly and make use of the bridging columns that accompanied the units.

(e) When informed by aviation that there is nothing ahead of them, the brigade advances, the light tanks in the lead; the reconnaissance detachment ensures the protection of an exposed flank.

(f) The armoured brigade moves along the road in column on several routes, always ready to deploy as soon as it encounters resistance and ready to seek immediately the first fissure capable of being exploited in the enemy's formation. Once the fissure has been found, the brigade continues its advance, neglecting temporarily the roads blocked by the enemy. Moving along with it are the reconnaissance and liaison detachments, artillery observation, elements of the antitank battalion, and elements of engineer troops capable of dealing rapidly with any terrain incident such as a road to be cleared, the preparation of detours, the improvement of fords, etc.

(g) In rear of it, in the second echelon, follow the brigade of riflemen, the artillery, the main bodies of the antitank battalion, the engineer battalion, and the services. This infantry brigade will be charged with the frontal attack, and the reduction and mopping up of the centers of resistance outflanked by the tanks.

(2) Should the terrain prove to be held in depth by a determined enemy, though not protected by a continuous line of obstacles:

Guderian: 'War will no longer be the war of aeroplanes and tanks; it will be the war of thousands of planes and thousands of tanks.' A German column advances towards Orel, Russia.

(a) The armoured division will maintain a formation in depth, tanks in first echelon, riflemen in second echelon. The armoured brigade will deploy on an extended front, regiments in line and each regiment in column of battalions. As the fight progresses and reveals new resistances in width, the battalions deploy their light companies, the heavy companies being held in reserve for overcoming more serious resistances.

(b) The battalion in the second echelon is held in readiness to intervene, either to extend the flank, or to relieve the leading battalion should it be held up or suffer heavy losses.

(c) Kept on the alert by its liaison and observation detachments, and advancing with the tanks, the artillery of the armoured division deploys and ensures to the tanks the most rapid, accurate, and intense fire support possible.

(d) Abandoning its motorcycles and detrucked from its cross-country vehicles, the infantry overcomes such points of resistance as the tanks have left behind by pinning them down frontally, outflanking them, and then mopping them up once they have been overcome. The assaulting engineer detachments assist with their flamethrowers and their explosives, and without loss of time reestablish the roads blocked or damaged by the enemy.

(e) In principle, the two echelons do not remain together, and the tanks continue to advance at their own pace. If the defence areas put up too energetic a resistance, the assault of the Stukas will neutralize them and will permit the riflemen—once more in their vehicles—to close up on the armoured brigade.

(3) Should the armoured brigade encounter a mechanized unit of a type comparable to its own and in good order:

(a) The armoured division will gain contact in such a manner as to determine the exact nature of the resistance encountered, its weak points, its flanks, and its support.

Observation aviation completes the investigation. Protected by its light elements, the armoured division deploys in line of regiments or battalions, maintaining proper intervals and distances between the tanks, with the heavy ones to the rear.

(b) The artillery deploys with a view to firing before the enemy antitank arms can open fire. The infantry organizes positions with a view to constituting an eventual line of support.

(c) Bombardment aviation prepares the attack by dive bombing on the enemy's supporting artillery and on his concentrations of tanks.

(d) The tanks move to meet the enemy tanks. The rule is to impose one's will by sheer boldness, by deploying first and being the first to open fire. In order not to be hit, a tank must fire first at the greatest possible range and with the greatest accuracy. The fire discipline so highly developed in the German mechanized arm is thereby justified.

(e) The combat must not degenerate into fragmentary individual combats. A team spirit must prevail down to the smallest units. From the brigade down to the section, tank leaders must continue to wage the combat as a whole, violently but with flexibility. The presence of the commanding officers at the front and the existence of good radio communications appear to be absolute necessities.

(f) Envelopment and attacks from the rear are sought as being the most profitable.

(g) Any weakening on the part of the enemy must be exploited at once. Here again, a weak place must be converted into a breach, the tanks forming a mass at the point disclosed. The widening of the breach must entail the disintegration of the adversary's formation and the lowering of the enemy's morale, and the assault of the tanks must then be converted into a pursuit.

(4) However, the armoured division may have to attack a fortified front, supported by concrete fortifications, bristling with barbed wire, protected by obstacles which the tanks cannot cross, and held by an enemy who is not disorganized.

Here the tanks become easy targets for well-emplaced and sheltered antitank artillery, and so may be destroyed. The desired speed of the armoured division can no longer be materialized. Therefore, the infantry must now precede the tanks. We have here a complete change in tactics. The commanding general of the armoured unit will then plan a classical attack:

(a) Preparation of the attack by bombardment aviation according to a coordinated plan prepared by the aviation and motorised units.

(b) Crossing the river in pneumatic boats under the protection of the last wave of dive bombers.

(c) Reinforcement of the infantry by assaulting elements of engineers armed with flame-throwers and explosives, as well as by elements of light antitank artillery.

(d) Support by the artillery of the divisions, reinforced, if possible, with heavy artillery and

The French Renault B1bis was a powerful tank but had significant design flaws, including the need for the driver to aim the main gun and the one-man turret housing the commander and the 47mm secondary armament. It also suffered from mechanical problems and of the 267 combat losses, half were abandoned by their crews. That fate, however, did not await the two shown here. These are *Beni Snassen* (right) and *Aisne* of 41ème BCC which were knocked out by the artillery of 2nd Panzer Division at Pogny on 12 June during fighting for a bridge over the Marne.

    kept informed by ground and aerial observers.

(e) A thoroughly energetic attack will be made and the casemates resolutely attacked by the engineers and antitank guns; the infantry will advance without regard to losses. Its objectives are in depth. At Sedan the Grossdeutschland Regiment penetrated as far as 8 kilometers from its jumping-off point, and into French artillery positions.

At this point the infantry 'turns the terrain over to the tanks.' The tank then becomes more an agency of exploitation than of penetration.

As soon as the breach is sufficiently widened and conditioned to enable the tank to pass, the tank resumes its place in the first echelon in order to ensure maximum speed to the advance of the armoured division.

These four situations, selected as being the most characteristic, are not the only ones encountered, for the possibilities are unlimited.

Defence against the armoured division

This study cannot be ended without endeavoring to determine the means of parrying the action of the motorised arm. Analysis of each method of attack will reveal a corresponding method of defence.

a. Morale – The tank demands of its crew a very high morale. The defender must be able to create a still higher morale. The action of tanks is based on speed. This speed must be checked.

b. Speed of Attack – The speed of tank units results in the conquest of objectives in depth. It must be parried by resistance in depth.

c. Obstacles – The advance of a tank is stemmed by obstacles. They must be placed not only in front of defence areas, but also in their depth and rear where they will constitute actual 'stopping lines' for the mechanized units already reduced and worn down by the defence.

d. Villages and Woods – A tank fears villages and woods. If these are organized for defence and offer a stubborn resistance, they can isolate the tank from its infantry, artillery, and means of supply.

e. Armour – The armour of the tank has proved to be superior to the fire of the defence. The shell must reconquer its superiority over the armour plate.

f. Antitank Guns – Too often the antitank guns of the defence have been submerged by the onrush of tanks. Prior to the war the Germans calculated that each antitank gun attacked by compact tank units could hardly destroy more than three tanks before being destroyed itself. On this basis, they had reckoned that a nonalerted defence could rarely oppose sufficient antitank guns to any massive attack (such as 60 tanks per kilometer). Therefore it would be necessary:

(1) To protect the antitank weapons effectively against observation and hits.

(2) To reestablish rapidly the balance between the attack and defence by opposing to the mass of tanks a flexible and mobile mass of guns on self-propelled mounts capable of strengthening the position of resistance at least in depth.

(3) It should be possible to oppose a mass of airplanes and tanks with an equally large mass of airplanes and tanks.

The morale of the German troops was high – particularly after their run of victories – first the political, bloodless victories in Austria, Czechoslovakia and the Rhineland; then on the battlefield in Poland. Here a column of PzKpfw Is (foreground) and IIs (sideways on an Ausf D) in France in 1940.

g. Lessons from Operations of a German Armoured Division – A study of the operations of the armoured division south of the Somme is instructive and comforting in this respect. It discloses

(1) The great difficulties encountered by the German armoured units which had penetrated deep into the position, far from their infantry and artillery which were held up by French centers of resistance that had been neglected or avoided by the tanks.

(2) The impossibility for armoured units acting alone to capture villages held by a resolute defence.

(3) The great difficulty the German command encountered in supplying the tanks and furnishing them with indispensable repair material.

(4) The vulnerability of the tanks thus slowed down and paralyzed, when counterattacked by airplanes and tanks.

Motorised Infantry

1. These units form the offensive infantry element in the armoured division. Their strength lies in their speed and cross-country performance, together with the possession of numerous automatic weapons and protective armour.

2. The possession of armoured personnel carriers enables motorised infantry units to overcome comparatively weak opposition without dismounting. They can follow up tank attacks on the field of battle without dismounting.

3. Motorised infantry is characterized by ability to alternate rapidly between fighting from carriers and fighting on foot, and also to combine these two methods of combat.

4. Mobility and the possession of numerous automatic weapons enable motorised infantry units to defend even a broad front against comparatively strong enemy forces.

5. Motorised infantry on wheeled vehicles moves faster than motorised infantry on APCs, although in difficult country movements on wheeled vehicles are restricted. Owing to lack of sufficient armour, motorised infantry cannot fight from their trucks.

6. The chief task of motorised infantry is close cooperation with tanks. By following up closely they can quickly exploit the tanks' success.

7. Motorised infantry units also prepare the ground for the employment of tanks by clearing a way through country difficult or impossible for tanks. They will then bear the brunt of the fighting. In this their main tasks will be the following: (a) Attack over tankproof sectors and rivers; (b) Attack on an enemy in or behind tankproof country; (c) Attack on a fixed position; (d) Fighting in villages and woods.

8. Their greater speed compared with tanks enables them at an early stage to take possession of important points and sectors, to carry out wide and deep enveloping movements, or to pursue the enemy rapidly.

9. Motorised infantry units are organized into brigades. In the accomplishment of their tasks they are often reinforced by other arms – primarily antitank guns and artillery.

In 1939 each Panzer division had a motorised artillery regiment of two Abteilungen increased to three in 1940. There were insufficient prime movers to haul the guns and they had problems keeping up with the tanks. Because of this they began to put guns onto tank chassis to make them mobile. This is the 15cm sIG 33 (Sf) auf Panzerkampfwagen I Ausf B (a 15cm gun on a PzKpfw I chassis). It served until around 1943 but had some drawbacks: no ammunition stowage and it was plagued by breakdowns. The 36 vehicles were split into *schwere Infanteriegeschütz-Kompanie (mot.S.)* (SP heavy infantry gun coys) numbers 701–706 and assigned to Panzer divisions.

The solar topees give the game away: North Africa is the location for this PzKpfw III Ausf J. Note the crew members taking the opportunity to get some fresh air by sitting outside their hatches – something, of course, only to be done in a safe environment behind the front lines.

2 North Africa

North Africa was the first victorious Allied campaign of the war and as such a turning point. It was also where they were blooded and battle-hardened in the ways of the new mobile armoured warfare. To the Germans it was an expensive sideshow that they were drawn into, an unwelcome distraction from the colossal Operation Barbarossa – the invasion of Russia. But Rommel's arrival and the initial startling success of the Afrika Korps seduced Hitler into expending valuable reserves and resources on the gamble for the glittering prize of the Suez Canal and the Iranian oilfields beyond. For both sides the campaign hinged on critical naval resupply and much of the struggle took place on and above the Mediterranean, but with German attention focused on the Eastern Front, ultimately it was the British, through their tenacity and naval power, and despite taking heavy losses, who were able to dominate. For a while the ground fighting, too, was a very close affair, see-sawing up and down the African Mediterranean littoral (mainly from Libya to Egypt), as following a successful resupply either side would launch a fresh assault that would eventually peter out the farther it went into enemy territory, lengthening vulnerable supply lines. Against the even more inexperienced Italians the British performed well, but German equipment and tactical superiority gave them the edge – at first, for it was the mindset of the British higher command that had to change. Tanks were used to cavalry charge defended positions or stretched out, defending 'boxes' that could be attacked individually. However, in the face of the experienced German war machine, sometimes with obviously inferior armour, the British and Commonwealth forces stubbornly persevered.

Fortunately, they were increasingly better supplied and resourced than the Germans, and other naval and air assets evened up the contest considerably. The open terrain of the desert well suited mobile warfare, with tanks, artillery and airpower proving the most critical assets and the campaign witnessed the arrival of various new designs – especially from the Allies, who were playing catchup. Although having some good armoured cars in the Humber and Daimler, British tanks were still divided into slow, well-armoured infantry-supporting tanks and lighter, faster Cruisers for tank-on-tank combat. They were still undergunned, with 2pdrs that couldn't fire high explosive shells to deal with dug-in infantry and antitank artillery, and most of them still suffered from endless automotive problems. The Matilda II had excelled against the Italians but by 1942 its slow speed, light armament and vulnerability to more powerful antitank guns (especially the 88mm) and the new upgunned PzKpfw IIIs and IVs rendered it virtually obsolete – for its turret ring could not be enlarged and therefore it could not upgrade its main gun. The Valentine was a slow infantry tank with 65mm-thick frontal armour porting a 40mm/2pdr main gun firing only AP ammo. By 1942 it, too, was also considered obsolete, although it was at least powered by a reliable bus engine. The polygon-turreted Crusader was a cruiser that suffered from constant automotive failures yet was the fastest tank in theatre, with the same 40mm/2pdr main gun and ammo as the Valentine, upgraded in 1942 to 57mm/6pdr (Crusader III) at the cost of a reduced turret crew. A small number of Churchills also saw action towards the end of the campaign. Another slow infantry tank with chronic engine problems, it was at least equipped with a 57mm/6pdr gun. In towed antitank capability the British had at first a 40mm/2pdr that was replaced in 1942 with a 57mm/6pdr gun and by 1943 the powerfully effective 72.6mm/17pdr had been rushed into service to counter the Tiger. They also had the excellent all-purpose Ordnance QF 25pdr (87.6mm) artillery piece.

American equipment was certainly critical for the British and Commonwealth forces and for the most part much appreciated, for the attrition rate during their combat learning curve was astounding, and the North African campaign plainly illustrated that this was, above all, a war of resources and production. The M3 light was named the Stuart by the British, and it was just about on a par with the Panzer III Ausf G in its armour and M5 37mm main gun. It had only a two-man turret crew and a limited fuel capacity and range; by 1942 it had been relegated to a reconnaissance role. The M3 medium Grant (as it was known with its British-designed turret; they dubbed the American model the Lee) was well-armoured (38–51mm) and had considerable firepower – a 37mm gun in the turret, and a 75mm in a right-hand sponson and up to four machine guns. It was certainly a shock to the Germans when they first encountered it, but to use its strange sponson-mounted 75mm necessitated dangerously exposing its vulnerable high silhouette and riveted construction, and it had a poor off-road performance. As the M4 Sherman became available the M3 medium was replaced.

Though also not without faults (a high silhouette and a propensity to catch fire when hit), the Sherman was one of the outstanding tanks of the war and was produced in large numbers. Its speed, rugged automotive reliability and 75mm M3 main gun made it a powerful danger to all Axis armour in theatre. Also from late 1942 some Allied self-propelled artillery began to appear in the form of the British Bishop (converted Valentine chassis with 25pdr gun-howitzer) and the American Priest (105mm Howitzer Motor Carriage M7).

On the Axis side was the Italian M13/40, whose light armour and bolted and riveted construction made it very vulnerable, although if did have a 47mm main gun.

The British armour didn't perform well in the desert against Rommel's Panzer divisions (the 21st and 15th) partly because of its equipment – such as the Mk VIB light tanks shown here – partly because of its poor tactics and leadership.

The British concept of cruiser and infantry tanks led to a number of vehicles that did not perform well. The Crusader was chronically unreliable, with poor armour and a peashooter. By the time the Mk III came along, the gun and armour were better but the commander had to act as loader in the reduced crew (necessitated by the upgunning and reduction of internal turret space).

American tanks made a huge difference to the desert campaign. The first to reach the beleaguered British in Africa were the M3 medium tanks, partly financed by Lend-Lease. Objectively, the M3 medium was a poor tank with a high silhouette, sponson-mounted main gun and poor, riveted armour, and it is no surprise that of the 2,855 that reached the British, 1,700 went to Australia for home defence and 900 went to India. However, in May 1942 it was a godsend, its gun better than any British tank gun and capable of knocking out any of the opposition from decent range, and its engine reliable. This (**Below**) is the Grant version, with an altered turret to allow space for a No 19 wireless set in the bustle. Monty is using it as a dais to speak to the troops. Luckily, waiting in the wings was the M4 medium (**Above**) dubbed the Sherman by the British. It arrived on the scene in October 1942: the British would end up with over 17,000 of this war-winning design. Note the sand shields on these Sherman IIs (the M4A1's British designation).

The PzKpfw III and IV were really different beasts to their Allied counterparts, for they were tried and tested designs with upgrade paths that enabled them to upgun and uparmour and so remain in use and be mass-produced. The PzKpfw III was designed for tank-on-tank combat, armed with a high-velocity 37mm gun that was later up-gunned in the Ausf F with a short-barrelled Kwk 38 L/42 50mm gun, and then later still a long-barrelled 50mm. It could also mount a short-barrelled 75mm, used to fire high explosive shells for infantry support – a reversal of roles between it and the PzKpfw IV. Under General Kesselring in Tunisia (1943), the Afrika Korps was rearmoured with PzKpfw III Ausf L and M. Originally intended as an infantry support tank, the PzKpfw IV was armed with a short 75mm gun and until the longer-gun variant began production, the tank was outperformed by the PzKpfw III in armour penetration. As increasing numbers of the PzKpfw IV were armed with the long-barrelled 75mm Kwk 40 from 1942, it swapped roles with the PzKpfw III as a tank killer that could penetrate all British and US armour in theatre at ranges of up to 1,500m and was used by Rommel to spearhead his offensives. In early 1943 the first Tiger Is reached Africa armed with a powerful 88mm gun. Superior to any Allied tank, fortunately their arrival was too little and too late to change the fate of the Axis forces in North Africa.

What the British also had was the Desert Air Force, which showed another important area of tactical air support. Unlike the dive-bombing that had assisted *Blitzkrieg*, Air Vice Marshal Arthur Coningham's Western Desert Air Force wrote the rulebook for air-ground cooperation. This groundwork was passed on to the Americans after Operation Torch and proved a significant benefit to the Allies: the RAF's 2TAF and the American IX and XIX Tactical Air Command would prove a serious thorn in the flesh of the German forces after the invasion of France.

Desert warfare

The campaign began when Italian inexperience and incompetence enabled a startling victory for the small British and Commonwealth army known as the Western Desert Force. They, in turn, were promptly taught the same lesson by Rommel's newly arrived Afrika Korps, when a similar probing armed reconnaissance turned into a full-blown offensive. Caught out by its speed and ferocity, the British were quickly overwhelmed, losing the whole of Cyrenaica except for the critical port city of Tobruk. They were only reprieved when the Axis advance was curtailed by shortages of fuel and ammunition. The British then responded with two retaliatory operations of their own – Brevity (15–16 May 1941) and Battleaxe (15–17 June), but both were against prepared defended positions and were defeated with heavy losses.

The British now reorganised, forming the Eighth Army in September 1941 with fresh equipment including 300 cruiser tanks, 170 infantry tanks and 300 of the new US lend-lease M3 light tanks, along with 34,000 lorries, 600 artillery guns, 240 AA guns, 200 antitank guns and 900 mortars. Operation Crusader (18 November 1941–31 January 1942) was then launched to relieve Tobruk. Although ultimately it succeeded in its aim, it highlighted the problems that the British were having in integrating and co-ordinating their armour, infantry and artillery. Fighting against high-quality German armour, the 88mm's excellent antitank capability and battle-hardened troops, mistakes proved costly in both men and matériel and so it was just as well that more Allied supplies arrived than did German.

Rommel, in turn, struck back hard and, though he still could not take Tobruk, some of his advance troops actually crossed the border into Egypt before fuel and water ran critically low and the need to safeguard his remaining forces prompted him to break off and withdraw. Both sides had fought tenaciously and now paused to resupply. British tank tactics needed rethinking in the face of terrible losses. Although Tobruk had been relieved the price was considered too heavy and various commanders' heads rolled. April saw both sides resupplied, the British now with 900 tanks including 200 new heavily armoured Grants compared to 320 German tanks and 240 poor Italian ones. As usual Rommel attacked first and it was the Germans' turn to be surprised by the Grants, which proved impossible to knock out except at close range. Rommel concentrated on encircling and destroying the British armour piecemeal or drawing them onto his antitank guns, while repeated British counterattacks threatened to cut off and destroy his own forces, but by shifting the emphasis of his attack he once again outmanoeuvred the British, forcing them into a hasty retreat eastwards while trapping the remainder at Gazala.

Taking advantage of the chaos and confusion, he next struck at Tobruk and finally succeeding in taking the port, along with 32,000 prisoners and huge quantities of much-needed supplies. This was the high watermark of his success, and on 22 June Hitler rewarded him with promotion to field marshal. However, the Führer was still intent on his colossal Russian operation and would not countenance any further resources for the African theatre. Realising that delay would only benefit the British who received many more regular supplies, Rommel continued with his offensive, storming heavily fortified Mersa Matruh and plundering more huge stockpiles of fuel and food, hundreds of tanks and trucks. He then chased the Eighth Army right back to the critical defence line at El Alamein, where the Qattara Depression creates a naturally defensive choke point that cannot be outflanked. Here at the end of July his attack, battered and contained by Allied air superiority, ground to a halt, and there was another pause in the fighting as both sides rested and regrouped. A frustrated Churchill took a few more heads and General Bernard Montgomery was made the new commander of Eighth Army. A cautious man, he succeeded in stalling Churchill while he built up his forces and trained fresh troops to the desert. Meanwhile, knowing time was not on his side, Rommel renewed his attack on 30 August, but pre-warned by the Ultra

Rommel gets forward in his SdKfz 250/3 command vehicle. He called it *Greif* (Griffin) and the G is visible to the left of the man sitting on the outside of the vehicle. Note the 'bedstead' tubular aerial frame.

The German component of the Axis forces in the desert – now enshrined in legend as the Afrika Korps – punched above its weight from its arrival in spring 1941 until defeat at Alamein in November 1942. Although much of Rommel's hype was down to German propaganda skills – the German high command despaired at the way he outran his supply lines – he came close at Gazala to inflicting a decisive defeat on the British by use of a concentrated tank attack around the British left flank.

cipher intercepts, Monty was able to thwart his final desperate attempts to achieve a breakthrough. An ill Rommel, worn out by the long campaign and fearing that it could not be won with the few resources he had left, flew home to Germany to recuperate.

The 8 October 1942 the Anglo-American Torch landings surprised the Germans, who were now trapped in Tunisia between two armies. Hitler foolishly rushed in reinforcements which were too little and too late, while Monty took his time to prime his hugely superior forces. Finally on 23 October 1942 he began his offensive and Rommel rushed back to Africa to immediately counterattack with his remaining 200 tanks. Monty responded with the bulk of his 800 in what became the biggest tank battle of the desert war. Inevitably, the Allied numbers told and so began the final retreat of the Afrika Korps, although by now it had been through a number of name changes. The Germans were fighting in small combat groups outnumbered by massively superior British and Commonwealth forces, who also enjoyed air superiority.

Right: M4A1 at Kasserine, 24 February 1943. The US Army's Armored Force was born on 10 July 1940 under General Chaffee. It was as well for America that it still had nearly two years before its tanks would first be involved in action as the Armored Force had obsolescent tanks: there were only 66 mediums as of June 1941. But in July the first M3 mediums started to roll off assembly lines, along with new halftracks. However, the defeat of 1st Armored at Kasserine in February 1943 was a rude awakening. The battle emphasised the need for combined-arms tactics and not cavalry tactics in a mechanised disguise. The Tunisian fighting also emphasised the importance of field artillery, clearly demonstrating the advantages of the new 1941 fire direction centre in massing artillery fire. Indeed, it was the artillery that stopped the German attack at Kasserine. American armour needed to get much better quickly: success in Sicily would show that it had done so.

The Tiger was introduced to the Tunisian campaign and first saw action on 4 December 1943. While it performed well, sPzAbt501 lost 7 Tigers (along with 19 PzKpfw IIIs and 8 PzKpfw IVs) to the British during Operation Ochsenkopf. This one, photographed some weeks later when American units passed by, was demolished by its crew as they retreated.

On 19–25 February Rommel turned briefly to badly maul the green American forces at the Kasserine Pass in what would turn out to be his last successful African battle. He then turned back to attack the Eighth Army, but once again forewarned by Ultra intercepts, the Germans were drawn into a kill zone bristling with antitank guns and after losing over 50 tanks Rommel called off the assault. On 9 March he was ordered back to Germany and never returned. Slowly and stubbornly the remaining Axis Forces fell back to their final defensive positions in Tunisia, but the Allies dominated the Mediterranean and isolated them from all hope of resupply or escape. Despite a tenacious last-ditch defence the entire force of 248,000 men – including the recently arrived reinforcements – surrendered on 13 May 1943 and Churchill's famous phrase caught the moment: it was 'the end of the beginning.'

German methods of armoured attack by small units

[From *Tactical and Technical Trends* 16, 14 January 1943]

a. Composition of a German Box (moving defence area)
The box is the part of the column which is inside the solid line in sketch C. The box varies in size, but if an armoured battalion is the basic unit, it might contain the following combat troops, in addition to the service elements:

- One battalion of motorised infantry, usually carried in halftracks
- One battalion of 50mm antitank guns
- One battalion of 88mm antiaircraft/antitank guns
- One battery of 150mm close-support infantry guns, sometimes on SP mounts
- One battalion of field artillery

On the move or in the attack, the guns within the box are disposed as shown in sketch C. Infantry guns and field guns are usually kept in the box only when the defensive is assumed.

In size, the box is approximately 2 miles deep and has a front of 800 yards. The 88mm gun, though it has proved a very effective antitank gun, is primarily included in the box to protect the lightly armoured vehicles from air attack.

b. The method of advance (see sketch A)
On very flat country, the distance between the reconnaissance unit and the leading echelons of tanks is from 5 to 10 miles; the distance between the 1st and 2nd echelon of tanks is 1 mile, and the distance between the 2nd echelon of tanks and the box is 2 miles. The whole force is directed towards some terrain feature, which, if captured, will force the enemy to fight on ground chosen by the attacker.

Over normal terrain, each portion of the column moves from high ground to high ground by bounds. Each echelon of tanks is supported by artillery which moves in the rear of the tanks.

c. Tactics if attacked on the move
When British tanks are reported to be advancing to a fight, the box halts and takes up a position for all-around defence. As the British tanks advance, the reconnaissance units fall back, and the two echelons of tanks deploy on a wide front (see sketch B). If the enemy continues to advance, the Germans continue the retirement to position B (sketch B), and force the enemy to attempt a breakthrough against one of the flanks of the box.

If the enemy decides to attack the German left flank, the troops on the left of the

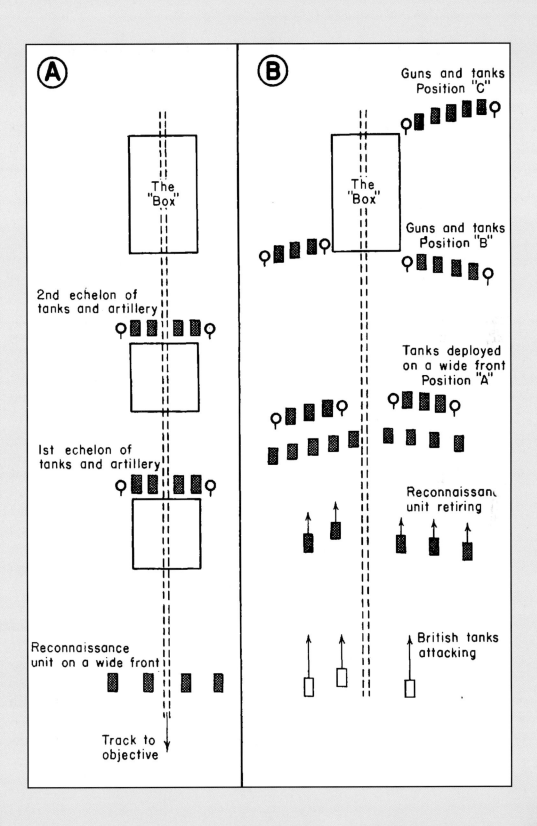

box at position B fall back to position C. The enemy tanks, if they pursue, are then not only engaged frontally by the German tanks from position C, but are caught in flank by AT and AA guns of the left side of the box. Finally, the tanks to the right of the box at position B swing around and engage the attackers in the rear.

If artillery has accompanied the tanks in the advance, it may either continue to support them, or enter the box to stiffen its antitank defence.

d. Attack led by tanks against an organized position
In general, the Germans assume that the defenders have seized and occupied the best positions, hence, they attempt to overwhelm him and take over such positions.

The German commander usually launches a frontal attack against one centre of resistance. The attack might be developed in the following way (see sketch C).

- Phase I: The German commander will reinforce his reconnaissance unit with tanks deployed on a wide front and drive in the covering force, until the enemy is approximately 2,500 yards from the main line of resistance.
- Phase II: A careful reconnaissance will then be carried out by a senior commander in a tank.
- Phase III: The German covering force deploys as follows:
  Tanks, generally PzKpfw IVs, take up a hull-down position on a ridge, or high ground, and with the fire of their machine guns attempt to pin down the defences. They may engage AT guns that are visible with their 75's. Under cover of this fire, 50mm AT guns, heavy machine guns, and close support 150mm infantry guns are also deployed in an attempt to knock out the AT guns of the defence, or to kill their gun crews.
  Under the cover of fire of this covering force, the attack forms in rear as follows:
  (1) Three rows of tanks about 50 yards apart, each row approximately 150 yards in rear of the one in front.
  (2) When the tanks are in position, the box forms up in rear as shown in sketch C, the infantry all riding in vehicles.
- Phase IV: At H-hour, the whole force moves forward at about 15mph, depending on the ground. As they pass through their covering force, the tanks begin to fire, not so much with a view to hitting anything, but for the psychological effect and to keep the defenders pinned down. On arrival at their objectives, some tanks drive straight through to the far side of the objective, while others assist their infantry in mopping-up operations. The infantry does not usually dismount until they arrive at the objective, when they fan out and use tommy guns extensively.
- Phase V: When the attack is successful the covering force moves forward into the captured area to stiffen the defence. The tanks are usually withdrawn and serviced near what has now become their rear area.

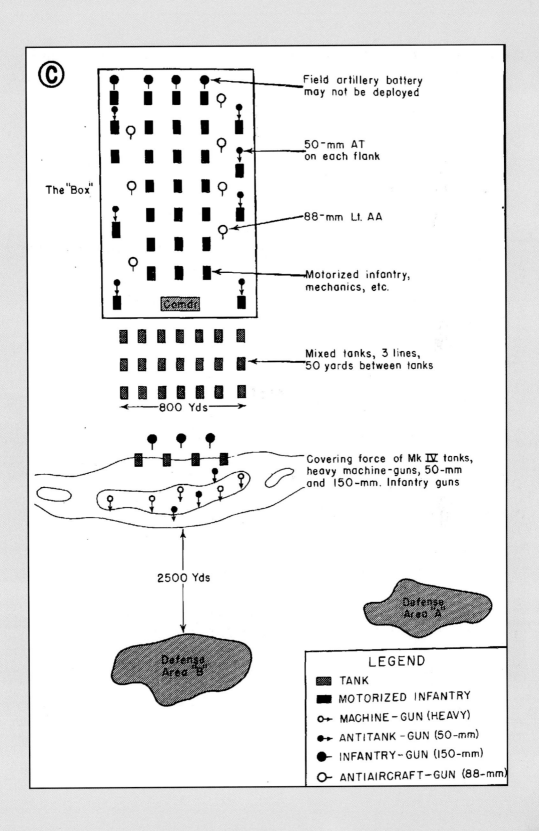

Ⓒ

Field artillery battery
may not be deployed

50-mm AT
on each flank

The "Box"

88-mm Lt. AA

Motorized infantry,
mechanics, etc.

Comd

Mixed tanks, 3 lines,
50 yards between tanks

← 800 Yds →

Covering force of Mk Ⅳ tanks,
heavy machine-guns, 50-mm
and 150-mm. Infantry guns

2500 Yds

Defense
Area "A"

Defense
Area "B"

LEGEND

▨ TANK

■ MOTORIZED INFANTRY

O→ MACHINE-GUN (HEAVY)

●→ ANTITANK-GUN (50-mm)

● INFANTRY-GUN (150-mm)

O— ANTIAIRCRAFT-GUN (88-mm)

In the early days after the invasion, Russian intermediate and lower command was very inexperienced. Tank losses were so high that replacements arrived directly from the factories, with mechanics or inadequately trained soldiers as drivers, and were then dispatched into combat right off the railway cars. By the time of Stalingrad, however, the Russian forces were more experienced and it was the Germans who came off worse as this Panzer graveyard at Peskovatka, on the Volga north of the city, attests.

3 The Eastern Front

The battles on the Eastern Front were some of the largest military confrontations in history, fought with such ferocity that they accounted for almost half the total deaths of the war – over 30,000,000 people, many of them civilians. On 22 June 1941, the Germans launched Operation Barbarossa, unleashing three massive army groups against their erstwhile Soviet partners. As in the invasions of Poland and France, the Panzers spearheaded the assault, with the front line extending 2,000 miles from the Baltic to the Black Sea. The Red Army retreated everywhere and lost more than 3,000 tanks. By the autumn the Germans had advanced 550 miles, occupied half a million square miles of Soviet territory, inflicted 2.5 million casualties and taken over one million prisoners. But it wasn't enough. The euphoria of those first easy victories and fast progress evaporated as winter set in and the Nazis failed to take Moscow, instead being pushed back and drawn into an increasingly desperate war of attrition, to be slowly worn down by the seemingly endless reserves that the USSR could produce to replace the whole armies that it lost.

Over almost four years, from 22 June 1941 to 25 May 1945, a series of titanic battles took place. Moscow (2 October 1941–7 January 1942) involved 3,500,000 combatants and 6,000 tanks; Leningrad (8 September 1941–27 January 1944) over 1,600,000 combatants; the most bloody of all, Stalingrad (23 August 1942–2 February 1943) involved over 2,200,000 soldiers and countless civilians; Kursk (5 July–23 August 1943) nearly 3,000,000 men and 8,000 tanks; and finally Berlin (16 April–2 May 1945) with over 3,500,000 combatants. In a such cauldron of combat, AFV developments and tactics were thrashed out and tested to extinction.

The Germans were as disconcerted when they met the KV-1 as they were when they first saw with the T-34; its heavy armour proved impervious to anything but their 88mm guns. It was armed with a 76mm M1941 ZiS-5 main gun – a modified version of that used in the T-34/76 – and the main differences between the two tanks were the KV-1's heavier armour, which made it slower, and a roomier but more expensive turret, making the main gun operation easier. The KVs were designed for infantry support rather than the T34's tank-fighting role and were made from 1939 until 1943.

The T-34 was the most-produced tank of the war and a contender for the best. Its sloping armour, powerful engine, efficient suspension and wide tracks made it deeply influential and it soon became the mainstay of Soviet armoured forces. It was armed with the high velocity 76.2mm F-34 main gun in a hexagonal turret, but because there were several manufacturers of the turrets across the USSR there was quite a bit of variation. Over the period January 1944 to April 1944 the T-34/76 m1942/3 was replaced by the T-34/85 at the three main T-34 production plants. The T34/85 was an upgunned response to the new German 88mm-armed PzKpfw V Panther and PzKpfw VI Tiger I which were appearing on the battlefield by 1943 and against which the T34/76 struggled. The T-34/85 had a new three-man turret and was armed firstly with the 85mm D-5 (a converted 85mm 52-K anti-aircraft gun) and then with the similar 85mm ZiS-53 or ZiS-S-53 gun, both of which were simpler, easier to operate and gave a higher rate of fire.

Although deservedly famous the T-34 was not without its faults, in design, manufacture and usage – up to 40% of its losses were operational rather than in combat but it still sustained more combat losses than most other tanks because of the build numbers. The early versions of 1941–43 were often badly made with a transmission prone to break down, poor armour welds, an engine that was sensitive to dust, an air-filtration system that never worked properly and tracks that used to regularly fall apart. The original turret was cramped and could only fit two, with the commander having to seek targets and aim and fire the gun simultaneously. The sloped turret constricted space and limited the amount of ammunition capable of being carried and the electrical mechanism for rotating it was weak. Initially, only one in ten T-34s – those belonging to company commanders – were actually equipped with a radio while every German tank had one. The rest of the Russian tank crews in each company signalled with flags. The Germans soon learnt to recognise and target the command tanks.

Russian tank tactics often contributed to the high losses they sustained, along with poor crew training and leadership. Overextended spearheads were surrounded, cut off and destroyed regularly, but tanks were encouraged to penetrate deeply without infantry support and fight for as long as they could. They were sometimes used bunched together en masse in suicidal charges – often with the deliberate intention of ramming an enemy and negating both vehicles. Despite this, like the M4 Sherman, it was produced in such numbers (over 57,000 of all variants were made during the war) that the combat losses were more than replaced. Faults were continuously corrected, production simplified and tactics developed that ensured its survival and prosperity.

The T-34/85 entered mass production in early 1944 and about 11,800 were produced in that year alone. It was heavily involved in Operation Bagration – the summer offensive that destroyed the bulk of the German army on the Eastern Front. By the end of the year it outnumbered older versions. Its high silhouette and broad turret were a disadvantage especially when attacked from the side, but the high-velocity and range of its 85mm gave it a powerful punch.

Tank battles against Japan in the 1930s taught the Russians lessons. The BT-5s (**Above**) and BT-7s performed well although they were vulnerable to antitank teams close-in. Soviet tank designers began to work on a new approach which led to the T-34 (**Below**). Its turret was located well forward to permit their own tank infantrymen to use it as a shield while riding atop and so provide local infantry protection. However, as a German report noted: 'every provision has been made to prevent unwelcome riders from getting aboard: a lack of external fittings, tools, sharp projections, etc., serves the double purpose of eliminating hand grips for enemy hitchhikers and the chance that a fire bomb or other missile could lodge on the tank. The mudguards are narrow so that tank hunters who seek to jump aboard run the risk of being caught in the track. As a further protective measure for the crew, the hatch in the top of the turret is so constructed that it cannot be opened from the outside. A special tool is required to open the hatch from the inside.' In later years the T-34 was equipped with ropes and other handholds to assist tank desant riders, particularly as the tank-hunting teams were equipped with Panzerfausts.

At the heart of the Russian armoured force that overran the German armies on the Eastern Front, the T-34 was a real all-purpose tank. With wide tracks and low silhouette, its performance in Russian terrain was frequently superior to that of German tanks, particularly with respect to cross-country mobility – German generals such as the influential Guderian thought it superior to German vehicles. The early models had their problems – initially, mechanical (particularly the clutch and transmission); certainly tactical (the commander had too much to do and lack of radios meant that tactical control was poor); and the calibre of gun was too small. Heavy losses in 1941 forced improvements that meant the M1943 was better armoured and had better fuel and ammunition capacity but it would take the T-34/85 before the upgunning gave the T-34 parity with the PzKpfw IV and StuGs.

Above: A late war development, the ISU-122 had an A-19S 122mm main gun. With 90mm/3.5in of front and side armour, 120mm/4.7in on the gun shield, it was a powerful heavyweight that proved a useful tank destroyer. Its companion ISU-152 was more effective as an assault gun.

Below: Tank desant is a useful way of transporting troops quickly and can help ensure tank-infantry cooperation – but it is a dangerous tactic: the men on the back make easy targets.

Introduced in mid-1943, around seven million Panzerfaust single-use weapons were manufactured during the war. Most were Panzerfaust 60s which had a range of 60m and could defeat 150mm of armour. It proved hugely successful in the last weeks of the war.

In the urban warfare that took place as the Allies entered Germany, a new threat emerged: the use by often untrained young defenders of the Reich of the Panzerfaust – a one-man, single-use, pre-loaded launch tube firing a high explosive antitank (HEAT) warhead that created massive internal spalling, killing the crew and destroying equipment. To cope with this crews took to improvising outer layers of protection on top of the tank's armour, even using welded bed frames.

The IS series was developed to succeed the KV heavy tank on which it was based, with thicker armour and a heavier main gun to counter the German Tigers and Panthers, but also to be used as a breakthrough tank firing HE munitions against entrenchments, antitank guns and bunkers. Based on a modified KV chassis, it kept the KV suspension together with the standard Model V-2 12-cylinder diesel engine, but by lowering the driving sprockets, idlers and return rollers and modifying the hull roof, space was made for a larger turret ring. The original IS-1 had an 85mm main gun, whereas the IS-2 mounted a massive 122mm A19 main gun fitted with a double-baffle muzzle-brake, whose two-part shells were so large only 22 could be carried at a time. It was also armed with three 7.62mm Degtyarev MGs – one coaxial with the main gun and two in ball mounts: one in the hull front and the other in the rear of the turret.

The SU-152 was a fully enclosed 152mm gun-howitzer built originally onto the KV-1S tank chassis but when that vehicle gave way to the new IS tanks, their chas-

Another Russian monster, the KV-2 heavy artillery tank was armed with a 152mm howitzer. It wasn't a great marriage, the turret being too heavy and making traversing difficult. Only 300 were built. It was designated PzKpfw KV-II 754(r) in German service and this one looks as if its been used for target practice!

sis was used instead for the now renamed ISU-152, which began production in December 1943.

German improvements

The PzKpfw IV was the most-produced German tank of the war after the PzKpfw III, with some 8,500 of all versions built. Variants included the Sturmgeschütz IV assault gun, the Jagdpanzer IV tank destroyer, the Wirbelwind self-propelled flak gun and the Brummbär self-propelled heavy assault gun. Robust and reliable, it saw service in all combat theatres and received continuous upgrades and design modifications – chiefly increases in armour thickness and the size of its main gun. The Ausf J was the final model of the series. Its survival was down to Guderian, who was reinstated as *Generalinspekteur der Panzertruppen* (Inspector of Tank Troops) in February 1943 after the fall of Stalingrad, making improvements and corrections that increased tank production. Guderian fought to retain the PzKpfw IV despite being outclassed by the Panther and Tiger and Russian tanks because the troops were so familiar with it and it was much more reliable.

The Panther was the German response to the Russian T-34 and was rushed into combat in July 1943 in the Battle of Kursk. As a result early versions were mechanically unreliable and often recalled for modifications and the Panther's first appearance was a disappointment. However, once these had been sorted out it went on to earn a deadly reputation as a defensive weapon, with its long-barrelled 75mm Kwk 42 L/70 main gun and a killing range at 2,000 yards. Its distinctive sloping armour was as a direct result of the T-34 and increased its overall effectiveness. The Ausf G was the final production model and was produced in larger numbers than previous versions, from March 1944 until the end of the war. Ausf G improvements included thicker side armour of 50mm and the modification of the gun mantlet's bottom edge from a circular profile to a

Above: The Panther was one of the best tanks of the war. Its wide tracks gave it low ground pressure, so it had a good cross-country performance. Some 6,000 were built in three versions (Ausf D 842, Ausf A 2,200 and Ausf G 2,961).

Below: The Flakpanzer IV Wirbelwind (whirlwind) SP AA gun married a quad 2cm Flak 38 with a PzKpfw IV chassis. It was effective both in its intended role and against ground targets. Around 100 were converted from the PzKpfw IV.

wedge shape. This eliminated a lethal weakness in the original curved design of the mantlet that enabled a deliberate frontal shot to deflect straight down through the thin driver's hatch deck armour plating, killing the driver instantly and brewing up the tank.

Tigers were primarily assigned to independent heavy tank battalions of 45 tanks each (on paper) that the high command parcelled out to help out in particularly tough battles. Originally designed for spearheading attacks, it was on the defensive that the Tiger really excelled. Hull down or hidden, it earned a fearsome reputation with a spectacular kill ratio of ten to one using its lethal 88mm Kwk 36 gun. However, it was rushed out early, its size and weight gave it problems with transportation and bridge-crossing, its tracks had a tendency to jam in mud or icy weather, it was finicky to maintain and it had a high fuel consumption. This meant that a Tiger battalion very rarely went into combat anywhere near full strength and losses from breakdowns halved the vaunted kill ratio. They were also slow and expensive to build – 1,347 were made between August 1942 and August 1944, after which it was phased out in favour of the Tiger II.

The Henschel-made Tiger II (aka the King Tiger) had thick sloping armour up to 185mm at the front and was armed with the long-barrelled 88mm Kwk 43 L/71 whose range was well beyond that of any enemy tank. Fortunately for the Allies, the Henschel factory was continually bombed and only about 500 were produced. Initial automotive problems were ironed out thus improving its reliability and for such a behemoth it had good tactical mobility, but could be destroyed in flanking ambushes by both Soviet T-34/85 and IS-2 tanks, and ISU-122 assault guns.

The evolution of Russian 'Deep Battle' doctrine*

When the Germans first burst Blitzkrieg upon the world it was entirely successful because there was nothing in the old forms of warfare to counter it. To do so required the evolution of new equipment and tactics that had to be learnt the hard way through trial by combat. However, Blitzkrieg was an expensive form of warfare to wage, requiring air superiority, mobile armour, artillery and infantry formations, and massive amounts of fuel and ammunition constantly supplied to keep an attack going. Success extended these vulnerable supply lines.

By 1943 the USSR had finally evolved the methods – learnt at great cost – with which to blunt Blitzkrieg. With its troops better trained, equipped and experienced the Red Army now deployed in much greater depth using a layered approach, so that a breakthrough would hit still more prepared defence lines, bristling with massed antitank guns and supported by infantry and artillery. Reserves of armour behind the front line were used to choke off an attack with flanking strikes or completely envelop it with a reversed pincer counterattack of their own. Finding these other layers

* This section makes heavy use of material from Connor, *Analysis of Deep Attack Operations*.

Above: The Tiger saw extensive use on the Eastern Front, with eight independent heavy tank battalions (sPzAbts) and elements of three SS-Panzer divisions (Leibstandarte, Das Reich and Totenkopf) and the army's Grossdeutschland Division. Note the size of the tracks and the **Zimmerit** applied over hull and mantlet.

Below: One of the best-known Tigers in the world, turret number 131 is today the only running Tiger and has been housed at Bovington Tank Museum since the early 1950s. Hit a number of times by the accurate shooting of B Squadron 48RTR on 24 April 1943, it was – unusually – abandoned by its crew (from sPzAbt 504) and captured. It provided the Allies with an intact example of the Tiger and was shown to both the king and Winston Churchill before being transported to England. Note the British First Army crest at left rear.

With industrial equipment and workforce relocated east, the city of Chelyabinsk was dubbed 'Tankograd'. By 1944 over 60,000 workers had been gathered there to build tanks. Massive economies of scale caused the production price to fall from 269,000 rubles to just 135,000, and man-hours to descend from 9,000 hours to eventually just 3,200 hours per tank. They built the KV series (as here), T-34/76 and -34/85, IS series, and SU-85. It was awarded with numerous patriotic honours for its work.

and avoiding attacking into such prepared kill zones forced the Germans to feint and constantly shift their forces looking for a weak spot to focus on. As the campaign progressed they no longer had guaranteed air superiority and gradually lost it to the Soviets, making their own armour much more vulnerable. As the tide turned and the Soviet version of Blitzkrieg – the Deep Battle doctrine – used in conjunction with deception (*maskirovka*) became more successful, whole German armies were kept off balance, isolated and then destroyed. It was right and proper that the western Allies left the Soviets to take Berlin, for they had truly paid the blood price.

Mikhail Tukhachevsky was a casualty of Stalin's purges of the Russian officer class. His Deep Battle theories were based on a close partnership of armour, artillery, infantry and air assets supported by strong reserves. Ahead of his times, he had an able proponent of his ideas, Georgi Zhukov, who put his theories into practice brilliantly against the Japanese in 1939 at the Battle of Khalkhin Gol. Like his British contemporary Montgomery, Zhukov became known for his build-up of numerical superiority, his careful logistical preparations and use of deception before an air and artillery bombardment was followed by an all-arms attack spearheaded by armour. The key to the Deep Battle concept was sustainability and longer-term goals. At Stalingrad, first the Germans' attack was slowed in the city and pummelled to a standstill. Next massive bombardments prepared for huge encircling pincer attacks that trapped German Sixth Army. Holding off rescue attempts, artillery pounding von Paulus's trapped men, the Russian forces squeezed until the remaining 90,000 men surrendered.

At Kursk, the German armoured thrust was slowed by the massive antitank defences – over 6,000km of trenches fronted by mines and wire defended by antitank guns and 20,000 artillery pieces – then held with large reserve forces plugging any holes that appeared, before Zhukov's counterattack took place after a huge artillery bombardment. He had held back three-quarters of his armour and 3,000 aircraft for this phase and while it proved impossible to encircle Fourth and Ninth Panzer Armies, the Russian attack drove the Germans back, taking the initiative and starting the advance to Berlin.

Offensively, the key to the use of tank forces in the Deep Battle was to create space through the depth of the enemy's position. Thus, assault rifle divisions, reinforced as necessary by a tank brigade, were expected carry out operations to the depth of the enemy's tactical defences. As soon as it was clear that the enemy's defences were crumbling, larger tank forces were committed to attack in the enemy's rear while the assault divisions might still be fighting their way through the tactical defences.

These larger Soviet force structures were organized to allow them to carry their operations progressively further into the enemy's rear. The tank corps could carry about 100km into the rear; the tank army or cavalry-mechanised group (CMG) could carry about 200km into the enemy's rear before it would need support. Moreover, the doctrine allowed these formations to run without maintaining connection with their following combined arms or rifle armies. Thus, the encirclement at Vitebsk was made by tank brigades and forward detachments, while that at Bobruisk was made by tank corps. However, the encirclement of Minsk, 250km deep, could not have been made without the CMG or tank army. More remarkably, those formations still had enough combat power to continue operations for another 150–200km, past Vilnius and Baranovichi, before they were used up.

Russian troops travel on the back of T-34s. For the first two winters of the war in the east the Russians had the advantage because the T-34 was better on snow and mud than its German equivalents. It also had an engine starting system that worked in the coldest conditions.

Russian tank tactics against German tanks

[From *Tactical and Technical Trends* 16, 14 January 1943]

a. Manner of conducting fire for the destruction of enemy tanks
(1) While conducting fire against enemy tanks, and while manoeuvring on the battle-field, our tanks should seek cover in partially defiladed positions.
(2) In order to decrease the angle of impact of enemy shells, thereby decreasing their power of penetration, we should try to place our tanks at an angle to the enemy.
(3) In conducting fire against German tanks, we should carefully observe the results of hits, and continue to fire until we see definite signs of a hit (burning tanks, crew leaving the tank, shattering of the tank or the turret). Watch enemy tanks which do not show these signs, even though they show no signs of life. While firing at the active tanks of the enemy, one should be in full readiness to renew the battle against those apparently knocked out.

b. Basic types of German tanks and their most vulnerable parts
The types of tanks most extensively used by the German army are the following: the PzKpfw 38, the PzKpfw III, and the PzKpfw IV. The German SP Sturmgeschütz III has also been extensively used. In addition to these, the German army uses tanks of all the occupied countries; in their general tactical and technical characteristics, their arma-ment and armour, these tanks are inferior.

(1) Against the PzKpfw 38, fire as follows:
(a) From the front – against the turret and gun-shield, and below the turret gear case.
(b) From the side – at the third and fourth bogies, against the driving sprocket, and at the gear case under the turret.
(c) From behind – against the circular opening and against the exhaust vent. Remarks: In frontal fire, with armour-piercing shells, the armour of the turret may be destroyed more quickly than the front part of the hull. In firing at the side and rear, the plates of the hull are penetrated more readily than the plates of the turret.

(2) Against PzKpfw III tanks, fire as follows:
(a) From the front – at the gun mantlet and at the driver's port, and the machine gun mounting.
(b) From the side – against the armour protecting the engine, and the turret ports.
(c) From behind – directly beneath the turret, and at the exhaust vent. Remark: In firing from the front against the PzKpfw III, the turret is more vulnerable than the front of the hull and the turret gear box. In firing from behind, the turret is also more vulnerable than the rear of the hull.

The Russo-German agreement meant that there was close cooperation between the two countries in the 1930s. This included the manufacture of weapons. The 1-K 37mm antitank gun for example, was developed by Rheinmetall and similar to the Pak 35/36. The 53-K 45mm model 1937 (as here) followed on, 37,354 units being built 1937–43.

Russian tank hunters armed with grenades, Molotov cocktails and satchel charges forced a closer cooperation between German tanks and infantry.

(3) Against the self-propelled assault gun, fire as follows:

(a) From the front – against the front of the hull, the driver's port, and below the tube of the gun.

(b) From the side – against the armour protecting the engine, and the turret.

(c) From behind – against the exhaust vent and directly beneath the turret.

(4) Against the PzKpfw IV, fire as follows:

(a) From the front – against the turret, under the tube of the gun, against the driver's port, and the machine gun mounting.

(b) From the side – at the center of the hull at the engine compartment, and against the turret port.

(c) From behind – against the turret, and against the exhaust vent. Remarks: It should be noted that in firing against the front of this tank, the armour of the turret is more vulnerable than the front plate of the turret gear box, and of the hull. In firing at the sides of the tank, the armour plate of the engine compartment and of the turret, is more vulnerable than the armour plate of the turret gear box.

Vulnerability of Tiger tanks

[From *Tactical and Technical Trends 40*, 16 December 1943
(as published in *Soviet Artillery Journal*)]

Tank mobility depends upon its suspension but these are all vulnerable to shells of all calibres. Firing armour-piercing shells and HE shells at the sprocket, idler and tracks will often disable a tank. Also use AT grenades and mines. If movable mines are used, attach three or four of them to a board and draw the board, by means of a cord or cable, into the path of an advancing tank.

There are two armour plates on each side of the tank. The lower plate is partly covered by the wheels. This plate protects the engine and the fuel tanks which are located in the rear of the hull, directly beyond and over the two rear wheels.

Fire at the lower plates with armour-piercing shells from 76mm, 57mm and 45mm guns. When the fuel tanks are hit, the vehicle will be set on fire. Another method of starting a fire is to pierce the upper plates on the sides of the tank, thus reaching the ammunition compartments and causing an explosion.

The rear armour plate protects the engine as well as giving additional protection to the fuel tanks. Shells from AT guns, penetrating this armour, will disable the tank.

The turret has two vision ports and two openings through which the tank crew fire their weapons. The commander's cupola has five observation slits. There are two sighting devices on the roof of the front of the tank, one for the driver, the other for the gunner. Also, in the front of the tank there is a port with a sliding cover.

The turret is a particularly important and vulnerable target. Attack it with HE and armour-piercing shells of all calibres. When it is damaged, use AT grenades and incendiary bottles (Molotov cocktails).

There is a 10mm slit all around the base of the turret. AT gun and heavy MG fire, effectively directed at this slit, will prevent the turret from revolving and thus seriously impair the tank's field of fire. Furthermore, hits by HE shells at the base of the turret may wreck the roof of the hull and put the tank out of action.

The tank's air vents and ventilators are under the perforations in the roof of the hull, directly behind the turret. Another air vent is in the front part of the roof, between the two observation ports used by the radio operator and the driver. Use AT grenades and incendiary bottles against these vents.

VULNERABILITY OF TIGER TANKS

Fire at the gun

Fire at the gas-tank

Use all weapons

Use all weapons

Use guns of all calibers

Use guns of all calibers

Above: This optimistic appreciation of the Tiger's weak points was originally produced in Russian. In many ways the weakest part of the Tiger was its overlapped wheel arrangement: *Schachtellaufwerk*. Govind Chavan summed it up well: 'an engineer's dream and a tank crew's nightmare.' A smoother ride but replacing wheels could involve removing lots of overlapping ones. On top of that, mud and detritus often got jammed between them.

Opposite: Two Tigers from sPzAbt (Fkl) 301 knocked out by 5th Battalion, King's Own Scottish Borderers at Waldfeucht, Germany. The antitank platoon responsible was under the command of Captain Robin Hunter, who won an MC for his display of bravery and command.

Infantry Cooperation with Tanks
[From *The German Motorized Infantry Regiment*]

When motorised infantry units have to clear a way for tanks through obstructed country, they attack on foot in advance of the tanks. Their object is, by constant concentration of their forces, to force a breach rapidly in the enemy main line of resistance and make lanes for the tanks. Engineers will be placed under command of the forward attacking companies.

The first objective is the far side of the tank-proof ground. When this is reached, the motorised infantry must push on to keep the exits open for the following tanks.

If motorised infantry and tanks have to attack simultaneously, the task of the infantry is to produce the maximum fire power of all weapons at the decisive moment by adopting a broad attacking formation. The main concentration of fire will be on the antitank weapons, to allow the tanks to gain ground quickly. Before the enemy position is assaulted, natural and artificial obstacles to the front will be cleared. The assistance of engineers will usually be necessary for this task.

The attack is carried out on foot. After the enemy has been disabled by the fire of the tanks, the motorised infantry will assault the enemy position. Mobile reserves on vehicles will be held ready to follow up and exploit rapidly a successful tank attack.

If the motorised infantry units have orders to follow the tanks on foot and to break through the enemy position immediately behind the tanks, they must take advantage of the disablement of the enemy, caused by the fire from the tanks, to make a determined assault. The same applies when tanks are sent through motorised infantry to help in their advance. Infantry units utilize the time before the tank attack to prepare themselves for the common battle.

The fire of all weapons must support the tanks by concentrating on the enemy antitank weapons.

While the tanks engage the enemy's attention, commanders must spur their men forward for the assault. Some of the heavy weapons (especially those on self-propelled mountings) and armoured carriers, join the tanks and move forward rapidly to alternative positions.

When, in collaboration with the tanks, the enemy antitank weapons have been accounted for, mobile reserves of motorised infantry advance, keeping in close contact with the tanks. The vehicles of the dismounted troops are moved up. Every unit entrucks on the battlefield and follows the tanks independently.

If tanks are put under command of motorised infantry to prevent an enemy recovery or to destroy particularly troublesome pockets of resistance, they must only be employed *en masse;* their offensive power must not be split up. They will clear the way for the infantry by short advances with limited objectives and in close cooperation with the infantry.

If the ground favours an attack by tanks and if no tank obstacles have been detected inside the enemy main line of resistance, the task of the motorised infantry units will usually be to follow the tank attack. They will remain on vehicles behind the tanks so that they can quickly exploit the success of the tanks. Narrow and deep formations, will be the rule, in order to avoid as far as possible the effects of enemy artillery fire and to retain a mobile reserve in rear of the foremost units. Pockets of resistance and defense areas which the tanks have not reduced will be dealt with as en- countered. For this, dismounting may be necessary. The remaining infantry will continue to follow up the tank attack in their vehicles. Contact with the tanks must never be lost.

Antitank troops will, as a rule, be used for the protection of an open flank.

Norway 1940: infantry and tanks working together. Norway had no tanks, and the Germans had few – the *Panzer Abteilung zur besonderen Verwendung 40* (Tank Battalion For Special Duties 40) formed on 8 March at Putloss in Schleswig-Holstein, three light companies assigned from three Panzer divisions: 3rd (probably 5th Panzer Regiment), 4th (36th Panzer Regiment) and 5th (15th Panzer Regiment). Some 50 tanks went to Norway: 30 PzKpfw Is, 15 PzKpfw IIs and 5 kleiner Panzerbefehlswagen Is followed by 3 NbFz PzKpfw VI heavies and 7–10 PzKpfw III mediums.

The US Army's *Armored Force Field Manual FM 17–10* of 1942 was superseded by *FM 17–100* on 15 January 1944. Both clearly state the role of the armoured division, the latter saying: 'its primary role is in offensive operation against hostile rear areas.' In *Military Review* Jan 1946, Lt Col Albin F. Irzyk, commander of 8th Tank Bn in 4th Armored Division reiterated this doctrine: 'In discussing tanks, many forget that the tank is not a vehicle built primarily to fight other tanks. Rather, its mission above all others is to get into the enemy's rear areas, to disorganize him, to destroy supply and communications, and generally to wreck havoc there.' This doctrine proved decisive in France (see page 91) and, to an extent, in Sicily – both times, incidentally, involving Patton. However, it was not possible to use tanks for exploitation in Italy because the Germans withdrew in good order from defensive line to defensive line. The only – albeit brief – opportunity for this sort of exploitation was after the fall of the Gustav Line, when Mark Clark went for the glory of liberating Rome rather than attempt to exploit the German retreat. Until the final stages of the Italian campaign in 1945, there would not be a simlar opportunity. Here Fifth Army M4A1s are greeted by white flags as they enter an Italian town.

4 Sicily and Italy

Following the conclusion of the North African campaign the Allies held a meeting in Casablanca and disagreed about what to do next. The Americans wanted to concentrate on an invasion of France and get the war over with, but the British didn't think it was yet feasible. US troops had only just begun to be blooded and a lot more practice and experience were required to take on the battle-hardened Germans in defended positions. In the end a compromise was reached – the Normandy landings were set for a later date and a stepping stone approach to Italy from Sicily was selected for the Allied forces currently in the Mediterranean theatre. This would keep Stalin appeased by opening another front, tie down German resources and, it was hoped, knock Italy out of the war. By and large these aims were achieved, but in reality the differences between the Allies would confuse the issue.

The landings in Sicily and Italy did much to prepare the Allies for the Normandy landings but the exceptionally difficult terrain would make the Italian campaign a very 'tough gut' rather than a 'soft underbelly'. In fact it would turn out to have the highest casualty rates of the whole war for the western Allies. It didn't help that the preparations for D-Day took precedence in resources and manpower, with some of the most experienced units being steadily syphoned off and that, later, more of the better troops were taken for the landings in Southern France. The Americans viewed Italy as a secondary theatre after the fall of Rome and it is surprising that the Allies made as much progress as they did, particularly after their main chance to crush the opposition disappeared as Mark Clark went for the glory of being first into Rome rather than attempting to trap the German forces streaming back from the fall of the Gustav Line.

The terrain precluded the unimpeded use of armour in Italy, which was often reduced to piecemeal supporting roles. The troops assembled were probably the most international of all Allied forces – British and Commonwealth, American, Canadian, Free French, South African, Polish, Australian, Brazilian, New Zealand, Greek, Belgian, Czechoslovak as well as some Italian royalists and partisans. Facing them was the German Army Group C, including two Tiger battalions.

Until the Normandy landings Operation Husky's invasion of Sicily was the largest amphibious operation in history, with some landings strongly opposed. 600 US, British and Canadian tanks were eventually disembarked – the bulk of them Shermans, which by now equipped all the Allied forces. The Axis possessed around 260 tanks, the Italians about 100 Semovente SP guns and ancient French Renaults; the Germans (Hermann Göring Panzer Division and 15th Panzergrenadier Division) about 150, mainly PzKpfw IIIs and IVs but also a unit with around 17 Tigers. The only real concerted use of Axis armour occurred on D+1, when the Hermann Göring Division attacked the US landing at Gela, almost pushing the Americans back into the sea until defeated by the combined firepower of artillery, bazookas, offshore naval bombardment from cruisers and destroyers and carpet bombing. The main operation for the US 2nd Armored Division was Patton's brief rapid dash for Palermo, while the British hit the German defence line centred on Mt Etna and were stalled. The rugged, mountainous terrain and primitive road network prevented any mass tank action, their role instead curtailed to occasional rapid pursuit but primarily just infantry support. Determined German resistance and the lack of integration between the US and British armies meant that it took six weeks before the Sicily was subdued, the victory soured by the escape of most Axis forces to the mainland. The Germans were puzzled by the Allied intention to march up the peninsula and reach the dead end of the Alps, but were perfectly content to run with it. In August 1943 Hitler sent Rommel into northern Italy with three corps headquarters, five infantry divisions and two Panzer divisions, making his headquarters at Lake Garda. Meanwhile, the defence of southern Italy was being overseen by the very able Field Marshal Albert Kesselring, who proceeded to give the Allies a two-year masterclass in a fighting withdrawal up the Italian mainland.

On 3 September 1943, a mere fortnight after the successful seizure of Sicily, the Allied invasion of Italy began. For this operation the 15th Army Group had been formed, containing the US Fifth and British Eighth Armies, the latter consisting of the British V, X and XIII Corps, 1st Canadian Corps and II Polish Corps.

In the end three simultaneous landings were made – the main one ('Avalanche') by US Fifth Army at Salerno, and two supposedly diversionary landings to tie down German forces by the Eighth – 'Baytown' aiming for Reggio de Calabria and 'Slapstick' for Taranto – 272 and 170 miles away respectively. Kesselring didn't contest either of these diversionary landings and so the Eighth had a long way to march up to the action. Meanwhile 'Avalanche' came very close to failure and required all available land, air and sea resources to maintain its beachhead against determined German Tenth Army counterattacks. The Americans had expected Italians not Germans. The grizzled veterans of 16th Panzer Division from the Eastern Front (equipped with 88 PzKpfw IVs, 42 Sturmgeschütz IIIs, 12 Wespe, 6 Hummel and 6 Grille SP guns) inflicted heavy casualties on the landing forces but eventually lost more than half of their tanks in the process to naval guns and bombers supporting the landing. Finally, after a fortnight of relentless combat and the arrival of the Eighth Army, the Germans withdrew to the southernmost of their defensive lines across the country.

US mobile artillery proved hugely effective in the desert and then in Sicily. The M7 howitzer motor carriage had a 105mm main armament and a gun crew of eight and was used by both American and British units (by whom it was called the Priest), although the latter eventually preferred to use the Sexton with a Canadian Ram or Grizzly chassis and a British 25pdr for ease of ammo resupply.

Italian SP artillery was stronger than its tanks, proving good enough for the Germans to incorporate into their inventory when Italy pulled out of the war. This is the Semovente da 90/53 mounting a 90mm gun on a M14/41 chassis. With an unarmoured gun platform it tended to be used from behind the lines rather than as a TD, its intended role.

If the Salerno landings had been hard what followed was worse. Fierce rearguard actions carried out by small forces maximising the potential of the landscape, bolstered with a series of in-depth defence lines continually blunted and held up the Allied advance. The German defence lines were constructed using slave labour and featured machine gun nests, casemates, bunkers, observation posts and artillery emplacements all supporting one another in a well-fortified in-depth network, protected by wire and thousands of mines. They also had gun turrets taken from old tanks atop a small metal or concrete sunken bunker, making them compact and easy to conceal. Chiefly PzKpfw Is and IIs and some Italian turrets were used, but from October 1943 Panther turrets were also incorporated. The two biggest fortified lines were the Gustav and the Gothic, both of which caused massive delays. Gustav featured the hellish, apocalyptic four-month battle of Monte Casino and the Gothic Line saw the largest battle of the Italian campaign with over 1,200,000 men participating.

The Germans proved elusive – cleverly concealed and exceptionally well organised in the mountainous terrain. The Allied infantry had to work its way slowly uphill and try to outflank these rearguard detachments, which then broke contact and withdrew to other prepared positions, demolishing bridges, culverts, tunnels, railroad tracks and trains, and laying mines as they went. Combat teams often consisted of just small infantry units operating with a minimum of support, while in autumn, winter and spring Allied armoured forces fought the terrain and the weather more than the enemy. Unable to deploy properly, they found it difficult to clear the villages and thickly wooded countryside.

The workhorse of the Allies was the Sherman, the backbone of most offensives from late 1942. Much has been said about its high silhouette (11ft off the ground), thin armour and propensity to burn when hit, but it was fast, rugged and reliable and its 75mm main gun could handle most Axis tanks except the Panther and Tiger, unless fighting in quantity. Crucially there were a lot of Shermans and, from 1944, the 76mm and 105mm (howitzer) armed versions became available, as well as the British modified Sherman Firefly (M4A4 or Sherman V), porting the excellent long-barrelled 17pdr main gun, and these improvements evened things up considerably. Another tank used by the British was the Churchill Mk IV NA75 – a modified variant similar to the Sherman Firefly, except this time an American 75mm main gun was put into a British tank. 200 of these were produced and saw service in Italy. Although slow, the Churchill reprieved itself with its climbing and sharp turning ability, enabling it to cope well with the difficult Italian terrain. Having armour thicker than the Sherman, Churchills were used to spearhead attacks and smash though defences with the faster Shermans then exploiting any breakthrough.

The Germans in theatre appreciated the Sherman for its cross-country and climbing ability as well as its speed and manoeuvrability. The grass is always greener: Allied crews wanted heavier tanks to cope with the heavy German armour they were coming across, while the Germans wanted lighter, faster ones but still keeping the same main guns. The Tiger had been seen in North Africa and the Panther began to be seen in Italy, but the Allies were unaware of the actual numbers being produced until statistical analysis of serial numbers from different parts of captured or destroyed German tanks revealed figures that were close to correct – and much higher than had been suspected: by February 1944, 270 Panthers were produced.

Both sides had some useful tank destroyers. The outstanding German ones were the Sturmgeschütz III and IV. The StuG III was produced in vast numbers up until the end of the war. It was based on the chassis of the PzKpfw III with a turretless armoured superstructure housing the powerful 7.5 cm StuK 40 L/8 main gun. The similar StuG IV was based on the PzKpfw IV, and also armed with the 7.5cm StuK 40 L/8.

The M18 Hellcat was the most effective US tank destroyer of the war with the highest kill to loss ratio of any US AFV, although its 76mm gun struggled against late war German tanks. It was famous for its speed but this was achieved at a sacrifice to its armour, which was paltry.

This Italian SP gun, the Semovente L. 40 da 47/32, married a Cannone da 47/32 antitank gun with an L 6/40 light tank chassis. It was typical of much of the Italian armour: undergunned and ineffective. It saw service in the German Army as the StuG L6 47/32 630(i).

Battle Lessons from a British Armoured Division
7th Armoured Division operations from North Africa to the River Volturno via Salerno, Mt Vesuvius and Naples

Document sent to US Staff College, Fort Leavenworth on 8 November 1943.

Prepared for Maj Gen George Erskine, CG 7th Armoured Division

General (referring to Platoon Training pamphlet)

You have rightly stressed 'manoeuvre in order to get control' which is of course vital and the age-old principle of fire and movement which is the basis of all tactics both armoured and unarmoured. I do feel however, that not enough stress is laid on gunnery. All our recent experience has shown that speed and accuracy in gunnery, in that order, are the most important things of the whole lot from the Troop Leader's and Tank Commander's point of view.

The second thing which you have not emphasised, and which is very nearly equally important, is the use of wireless. Complete familiarity, constant practice and brevity must be very highly developed in each commander. This has been amply proved during our operations in this country [Italy]. Every troop has been deployed practically the whole time and troops, even individual tanks, can seldom see each other. It is obvious from this that the whole control of the troop, squadron and regiment devolves on wireless and unless wireless training and discipline is first class, there will obviously be a shambles.

The only other things which I think should be stressed are map reading, choice of ground and an eye for country. This very close country is damned difficult for tanks, and choice of ground is vital.

Amphibious landings: Problems with loading

[Of the division's landings at Salerno] Owing to lack of space in the LSTs and lack of other shipping the infantry were left out by the Movements Staff. This was most unfortunate and might have had disastrous results. … Instead of landing on the evening of the 15th [September 1943] with a Bde Group ready at once to fight I had one Armd Regt, one Bty RHA, one Tp of RE and the transport of two Inf Bns.

There is no doubt that the LST is the perfect ship for the sea transport of an armoured division. The whole division was moved by this means except for the infantry of the Lorried Inf Bde. Personnel accompanied their vehicles which is very convenient and important – it simplifies embarkation and concentration. If men are separated from their vehicles and the landing is on an open beach it wastes much precious time joining them up.

Radio was important when tanks were dispersed and couldn't see each other and because of this wireless discipline was essential. The British had learnt to their cost that communications indiscipline provided German listening stations with vital tactical information.

A strong body of Divisional Police directed by the APM [Assistant Provost Marshal: 2IC Divisional Military Police] was invaluable. In spite of much transport landing at the same time for corps and other divisions it was easy to pick out and route correctly your own vehicles with your own police on the spot.

If a dry landing is possible it is a very great advantage not to have to waterproof. Waterproofing must be carefully done if it is done at all and it must be thorough. There is a tendency to slap grease and pitch everywhere and unless this is carefully supervised vehicles will be rendered unserviceable.

The design of military vehicles should take into account the possibility of having to be waterproofed. For instance, it is practically impossible to waterproof the petrol (radial) Sherman. The design of tanks should aim at the highest possible fording level since their weight for bridging purposes presents a most difficult problem and a ford is a far easier solution.

Tank-infantry cooperation
In close country tanks must have available more infantry to work with them than the one Motor Bn in the Armd Bde. The Motor Bn was just sufficient in open country. In close country there must be plenty of infantry for clearing, surrounding and searching villages and also for clearing thickly wooded country. The tanks themselves are much restricted to

roads and tracks if there is an abundance of ditches and tank obstacles. Tanks are remarkably blind when vines and trees just cover the turret. The probability of these conditions was appreciated and for this reason much training was carried out by each Armd Regt with Bns of 131 Infantry Bde. A technique was worked out by 131 Bde for such conditions assuming one Armd Regt under command. This was applied from CAVA to SOMA VASUVIANA and was most successful since it led to the capture of the crossings over the R SARNO at SCARFATI intact, opened the road to NAPLES and got the division round VESUVIUS. The training had been basically sound. The tanks play a predominant role until contact and thereafter a supporting role to the infantry. Success is dependent on a very intimate understanding between the tanks, the infantry and the artillery.

It is considered that the infantry in an Armoured Division is sufficient. The Divisional Commander can either lead with the Lorried Infantry Bde and some tanks (as was done up to SOMA VESUVIANA) and the infantry is then adequate but the pace after contact will be that of infantry on foot. Or the Divisional Commander can lead with the Armd Bde whose infantry may not prove sufficient unless augmented by the Lorried Infantry Bde. Infantry sent forward in such circumstances to work with the Armd Bde cannot be satisfactorily sent forward in 3-ton lorries – if they are sent in 3-ton lorries they will have to debuss well behind the tanks, they will have no wireless communication to the tanks and the object of quick working infantry in close cooperation with the tanks will not be achieved. The ability to send forward an infantry coy in semi-track Armoured White Scout Cars would be invaluable This coy would not require anything beyond the usual coy weapons since the supporting arms with the tanks and the tanks themselves would provide all that is required.

The solution offered is to mount one coy of each Lorried Infantry Bn in semi-track Armoured White Scout Cars. These cars should be on the establishment of the troop-carrying coy RASC which works with the Lorried Infantry Bde and should comprise one section of each transport platoon. The Coy and Pl Comds must have No 19 Wireless Sets so that the whole party can link on to the Armd Regt Comd's net – this is most important as the infantry must be fully in the picture of the battle the whole time.

Junior Leadership

In open country the more senior commanders can exercise control and give suitable directions and orders. In close country this is far more difficult. Much more responsibility is thrown on the junior leaders whose standard of tactical training must reach a very high standard. This standard will only be reached by constant attention and education by commanding officers. This education must be regarded as part of operations and not a matter which can be shelved until the next training period. Under the heading of leadership the training in recce duties is most important, particularly in the recce troops of the armd regts. The study must be appropriate to the immediate theatre of war.

Notes on the command and control of an armoured division

Both in the desert and in close country it has been found advisable to operate three HQs:

• Tac HQ This always includes the Comd, ADC, GII (Ops) and a LO. It is mounted in what happens to be the most suitable vehicles for the occasion. It is prepared to stay out indefinitely but it must be backed by a Main HQ for replenishment, replacement of batteries and written clerical work. It has no cipher personnel and can only keep continuous watch on the wireless by day. It must get onto a telephone by night. The LO always travels in a jeep (with a W/T set). There is also a small signal party in a White Scout Car carrying spare batteries, cable and charging plant. A three-ton lorry carrying replenishment fuel either accompanies or visits daily. The alternative means of conveyance of the Comd and his staff officers is drawn from a combination of the following vehicles.

(a) Command Grant fitted as an office with two wireless sets. It has good cross-country capabilities, is armoured and can follow where the tanks go.

(b) Cut down Grant [M3 medium] – same as Comd Grant but with a better view and more roomy – not suitable at night or in very inclement weather.

(c) Cut down Honey [M3 or M5 light]: there are three of these so that one can be loaned to CRA or CRE when required. These are very good recce vehicles – fast and handy with good cross-country ability. Fitted with two No 19 Sets.

The report emphasises the importance of motorised infantry in the armoured division. Usually this meant lorried infantry in the British/Commonwealth forces, although Universal carrier usage was also important (as here in the desert). The advent of the real APC came in Normandy as Canadian troops used 'defrocked' Priests (M7 GMCs without their guns) and turretless tanks.

(d) White Scout Car – fitted as an office – suitable for long distance road work.
(e) Two Jeeps each fitted to take a No. 19 Set.

Tac HQ moves about in accordance with the requirements of the battle usually near the Bde Comd most involved. The CRA may accompany it or attach himself to the leading Bde. The CRE generally moves during the day but joins up with Tac at night.

There is no need to put Tac on the telephone by day but at night it is always hoped to get a telephone to Main and this is usually done by placing Tac near a Bde HQ. This is necessary for several reasons (i) the signal personnel and staff are not sufficient to maintain continuous wireless watch; (ii) discussion of future plans by Comd with GI and A/Q is facilitated; (iii) discussion by the Comd with the Intelligence staff is often important and this is must for security reasons be done by telephone.

• Main HQ This is run during operations by the GSO I. It is the co-ordinating centre for the Comd's orders and decisions. It is also the receptacle for orders from above. It therefore includes the full staff of Ops, Intelligence, Signals, RA and RE. It has an air support tentacle if allotted to Div. It can operate on the move. The Div Comd is very dependent on his Main HQ, and can only function independently of it for a short time or with great loss of control and efficiency.

• Rear HQ This is run during operations by the AA and QMG. It includes all the administration staff and the heads of services. It can work on the move. All planning of the Comd is dependent on the administrative staffs and services being able to meet his requirements.

All HQs can be independent of buildings but in a country full of buildings, and when the weather is inclement, it is often convenient to make use of buildings and the hard standings adjacent to them. Siting HQs in wet weather is not easy and the dispersed methods of the desert are not suitable on wet and boggy fields. The location of HQ is important since it must be convenient to the control line and capable of developing good communications. The Comd and GI will be continually thinking out their next move.

Armoured Division tactics
The development of an advance
Sometimes the advance may go without pause or hindrance until the final objective is reached but if the enemy resists the advance he must be overcome. The first card to play is more artillery and that is why the Armd Div should always move in such a way that this card can be played in full and quickly. Medium arty well up behind the leading Bde will often make the enemy decide to quit. More and more arty is the best and

The armoured division denies ground to the enemy but should not be used to hold ground, Erskine opines. Tanks need to be mobile so that they can go where they are needed and not be forced into static defence. However, terrain makes a significant difference. In the desert, armour, such as these Lees and Shermans, can operate en masse. In Italy, as the *Historical Report of the 760th Tank Battalion for January 1944* summarises: 'Due to the nature of the terrain and the weather conditions . . . the employment of tanks en masse was not practicable. Movement was restricted to rearward ridge lines and cross-country movement was impossible. The most effective employment of tanks of this unit was in small groups used as accompanying guns in support of infantry . . . 500 to 1500 yards in rear where they have the protection of the infantry against antitank guns, where the heavy concentrations of artillery fire drawn by the tanks do not cause casualties among the infantry.'

surest answer to eject the enemy. The flanks must be found and any way of surrounding these must be exploited without delay. If the enemy has an intact front on a prepared position it may be that an Armd Div will not be able to penetrate his front or envelop his flank. It then becomes a matter for assault or large-scale manoeuvre. At this stage it is wise to get close enough to your enemy to observe him closely but not so close that you yourself are pinned to the ground. Infantry whose task will be to assault the enemy will have to get very close in order to develop their patrolling, and gain the most intimate knowledge of the enemy's defence and his dispositions. The Armoured Brigade at this stage should stand back sufficiently to maintain observation and retain the power of manoeuvre while the cross probing of the enemy's position is undertaken by the Lorried Infantry Brigade.

Holding ground
By its presence in any particular area an Armoured Division will deny this ground to the enemy. In this manner armour can hold ground but this is not an economical way of holding ground for any length of time. The same ground can be held far more effectively by ATk guns, infantry and Arty and if the need for holding ground is likely to continue for any length of time it is important that the ground should be taken over by a force

Infantry is a vital component of the armoured division – both in defence and in attack. In defence it needs to stand firm, holding ground until armour can help; in the attack it needs to work with armour to protect against antitank teams. As the 760th Tank Battalion report for January 1944 says, 'The presence of tanks in support of the infantry is a very great morale factor to the infantryman whether or not the tanks are actually giving effective support.'

of all arms, without armour, so that the armour can be released to play a more mobile role. In the first place the Armd Div can relieve itself with its Lorried Infantry Bde and restore mobility to the armour. Mobility is not restored to the armour in order that the armour can go away and have a rest. When mobility is restored to the armour the forces holding the ground in front of it can be sure of quick and rapid support at any threatened point. Without mobility of this kind armour will not dare move for fear of uncovering a vital point in the battlefield,

In defence
On ground where armour has any freedom of manoeuvre it can play an important and even vital part in the system of defence.

The system of defence must be built up without armour. That is to say the disposition must depend on ATk guns, infantry and arty and perhaps natural and artificial obstacles. Behind this screen the armour must be ready to move up and immediately strengthen the threatened point. This can usually be done by holding the amour centrally and having various alternative battle positions to which it can move. By judicious selection such positions are not difficult to find. The armour can quickly give depth to the defence and intervene in the battle. It does not matter to the armour whether the defence position is being attacked by infantry or armour or both – it is equally capable of dealing with either or both by day.

By night or during fog or mist its value is almost nil since the armour depends on its firepower to produce results and this cannot be developed in conditions of bad visibility.

It is very important that the infantry working with the armour should recognise that the armour is best used in this way. If the infantry are of weak morale and ask for tanks to stand close to them in defence before an attack has opened they must realise that it limits the scope of the armour to assist in strength at the threatened point when the attack of the enemy is developed. Infantry of high morale and good training will be quite happy to rely on their own resources and ATk guns to repel at least the first fury of an enemy attack.

The infantry must have had a reasonable time to prepare their defence system. Modern weapons enable the infantry to do this very well and very quickly. When tanks come up to support infantry they do so by using their weapons. The chief tank weapon is the 75mm and the main concern of the armour will be to find good hull-down positions from which to develop this weapon. Careful recces of all likely areas must be made.

Support of an infantry attack

The armoured division is not designed to support the infantry assault in a prepared position but in some ways and to some extent it can help. The enemy will defend himself against armour – that is to say he will stand behind a natural or artificial tank obstacle. The infantry will have the task of throwing him out of such position. The infantry will be able to do this with the assistance of properly coordinated and adequate artillery support. The greatest difficulty the infantry will meet is in overcoming the enemy's counterattack which must be expected within a few hours of their assault and which will include armour. The attacking infantry must get up their own supporting antitank weapons but this is often extremely difficult to do quickly and before the enemy counterattack develops. At this time the armoured division may be required to stand in with the assaulting infantry and help them to repel this type of counterattack until the infantry themselves have been able to bring up their own antitank weapons. At this time the armour often has to stand out in exposed and highly unsuitable positions to support the infantry. But this must be done until the infantry have put their defences in order.

Air support

The greatest blessing which the RAF can confer on an armoured division is immunity from the enemy's air. This gift is priceless since it enables the armoured division to move in a far closer and more compact manner than could be done if wide dispersion was necessary.

The armoured division can often clear enemy airfields and get them deloused and operational for the RAF. An armoured division, particularly when it appreciates the blessings of air superiority, will do everything in its power for the RAF who will be anxious to shin forward their landing grounds in pace with the army.

Tactical recce is vital in a fast moving battle and may often give the earliest clue to the enemy's intentions. The information must be received quickly and broadcast quickly.

Close bombing in support of the advance is a more difficult problem owing to the speed of the advance of the armour, the definition of the bomb line is often difficult and the tendency is to allow a little margin of error. The best results are obtained by directing the air force on targets found by the air outside the close support of the advance – this indirectly assists the armour very materially, Complicated arrangements for close bombing support do not work during a rapid advance and the type of thing which holds up the armour, such as the ATk gun, is almost impossible to spot on the ground sufficiently accurately to describe to the air. Therefore do not expect pin-point bombing but be grateful for the loosening effect of bombing further back which you may not even see.

Equipment of an armoured division

(a) Must be able to deal quickly and effectively with the unarmoured enemy and his vehicles including the ATk gun. For this purpose the machine gun and HE shell such as the 75mm is a very good answer.

(b) Must be able to take on the normal enemy armour on at least equal terms and have the means of dealing with monster tanks such as the Tiger.

(c) Must be kept down to Class 40 bridging, be capable of rail transport, be capable of loading on LCT and LST, and be amphibious or at least have a very high fording level.

(d) Radius of action approx 80–100 miles without refuelling.

(e) Maximum immunity from catching fire.

(f) Must be mechanically reliable and easy to maintain.

(g) The body of the tank should not so low that it is easily bellied and grounded.

(h) The equipment of the two Arty Regiments should be self-propelled and armoured.

(i) The ATk Regt must include SP ATk guns of the highest weight capable of knocking out the largest enemy tank at 1,500 yards or better. In fact a tank whose sole object is to destroy the largest enemy tank at the longest possible range. All the ATk guns should not be SP since in defence it must be possible to dig in the smaller type of ATk gun and form an inconspicuous ATk gun screen. The smaller type of ATk gun must be able to kill up to 600 yards. The proportion of small to large ATk guns and the number which should be SP will vary according to the enemy's superiority in the tank which is impervious to the gun mounted in our own tank.

(j) Fighting troops liable to operate closely with Armd Regts must themselves be conveyed in splinter-proof, bulletproof armoured vehicles. This applies to RE, motor infantry, and a proportion of the Lorried Infantry Bde.

(k) The Tank will be too large and slow to perform its own recce – a small tracked vehicle with speed, 100-mile radius, good cross-country performance, and low inconspicuous design will always be required for various recce duties. At present the Carrier Universal is used but this is not ideal.

(l) The ATk mine and the anti-personnel mine must be overcome by better methods of detection and destruction. Our own mine requires development to defeat detection.

(m) Development of methods of knocking out tanks from the air and counter action against this danger should be studied.

A heavily laden Sherman in Italy. 7th Armoured Division was most unhappy to have to relinquish its M4s and take up the Cromwell for the Normandy landings. It is said that some came close to mutiny – but their attitude was complicated by other factors, including their length of time in combat.

The Churchill was dismissed by the Germans, who captured a number in the 1942 raid on Dieppe. It wasn't fast but it could climb well, turn quickly, and was better armoured than many Allied vehicles. It also proved an excellent and adaptable platform for a range of 'Hobart's Funnies'.

5 Normandy to Germany

The Dieppe Raid, which took place on 19 August 1942, was an expensive disaster, but it taught the Allies many lessons – in particular, that trying to capture a heavily defended port was likely to fail and that specialist vehicles would be necessary to help attacking forces land and negotiate difficult coastal terrain as well the German strongpoints, obstacles and antitank defences that made up Hitler's Atlantic Wall. In early 1943 the British 79th Armoured Division, under the command of Maj-Gen Percy Hobart, had been given the responsibility to develop specialised vehicles and tactics to support the Allied troops for the D-Day landings on 6 June 1944. The distinctive and unusual vehicles that were produced became known as 'Hobart's Funnies' and the 79th, rather than operating as a single division, was distributed in smaller units across other the Allied divisions taking part in the beach landings and subsequent operations. The vehicles themselves were made by modifying existing AFVs: primarily Sherman, Churchill and Grant tanks. The Sherman Duplex Drive was an amphibious swimming tank that was used on all five beaches during D-Day, whereas the Sherman Crab was a mine flail. The Churchill was also fitted with either an anti-mine flail, a flamethrower (the Crocodile) or as an AVRE with a mine plough, a bunker-busting spigot mortar, fascines, a bobbin carpet layer (for tanks to drive over soft sand) or an ARK (armoured bridge carrier). The CDL (canal defence light) was a Grant fitted with a searchlight in its turret, to provide light during night operations or temporarily blind enemy forces. Although there were problems, primarily in the lack of training time and therefore confidence in these vehicles, they soon proved their worth in the assault phase of the invasion and continued to be invaluable afterwards in the progress across Europe to the German homeland.

Two new cruiser tanks were introduced in time for the invasion by the British: the Cromwell and the Centaur. The Cromwell was armed with the QF 6pdr (57mm) firing the new APDS round which could penetrate 100mm of steel armour at ranges of 1,000 yards (910m), but it could not fire HE. Its turret ring size precluded upgunning but eventually the main gun was bored out to 75mm so that it could fire unmodified US HE and AP ammunition. Because of its speed and low profile it was used in armoured reconnaissance or (along with Sherman 75s) supported by the heavier-gunned Sherman Firefly and Challenger. The Challenger was a Cromwell chassis modified to

The Churchill proved an adaptable frame for the range of 'Funnies', this one an AVRE armed with a 290mm Petard spigot mortar that could fire a 'Flying Dustbin' 26lb demolition charge some 80 yards. *Bulldog* is seen in Place du Cuirasse Courbet around D-Day as 3rd Division's carriers pass.

carry the same QF 17pdr as the Firefly, but in the end it was cheaper to convert existing Shermans than to produce a new tank and so only 200 were built. The Centaur was armed with the same main gun as the Cromwell (both were based on the previous Cavalier) and was another stop-gap design that would never fulfil its potential. Only specialised versions were used in combat. The Centaur IV was the definitive battlefield variant with a 94mm howitzer.

The Canadian Ram tank was only ever used as a training vehicle and was more successful modified – particularly as an armoured personnel carrier (the Kangaroo); without a turret as an ARV, as a flamethrower, ammunition carrier, artillery tractor and, when equipped with a 25pdr, the Sexton SP gun.

The Sherman was also upgunned. The M4A1(76)W was the first of the 76mm-armed series to be used by US troops themselves – the 76mm gun was produced from February 1944 and so was available in time for the Normandy landings and combat in NW Europe. The W (= wet) was an attempt to reduce the Sherman's propensity to brew up when hit. In fact moving the ammunition to the floor of the tank was more successful than the containers that surrounded them. These were filled with water, ethylene glycol and a rust inhibitor. The M4A1 carried 71 76mm main gun rounds, 35 of them (7 x 5-round racks) on the left side of the propeller shaft behind the driver; 30 (6 x 5-round racks) on the right side of the shaft behind the bow gunner and 6 rounds in an armoured ready rack at the loader's feet. The British also received it as the Sherman IIA but preferred the Firefly, armed with the QF 17pdr. Because of this, the British gave the M4A1(76)Ws to the Poles and other Commonwealth Allies fighting alongside them. To fit the larger gun the original M4 chassis required a new turret design that was cast in a single piece as was the hull and because of muzzle flash problems a muzzle brake was fitted in the M1A1C and later M1A2 versions. Subsidiary armaments included the usual coaxial .30 machine gun, a .50 machine gun mounted on top of the turret and another .30 machine gun in a hull ball turret in front of the assistant driver. It was powered by a Continental R975 C4 nine-cylinder radial engine with a top road speed of 30mph (48km/h) and a range of approximately 120 miles (193km).

The M10 was the most-produced US tank destroyer of the war and was in use right up to its end. It was based on a Sherman M4 chassis with an open-topped turret mounting a 3in (76.2mm) M7 Gun firing HE and AP rounds. There was also .50 M2HB Browning machine gun. It had a crew of five (commander, driver and three gun crew) and was powered by a General Motors 6046 diesel engine with a top road speed of 32mph (51km/h) and an operational range of 186 miles (300km). When first used in the Tunisian desert in 1943 the M10s could handle any German tanks that came their way and with their speed they were highly manoeuvrable and liked by their crews for the ease of observation and escapability. However, by late 1944 the M10's disadvantages had become more apparent. They were too thinly armoured and the open turret left the turret crew highly vulnerable – as evinced by their attrition rate in the battle for Europe. Armoured tops were improvised in an attempt to cope with threats from urban, bocage and forest environments where snipers, grenades, *Panzerschreck* and *Panzerfaust* teams began to take their toll. The M10's firepower now had little effect on the armour of the latest more heavily armoured Panthers and Tigers unless up very close and the hand-operated turret took two minutes to fully traverse.

The M10 was supplied to various Allied armies including the British and the Free French. The British called it the Wolverine and later modified it, adding a heavier 17pdr gun which made it a more potent tank destroyer, the 17pdr SP Achilles.

It's a very simple idea: you take bits of the German beach defences, cut them into points and weld them to a frame you can attach to the front of a tank. Then you have a device that can uproot a hedgerow, hitherto a serious obstacle. Whether they were quite as effective as modern writers would have you believe is debatable, but hats off to Sgt Curtis G. Culin III whose name is forever associated with them.

The Sexton was a British version of the Priest 105mm SP gun that had been provided originally by the USA, but with which they had operational problems mainly because the gun was not of a calibre used by Britain and required unique ammunition. Instead they had their own version made using firstly a Canadian Ram chassis based on the M3 Lee and then with the Sexton II using the chassis of the Canadian version of the Sherman M4 known as the 'Grizzly'. The Sexton mounted a British Ordnance QF 25pdr Mk II howitzer that had full elevation, a traverse of 25° left and 15° right with a range of 12,200m. It was intended for indirect fire support directed by forward observers. The six-man crew of driver, commander, radio-operator and the three-man gun crew all rode in the fighting compartment. The 86th (Hertfordshire Yeomanry) Field Regiment, RA began using their guns while still in their landing craft, continuing on the beach directed by forward observers far ahead with the advancing infantry.

Once the Allied bridgehead had been secured, a vast river of men, equipment and fuel were unloaded to keep the invasion supplied; by the end of August over two million men had been landed. Nevertheless the German forces held up the Allies for some seven weeks before the combination of overwhelming air superiority and resupply began to tell against their tenacious in-depth defence, while their critical armoured divisions in the west were consumed in the process, fed piecemeal into the line to shore it up. Although the Germans were experts in the art of fighting withdrawals, Hitler's constant interference was also crucial. His insistence that the bulk of German armour be held back until the exact point of invasion was confirmed, his refusal to let his commanders make tactical withdrawals when required and his most able commander Rommel being wounded and then implicated in the July plot and forced to commit suicide, ensured that the bulk of German forces employed in the defence of

British Sherman tank units in Normandy benefited from the arrival of the upgunned Firefly – which was doled out on the basis of around one a troop. It's the third tank here in front of a Sherman Crab, an M4A4 with a flail drum attached. It was used by three regiments under 30th Armd Brigade.

The thing the Cromwell did best was motor. Reliable if somewhat undergunned, it proved its worth in the drive to Antwerp. However, the limited resources available to the UK meant that only 6,000 Cromwells were built. They served primarily in armoured reconnaissance regiments and the famous 7th Armoured Division.

France were ultimately either wiped out or reduced to remnants, with some 400,000 troops being lost. 25 July saw the launch of the US Operation Cobra and on 30 July the British launched Operation Bluecoat. Having broken out of the difficult Normandy bocage, Patton's Third Army was introduced to exploit the gap created by US First Army, racing round to cut the Germans off, then pushing on to liberate Paris (19–25 August), stopping only when it ran out of fuel. The Allies were at the Belgian border by early September.

It's worth emphasising here that Patton's Third Army, introduced to exploit the gap created by Operation Cobra, then used its tank devisions exactly as US doctrine intended it should do, as expounded in *FM 17-100, Armored Command Field Manual, The Armored Division*: 'The armored division is organized primarily to perform missions that require great mobility and firepower. It is given decisive missions. It is capable of engaging in most forms of combat but its primary role is in offensive operations against hostile rear areas . . . The most profitable role of the armored division is exploitation.'

In the end though, this rapid Allied advance could not be sustained, which in turn gave the Germans time to regroup with resistance consequently becoming more dogged as the Allies reached the borders of the Reich itself. Montgomery's daring Operation Market Garden (17–25 September 1944) was thwarted and with it the chance of an early end to the war. However, with the Germans now fighting on two fronts the end was inevitable. Their last attack in the west – the Battle of the Bulge – was an expensive failure that used up the last of their resources.

In these final battles across Europe protection became more of a problem as anti-armour weapons improved and means of penetrating armour became more varied. In addition to conventional KE penetration by solid shot, a new method, HEAT,

New kit 1: The M24 Chaffee light tank entered production in April 1944 and service in winter 1944. It was an immediate success, the 75mm main gun being a great improvement on the 37mm of the M3/M5 light. However, the vehicle was slow reaching Europe and many units hadn't received quantities before the war ended.

was introduced. This relied on the chemical energy generated by a high velocity, high temperature jet of HE. This was fired at low velocity and was thus most accurate at shorter ranges (eg in hand-held weapons like the bazooka), leading to the fitting of stand-off armour to protect suspensions and turrets, whilst front glacis and turret frontal arcs became ever thicker. Other methods of protection included painting with anti-magnetic mine paste (Zimmerit), and fitting local smoke dischargers which fired a pattern of local smoke allowing a tank to escape to cover. Internal protection was improved by not storing ammunition above the turret ring (apart from ready rounds) and by the fitting of ammunition bins with water jackets. Engine and track performance improved, but in many cases petrol engines still had to be used instead of the more robust (and less flammable) diesels, because the majority of diesel fuel was needed for

New kit 2: The 76mm-armed Sherman came in various forms, but the M4A3E8 'Easy Eight' and M4A3(76)W HVSS versions were probably the acme of the Sherman as a tank hunter (the 76mm's HE shell being poor). HVAP rounds, when they were available – which was rare – also helped. The HVSS and twin road wheels on each axle considerably improved manoeuvrability.

New kit 3: The 90mm-armed M36 was the best-equipped of the tank destroyers. Based on the M10 chassis, with a large new turret, the M36 was well-received by its crews from October 1944. It achieved long-range kills against most German tanks although the frontal armour of the Panther (sloped) and Tiger (thick) proved tricky.

the navies. 'Duckbills' (track extensions) were fitted in some cases to improve traction in muddy conditions, whilst the invention by an American NCO of a device that could cut its way through the thick bocage hedgerows of Normandy – the Culin hedgerow cutter – was a brilliant invention that won its inventor a well-deserved medal. Undoubtedly the biggest continual threat to German assets came from the air, with the 'Jabos' (*Jagdbombers* = fighter-bombers), constantly searching out and destroying tank columns, thanks to the Allies' almost complete air superiority.

New kit 4: The M26 Pershing had a difficult genesis as inter-arm politics played an uncomfortable role in keeping the tank off the production lines. In the end, 20 reached the front in January/ February 1945 and were allocated to 3rd and 9th Armored Divisions of First Army. They performed well enough to show what the US tankers had been missing.

US 7th Armored Division: a month in action October 1944

[*After Action Report, 7th Armored Division,* 1–31 October 1944]

After nearly a month pounding the fortress of Metz with US Third Army, on 26 September 1944 7th Armored Division transferred to XIX Corps of the US First Army. It was given the mission of clearing enemy resistance from the area west of the Meuse River in the Peel Swamp region. It was a new type of country for the 7th. The terrain was level and open with patches of scrub pine and oak woods, but the ground was low (from below sea level to 20ft above) and swampy. Enemy resistance in that region had been reported light and not well organized. Subsequent events proved how false these reports had been.

The division attacked towards Vortum and Overloon, the latter attack made by CCA commanded by Col Dwight A. Rosebaum and made up of Task Force Brown and Task Force Chappuis.

Task Force Brown

(Maj John C. Brown, CO 40th Tank Bn)
40th Tank Bn, (-A & D)
B Co., 48th AIB
1/ A Co., 814th TD Bn
C Co., 82nd Engr Bn
489th Armd FA Bn

Task Force Chappuis

(Lt. Col. Richard D. Chappuis, CO, 48th AIB)
48th AIB, (-B),
A & D Cos., 40th Tank Bn
A Co., 33rd AEB
A Co., 814th TD Bn, (- 1 plat)
440th Armd FA Bn

CCB

(Brig Gen Robert W. Hasbrouck)
Divided into two:
Force #1 (Johansen, later Rhea)
23 AIB (-B)
C/31 Tank Bn
B/33 AEB (- 1 plat)
1/B/814 TD Bn
434 AFA Bn (-C)
1/A/82 Engr Bn

Force #2 (Erlenbusch)
31 Tank Bn (-C & D)
B/23 AIB
1/B/33 AEB
C/434 AFA Bn
  B/814 TD Bn (- 1 plat)
  1/A/82 Engr Bn

CCB Reserve
Tp B of the 87th Cav Recon Sqn, Mechanized,
Co D, 31st Tank Bn,
Co A, 82nd Engr Bn (-2 platoons)

Force #1 was supporting the attack on Overloon while Force #2, proceeded against Vortum. The attack opened on 30 September and was slow in the face of determined resistance from dug-in positions and pillboxes. The enemy was firmly entrenched, especially in wooded and populated areas, armed with AT guns and bazookas, and strongly supported by artillery and Nebelwerfer fire. Our own artillery, 434 AFA Bn, assisted by British 11th Armoured Division, supported the advance.

Force #2 of CCB cleared minefields along the route of advance and in spite of strong AT gun and bazooka fire, reached Vortum by the evening of 2 October, encountering little resistance in the town itself.

CCA attacked Overloon from the west and northwest, aided by Force #1 of CCB, who reached the southern edge of the woods northwest of Overloon, by 2 October. The town and its defences were bombed and strafed by air support (P-47 fighter-bombers), and artillery was fired into the town. The attacking forces of CCA (48 AIB supported by the 40th Tank Bn) reached positions to the west and northwest of Overloon, but were forced to dig in under heavy artillery and Nebelwerfer fire. On 2 October a fierce enemy counterattack was repulsed.

On 3 October, two enemy counterattacks were made from the woods southwest of Overloon, and were beaten off by elements of CCA from entrenched positions. During 3 October, relief of CCB by CCR was completed.

CCR was divided into two task forces composed as follows:

Task Force Wemple	Task Force Fuller
17th Tank Bn (-C)	38 AIB (-C)
C/38 AIB	C/17 Tnk Bn
1/C/87 Cav Rcn Sq Mecz	

CCR advanced with tanks and infantry towards Overloon from the north. In this sector, artillery, Nebelwerfer, and mortar fire from well-concealed and dug-in positions

A heavily laden 81mm mortar halftrack of HQ Coy, 48th Armored Infantry Battalion. Note the open storage bin next to the driver's door, the rack for mines and the skate rail for the MG.

A 10-ton power wrecker drops a new Wright Continental R-975 radial engine into a 31st Tank Battalion Sherman. The M4, M4(105), M4 Composite and M4A1 all used this engine – one reason why the Sherman was so tall. The other engines used were the GM 6046 (mainly M4A2), the Chrysler A57 Multibank (M4A3 and M4A4 – mostly used by the British), and the Ford GAA V8 (mainly used by the US Army). Maintenance was handled in an echelon system:

FIRST (Company)	Daily/weekly service by driver and asst driver
SECOND (Company)	Monthly by Company mechanic; also minor repairs/adjustments
SECOND (Battalion/Regiment)	Semi-annual maintenance at Bn/Regt level
THIRD/LIGHT (Division)	Lt Maint Coy performs repairs as necessary
THIRD/MEDIUM (Army/Corps)	Med Maint Coy performs repairs as necessary
FOURTH/HEAVY (Army)	Hy Maint Coy performs repairs/cannibalisation as necessary
FIFTH (Motor base)	Faulty assemblies are returned here for rebuilding as necessary

caused heavy tank casualties and prevented advance beyond the original position.

On 4–6 October, repeated counterattacks from the town were thrown back with heavy loses to the enemy – hard fighting paratroops and fanatical air corps personnel fighting as infantry. These counterattacks resulted in bitter hand-to-hand fighting and were stopped with the aid of artillery and air support. The town was half encircled from the southwest to the northeast. Entrenched positions were often within grenade-throwing distance of similar enemy positions, and in the fighting, fox holes changed and re-changed hands. During the night 5–6 October, CCB relieved CCA, and in the afternoon of 6 October received another counterattack.

7th Armored Division moved to another sector, being relieved by British 11th Armoured Division during 6–8 October. The Overloon battle had been a costly one for the division. During the first six days of October the division suffered 452 estimated battle casualties (killed, wounded and missing). 29 Medium Tanks, 6 Light Tanks and 43 other vehicles were lost during this same period. The importance of artillery during the battle is indicated by the following statistics. In one day (4 October), 489 AFA Bn fired 2,762 rounds. On 2 October, seven battalions (British and American) coordinated their fire, to fire 1,500 rounds in two minutes. Estimated heavy personnel casualties were inflicted on the enemy during the repeated fanatical counterattacks.

Training
Between 8 and 23 October when the 7th Armored Division was reassigned to the US Ninth Army during the entire period the following training schedule was carried out by the units not engaged in active patrolling and when in reserve. Instructions for at least four hours a day was ordered in the following subjects:

1. Tactics of small patrols, squads, platoons, and companies.
2. Operations of the individual soldier and his part of the team.
3. Use of small infantry units with tank units.
4. Terrain appreciation with respect to tactical operations of small units.
5. Proper use of arms with respect to suitable targets.
6. How to observe.
7. How to assault (emphasis on movement by infiltration).
8. Night patrolling.
9. Advancing by bounds.
10. Making use of maximum support in the advance,
11. Planning of any advance or operations of small units (emphasizing plans that must be made by individual soldier).
12. Sanitation and hygiene in the frontlines.
13. Necessity for relief of units.
14. Necessity for alertness on night operations and guard.
15. Certain tactics of the Germans (illustrate with specific personal examples).

A progress report showing the subject covered and progress made was to be sent in to Division Headquarters. It was suggested, that practical problems be worked on small German units in static sectors and that target practice be conducted against actual German positions.

The Counterattack

On the morning of 27 October a heavy artillery barrage preceded a coordinated German attack across the Deurne Canal and Canal du Nord. The initial thrust was toward Meijel held by C/87th Cav Recon Sqn (Mecz). The infantry attack was followed by Panther and Tiger tanks at approximately 11:30. Superior enemy numbers forced Tp C to withdraw from the town to the west. Here they met Tp B and the two troops organized a counterattack to retake the town. Co F, the Light Tank Co, joined in the attack which failed in the face of increasing enemy strength and strong AT and bazooka fire.

In the vicinity of Heitrak, D/87th Cav Recon Sqn (Mecz), received an attack from across the canal that broke their defensive line. Support was sent from CCR and Task Force Wemple was formed to hold the area. It consisted of C and D/17 Tank Bn, C/814th TD Bn, D/87 Cav. The attack was launched by 9th Panzer and the 15th Panzergrenadier Division. The enemy was supported by tanks (Panther and Tiger) and ample artillery. At first the strength of the enemy was undetermined, but as information was collected, the seriousness of the counterattack became clear.

Upon order of VIII Corps, BR 11th Armoured Division relieved CCB of the bridgehead zone, completing the relief by 20:45. Task Force Wemple was assigned to CCB from CCR, and CCB was given the mission of attacking astride the Liesel–Meijel road to converge with CCR to seize and hold Meijel. CCR was to attack Meijel from the Asten–Meijel road. Further to the south in the Nederweert sector, an attack forced A/87th Cav Recon Sqn Mecz to withdraw slightly. This troop fought all day and held the enemy on an extended line until reinforced by Task Force Nelson at 17:01. This task force consisted of a company of tanks, a platoon of infantry (1st Pl, A/38), and a platoon of TDs from CCA was attached to CCR at 15:30.

On the morning of the 28th, CCB began its attack astride the Liesel–Meijel road. TF Olmstead (B/23 AIB, C/31 Tank Bn, 1/C/814th TD Bn, AG Platoon of 17th Tank Bn, and the mortar platoon of 31st Tank Bn) attacked toward the canal down the Hoogebrug road. Both efforts met opposition and made little progress. At the same time the 48 AIB (-), 2 Med tank companies, 17th Tank Bn, 87th Cav (-), 1/C/33 AEB, and 2/B/814th TD Bn, of CCR, operating as a Task Force under Col Chappuis, attacked down the Asten–Meijel road meeting stiff opposition. Little progress was made that day, and defensive positions were taken during the night when, besides the usual artillery fire, the Luftwaffe bombed and strafed Asten and vicinity. Task Force Nelson reverted to CCA control at early on 28 October and continued to attack eastward toward Horik, but made little progress.

Recovered from a range at Oldebroek in 2010, 'Able Abe' was reconfigured as an M4A1 40th Tank Battalion, 7th Armored that was knocked out during the battle. Today it sits outside the excellent Overloon museum.

On the morning of 29 October, the enemy attacked in force from Meijel up the roads toward Liesel and Asten. Tanks also infiltrated across the canal to the east of Liesel. An attack on CCR forced the infantry back about half way up the road to Asten where the enemy attack was halted with the aid of artillery. In the CCB sector, Liesel was taken by the enemy. Enemy casualties in these attacks were heavy both in men and tanks.

After a conference between the Commanding General, VIII Corps and Maj Gen Lindsay Mcdonald Silvester, commanding the 7th Armored Division, arrangements were made to relieve the division in the Meijel–Liesel sector. The 15th (Scottish) Division was to take over that sector and operate toward Meijel while the 7th Armored Division was to move south to the vicinity of Weert to defend a narrowed sector and attack northeast to coordinate with the 15th Division's attack. The relief was carried on during the night of 29–30 October and was completed early on the 30th. CCB and CCR closed into assembly areas in the rear of the lines while CCA held in place. CCB moved to relieve CCA in its positions south of Canal du Nord while CCA reassembled along the Canal le Duc and prepared to attack to drive the enemy from the territory north of the Canal du Nord to a position south of Meijel. CCR was in division reserve.

It was decided to narrow the division's sector still further after a conference between the VIII Corps Commanding General and General Silvester. As the result of this decision,

CCB was relieved by BR 4th Armoured Brigade at 31 October and moved into division reserve. CCR moved into the Nederweert area and outposted and occupied positions northwest of the Nord and Nederweert Canals.

The month closed with the division poised to attack to regain the ground lost in the counterattack north of the Canal du Nord. BR 15th (Scottish) Division was on its left flank and BR 4th Armoured Brigade on its right. The First Belgian Brigade was relieved from assignment to the division on 31 October.

The counterattack had a far-reaching significance. The enemy's Venlo bridgehead over the Maas River was the key that the Germans held against allied entry into the Ruhr district.

During the month the division was assigned to two armies and operated under a third. It was commanded by Maj Gen Silvester who was relieved of the command at

Another 31st Tank Battalion shot. 7th Armored arrived in the ETO on 13 June 1944, reached the Continent on 10 August over Omaha Beach, and entered combat on 13/14 August. The division took part in the encirclement of the Ruhr before attachment to British Second Army, ending its 172 days in combat on the Baltic Sea. Note the markings on the glacis.

7th Armored suffered 5,799 casualties during the war, including 898 dead. It will always be remembered for its defence of St Vith during the Battle of the Bulge, but it also fought hard in the Peel marshes. Here, engineers work on Sherman casualties.

midnight on 31 October. Estimated enemy losses for the month included 12 Panthers; 23 Tigers; 9 x 88mm guns; 6 artillery pieces; 8 AT guns; and 16 vehicles of all types. The division's losses were 28 light tanks; 52 medium tanks; 2 M8 armoured cars; 7 M10s, 9 halftracks; two artillery pieces; and 81 vehicles of all types.

Personnel losses were 125 killed; 734 wounded and 364 missing for a total of 1,223 battle casualties. Non-battle casualties totalled 684. Estimated enemy losses were 1,426 dead and 1,627 wounded. 583 prisoners were taken during the month, to make a total of 6,009 prisoners taken since the division began operations.

During the period 1–31 October, the division used the following amount of supplies:

355,826 gal. fuel		105mm, all types, (How)	68,887
6,580gal oil		60mm, mortar, all types	1,150
10,940lb grease		81mm, mortar, all types	7,097
837 tons rations		76mm, gun, all types	5,335
1,000,000gal water		Rockets, HE, AT, M6A1	1,080
Ammunition:		Grenades, all types	4,350
Cal .30, all types	1,024,716	Mines	72
Cal .45, ball	44,400	2in mortar smoke bombs	522
Cal .50, all types	12,470	3in gun, all types	4,212
37mm, all types	5,260	4.5in proj, C/R	4,950
57mm, all types	450	Flare, trip	656
75mm, all types, G & H	15,541		

Japanese tankers at Khalkhin Gol in 1939. The tank is a Type 89 Chi-Ro medium, weighing 12 tons and armed with a 57mm main gun. The Japanese had a strong tank force but never learnt how to use it, and wartime developments passed them by. Their best design, the Type 3 Chi-Nu, never saw action because it was reserved for use defending the homeland.

Allied tank forces in India and Burma performed their part in the defeat of Japan, holding firm at Imphal and Kohima before racing to Rangoon. There was little of the tank action seen in western Europe: the terrain didn't suit it and the Japanese made little use of massed tanks to spearhead their assaults. This is a Stuart – an M3 light – that saw extensive service in India and Burma.

6 Tanks Against Japan

On 7/8 December 1941, Japan bombed the American fleet at Pearl Harbor and invaded British territory in Malaya through Thailand. By May 1942, the defeated British army crossed the Chindwin River having retreated 900 miles and lost 13,000 men. During the retreat Stuarts of 7th Armoured Brigade had certainly helped hold back the Japanese to allow the British forces to reach India, but Burma was in Japanese hands. Elsewhere, the story was the same, and Japanese forces had advanced to New Guinea and the Solomon Islands threatening Australia.

Tanks had played their part. The Japanese had begun designing its own tanks – mainly for infantry support – in the 1920s, and by 1937 they had over 1,000 in eight regiments. Their army was the fifth largest in terms of tanks but they proved no match for the Russians under Georgy Zhukov at Khalkhin Gol in August 1939. He destroyed the Japanese forces with his brand of Blitzkrieg, using tanks and supporting aircraft. The Russians lost half their 500 tanks, however, mainly to antitank guns (75–80%) and the Japanese were spurred on to double their tank production. That didn't add up to a great deal. Japanese tank and SP gun production through the war totalled less than 5,000 – and the best ones were kept at home to defend Japan and consequently never saw action.

The Japanese were slow to develop their approach to armoured warfare. They set up a Mechanisation Headquarters in April 1941 and three tank divisions in China in June 1942 – but never used them against Russia, slowly pulling regiments south until the Mechanised Army was disbanded at the end of October 1943.

While tank-on-tank action would be rare in the American island campaigns against the Japanese, when it happened the Japanese came off second best. This is unsurprising when one compares the heaviest Japanese tanks – the Type 97-Kai Shinhoto Chi-Ha (15.8 tons, 47mm gun, 1-inch armour) – with the American M4A3 (33 tons, 75mm gun, 2.5-inch armour). Their fighting techniques also lost out to the Americans' combined-arms doctrine. Fighting in small numbers, with poor radios, the most success the Japanese tanks had was in the original Malayan campaign. They ended up usually being used as artillery. Right at the end of the war, when the Red Army invaded Japanese Manchuria with T-34/85s supported by Sturmovik ground-attack aircraft they blew the Japanese opposition away.

India and Burma

The British turnaround on the borders of India was a remarkable achievement engineered by General Bill Slim's Anglo-Indian Fourteenth Army. The 'Forgotten Army' inflicted on the Japanese their biggest land defeat of the war, holding them at Kohima and Imphal before retaking Burma and outfighting them in the jungles. They were, to use Michael Calvert's words, 'spruce, streamlined, could move fast needing few orders, knew how to look after their tail, had the measure of their enemy and his tactics, understood how to use air supply . . . and knew how to curl up their strength into a coiled spring ready for the next advance.'

India Command had seen its first armoured division created in July 1940, but mechanisation was slow. There were few tanks, a lot of horses, and anyway the Indian armour was destined for use against the Italians and Germans in the Western Desert where it was badly mauled. Further units were created, and in May 1943 the 44th Indian Armoured Division formed, with one armoured brigade (255) and one infantry brigade (268). Elements of this division would see action at Kohima in 1944.

Following the abortive attempt to attack into Burma in the First Arakan campaign of 1942/43, the renewed advance in January 1944 was met by a swift Japanese response – Operation H-Go, part of the Japanese offensive against India – which led to the Battle of the Admin Box where two squadrons of the 25th Dragoons, equipped with M3 Lees, blunted the Japanese assaults and helped hold the position, in so doing providing Fourteenth Army with a morale-building victory.

In March–April 1944 the Japanese launched Operation U-Go, attacking India though Kohima and Imphal. There 254th Indian Tank Brigade supported IV Corps and provided crucial assistance in the defence. Tanks of 50th Indian Tank Brigade supported the British 2nd and, later, 7th Indian Infantry Divisions breaking the siege of Kohima and handing out one of Japan's most significant defeats. The Stalingrad of the East proved the turning point of the British war against Japan. As Robert Lyman says, 'The Japanese regard the battle of Imphal to be their greatest defeat ever … And it gave Indian soldiers a belief in their own martial ability and showed that they could fight as well or better than anyone else.'

The Allies went over to attack, Fourteenth Army advancing into Burma and entering Rangoon a few hours before the monsoon started in earnest, their advance spearheaded by armour.

American armour in the Pacific Campaign

The Pacific theatre wasn't the best place for tanks, particularly the rocky islands that were assaulted by the US Marine Corps. The Japanese didn't use their tanks en masse and most of the Allied military thought tanks and jungle didn't mix. However, it quickly became obvious that tanks provided very real support to the men on the ground

One of India's great regiments, the Royal Deccan Horse (today, the Deccan Horse) fought with distinction as part of 255th Armoured (later Tank) Brigade. Its motto *Laro aur larte raho* (To strike and strike again) could be found at the battles of Meiktila, Pokoku, the Irrawaddy operations and the advance on Rangoon.

Rumble in the jungle: Shermans and Lees are well camouflaged in this scene. The Lees are from 254th Indian Tank Brigade which was supporting 2nd Division during the advance to Kohima in 1944. The Sherman is an OP tank for 18th Field Regiment, RA who used M7 Priests.

Sherman V *Punjab* of the Sikh Squadron of the Royal Deccan Horse – one of 255th Indian Tank Brigade's regiments. They were involved in the race to Rangoon.

Kohima was voted the title 'Britain's Greatest Battle' in a 2013 National Army Museum poll and there's no doubt that the invading Japanese were stopped in their tracks at 'The Stalingrad of the East'. This after the battle view shows a Lee in the British positions. The Lees of the 3rd Carabiniers and 150th RAC Regiment of 254th Indian Tank Brigade distinguished themselves around Imphal.

The Lee had a smaller turret than the British Grant (see page 42) – of 50th Indian Tank Brigade in the Arakan. The Lee was used by the 25th Dragoons and 146th RAC (9th Duke of Wellington's Regiment (West Riding). The battles in the Arakan lasted 1942–1944 as the Japanese were held and, finally, routed.

British Tanks in the Far East October 1942–March 1944*

Type	Combined 31/09/42	India 31/03/44	SE Asia Command 31/03/44
Light tanks	126		
Sherman		221	18
Stuart	146	719	106
Lee/Grant	249	325	267
Valentine	207		
Churchill	27		
Total	754	1,265	391

*Source: Jeffreys, Alan: *Battle Orders 13 The British Army in the Far East 1941–45*; Osprey, 2005.

– certainly psychologically – and were hugely helpful when attacking Japanese strong-points, bunkers and caves. The infantry kept away the Japanese tank hunters – usually using satchel charges – and the tanks, especially when flamethrower variants came in – provided the power the infantry needed. There were logistical problems, and wear and tear (tracks in particular) was always a factor, but tanks proved their worth in the island-hopping campaign. The USMC divisions included a tank battalion – initially light tanks, the M3 or M5 light. In fact, the Marines was the only American force to use the precursor of the M3, the M2A4 light, in combat. In 1944 they started to use the diesel-powered M4A2 in the divisional tank battalions, and there were also a number of US Army independent tank and TD battalions in theatre.

Above: Two M4A1s of 7th Infantry Division, with wading equipment still mounted, arrive on Enubuj Island, Kwajalein Atoll, Marshall Islands, 2 February 1944. The two deep wading ducts were for the engine air intake (front) and exhaust (rear).

Below: Antitank rifles had been used in Europe at the start of the war, but most were smaller calibre than this Type 97 20mm monster. The whole receiver and barrel assembly slides while firing like an artillery piece. Its hefty 150lb weight required a nine-man crew: note the carrying handles (one visible at left of barrel. The magazine took seven rounds. It could penetrate 30mm of armour plate at 250 yards, but when first used against the Russians at Khalkhin Gol it was disappointingly ineffective. 1,100 were produced at Kokura Arsenal 1938–41 and, later, a few more at Nihon Seikosho.

A bridge has collapsed under an M4 and a bulldozer of the 117th Engineer Bn, 37th Division and an M4 of Co B, 775th Tank Bn attached to 32nd Infantry Div are doing their best to help: Luzon in the Philippines.

Mud isn't good for tanks. This M4 of Co B, 716th Tank Battalion is stuck in the Timuquit River. Infantrymen of the Americal Division are passing on 8 May 1945. Fighting continued in the Philippines until August.

OPERATIONS ON IWO JIMA
[Maj Samuel D. Littlepage, 16 March 1945.]

Tactical use of armoured units

1. Tank Companies were assigned to Regimental Landing Teams (RLTs) for the assault of the beach and landed from the seventh wave (H+60). These companies formed their own reconnaissance units, which went in with the third wave to report on the conditions of the beach, minefields and assembly areas for the tanks. In at least one company effort was made for the LVT(A)s in the first wave to report on beach conditions but communications broke down. Company commanders of the Assault Tank Companies – A and C – agreed that the reconnaissance units had not been able to perform their missions before the tanks were ordered in to the beach. The result was confusion and needless loss of tanks at the water's edge. For example, C/4th Tank Battalion beached in four different places before it could land.

2. Tank action on this island might be termed 'Platoon Action' as a platoon was the largest unit used except for operations on the airfields where whole companies were employed at times. This was necessitated by the character of the terrain and the fact that only about half the tanks of any company were operational at any one time after D-Day.

3. On D+5 an armoured push by all tanks available in the three tank battalions was supposed to sweep Airfield #2 and the ground adjacent to it. The result was that all tanks were canalized onto the airfield by the terrain and they got there by a single cut made by a tank-dozer. However, the tanks dominated this airfield and by knocking out its surrounding pillboxes, allowed the infantry to take possession of it.

4. A certain neglect of basic tactics was noted from time to time, an example of this is that on several occasions a whole platoon (three tanks) would push into an operation suspected of feeing covered by antitank fire without leaving any tank in defilade to cover it. The result was sometimes fatal and the only reason it was not more so is the fact that the Japanese did not use an antitank gun strong enough to penetrate the front slope plate of a medium tank.

5. The use of smoke as an offensive weapon to screen the movement of tanks and infantry was particularly neglected. Not a single example of this means of protection while closing with the enemy was noted.

6. On several occasions infantry commanders objected to the tanks firing over the heads of infantry, although the tanks were firing on the very weapons holding up the advance. The effect was that the infantry indirectly protected the enemy antitank and machine guns from the tanks.

7. The tanks seemed to draw mortar fire and the infantry leaders, particularly company commanders, disliked having the tanks around. A conflict of orders would occur where an infantry battalion commander would order the tanks supporting his unit into action

The soft volcanic sands on Iwo Jima proved difficult to negotiate for both LVTs (**Above**) – which include a number of LVT(A)4s – and tanks (**Below**). Note wooden side armour and welded nails to hatch covers. The spikes were to stop magnetic mines.

Because the M4A3s were heavier than the M4A2, for the Iwo Jima operation LSMs – landing ships medium – were used rather than standard LCMs. Only A/5th Tank Battalion was different, ferried from its LSD (landing ship, dock) by LCTs. Of the three battalions, 4th and 5th had M4A3s and the 3rd had M4A2s. These included flamethrower tanks (see below), tank dozers, flails and M32 ARVs.

The Marines had eight M4A3 flamethrower Shermans on Iwo Jima – four in each of the 4th and 5th Tank Battalions –and they proved very effective. They were armed with the US Navy Mk I flamethrower and were known as 'Ronsons'. Ironically, the 'Ronson lighter lights first time every time' nickname is said to have been accorded to Shermans in Europe before the 'wet' ammunition stowage was introduced.

at a certain point and the infantry company commander on the ground would order the tanks away.

8. Target designation by infantry units who have been fighting previously in an area of a tank attack was not good. Since a tank is practically deaf and has poor vision, it must depend on the units it supports to point out targets. Far too much time was wasted by tanks standing idly, in the front lines looking for targets at which to fire.

9. Mine reconnaissance and removal is very difficult and at times impossible for a tank crew, therefore they must rely upon those on the ground for this service. There were far too few engineers available for this work and even those had too many tasks.

10. Much of the success of tank operations on this island was due to the spirit of the individual tank commanders and their will to take more than a normal risk to aid those they were supporting. There was much discussion as to whether or not certain area was tank terrain for them.

11. In close country the tanks did not rely upon the infantry to protect them but covered each other from a column formation. This action was quite successful,

12. Infantry unit commanders did not use tanks for personal reconnaissance although this use was offered to some.

13. The tank-dozer was used to push trails through minefields in sand and around minefields bordered by thick vegetation. This action was very successful and greatly facilitated the passing of such barriers.

14. Antitank measures used by the enemy are listed in order of their importance: mines, antitank guns, antitank trenches, hand-placed charges.

15. The enemy practice of tying aerial bombs to yardstick mines is an expensive method of mining. Their policy is to completely demolish the tank with the mine as distinguished from the German policy of merely stopping the tank with the mine and destroying it by gunfire.

16. Japanese mining was erratic. In one case the mines were marked with stakes. In another case a complete field beside road was mined while the road was left untouched. Tanks on the beach were able to pick their way through fields because the mines were spaced too far apart.

Communications

1. Radio was the standard means of communication by tanks in the field. Each company and platoon command tank was equipped with a SCR508 and all tanks had SCR528s. Each platoon command tank was equipped with a SCR300 and all tanks had a telephone installed on the rear of the tank which was cut into the intercom system of the tank. Liaison parties at infantry regiments and battalions had SCR509s.

2. Contact with the infantry on the ground was established by placing the SCR300s in the infantry battalion command net. This kept the tanks informed at all times of all the

companies in that battalion. At times it was necessary to relay messages from one company to another but the system proved reliable. One objection to this system is that the infantry battalion command net is 'hot' and urgent messages are frequently delayed.

3. The telephone installed on the rear of the tanks worked very well. Although it was of great value, it was not used more because of the tendency of the tanks to operate independent of the infantry which could not follow the tanks in certain areas.

4. No means of visual signals, such as hand signals, flag signals or audible signals, such as tapping on tank with rifle butt, racing tank motor were noted.

Supply

1. The problem of supply was minimised by the fact that the tank company bivouacs were moved only once during the operation and then only for a few hundred yards.

2. By nightfall on D-Day 60% of the tanks operating were without fuel or ammunition. This deficiency was caused by the heavy fire falling on the beaches and it was remedied by salvaging from disabled tanks. After D+1 there was plenty of supply of all types.

3. All tank unit equipment was preloaded in vehicles thus minimizing the transportation problem.

4. Tank companies were resupplied by Regt QM until D+7 when tank battalion supply officer started a battalion dump.

5. LVTs performed a quick and efficient delivery of supplies from ship to company area and the Weasel was outstanding in getting supplies across sand areas.

Ammunition

1. Shell HE with an M48 fuse was the most used and best liked on the operation. All officers and tank crews that were asked complained about the lack of HE ammunition.

2. The T105 fuse gave good results against concrete and seemed to give better performance than the APC ammunition. The only appreciable need for APC was overhead fire in wooded areas. No steel embrasure shutters were found.

3. The only use of smoke noted was for protection of a crew while abandoning a disabled tank.

4. There were plenty of targets for canister but none was available.

5. All tanks were equipped with an extra ammunition rack on the floor of the turret and between the assistant gunner's knees. This allowed a 25% increase in the load.

Tracks

1. Track trouble was the most frequent reason for vehicle casualties. In the first half of the operation when the tanks were operating in deep sand and even trails were scarce, it is estimated that at least 50% of the track disabilities were caused by snapping. This condition was prevalent in all companies.

2. The extended end-connectors used on the tracks were of great value and allowed the tanks to traverse otherwise impossible terrain. It did not produce ill effects on the bogie wheels in this operation.

Conclusions

a. LVT(A)s in the first wave of a landing assault can give much valuable information about the beach conditions to tank units following.

b. Conditions of beach, minefields' passage and assembly areas must be known before tanks are landed.

c. Basic tactics must continue to be a training for veteran troops.

d. All tank and infantry troops and their possible replacement personnel should be trained in the use of smoke.

e. Target designation to tanks by infantry is a vital problem and should receive prompt attention.

f. Mine reconnaissance and removal is an infantry function as the engineers have too many other tasks.

g. Infantry unit commanders should use tanks for personal reconnaissance of ground over which they intend to operate.

h. The tank-dozer is too valuable to be used for firing purposes except when no other tanks are available.

i. SCR300 is the most appropriate means of contact with infantry.

j. All units should have means of communication other than radio.

k. Infantry commanders should use the radio themselves when giving important orders to tanks. This will eliminate possible misinterpretation by liaison personnel.

l. LVT and Weasel are essential to supply in sandy areas such as this island.

m. There is insufficient HE in our present unit of fire.

n. T105 fuse will greatly reduce the need of APC.

o. The performance of the MI Flamethrower was greatly hampered by the following factors:

    1. Lack of maintenance and operational schooling of operating personnel.

    2. Lack of tools and spare parts.

    3. Poor fuel mixture

    4. The present construction of the weapon will not withstand the pounding of a tank operating in the field.

p. The steel track has a very high disability rate in coarse sand. (It is believed that the rubber track will give better performance under such conditions.) The packing of the sand behind the rear idler is believed to be the cause.

q. The extended end-connector was a valuable asset in sand but it is a substitute remedy for a bad condition.

Japanese Armour

[From Japanese Tank and Antitank Warfare, 1 August 1945]

The Japanese paid no real attention to mechanised warfare until after their disastrous experience with Russian armoured units on the Manchurian border in 1939. Prior to this, their armoured forces consisted of independent tank regiments and tank groups comprising three or four tank regiments, a signals unit and an engineer unit. After 1939 the Japanese apparently planned the creation of an armoured army under an independent command. In pursuance of this new policy, two armoured divisions were activated in 1942. An additional armoured division was also activated in 1942, but not as a part of the armoured army command.

In 1943, it is believed, the Japanese realised their inability to create the armoured army as originally planned. This may have been primarily attributable to shipping difficulties and the higher manufacturing priorities of other items such as aeroplanes. The armoured army accordingly was deactivated in November 1943, and its organic divisions were placed under new commands. Nevertheless another armoured division was activated in 1944 subsequent to the deactivation of the armoured army.

Organization of armoured units

The original armoured divisions were organized as square (brigaded) divisions. These divisions were triangularised in early 1944, and the new division activated that year was triangular. Estimated strength of such a triangular armoured division is 12,950 officers and men, 175 medium tanks, and 141 light tanks. But armoured divisions, like all Japanese units, deviate from the established table of organization. Thus far, two divisions have been encountered in combat without either their antiaircraft defence units or their reconnaissance units.

In addition to the armoured units included in the triangular armoured divisions, the Japanese have several types of independent units. There were originally nearly 20 independent tank regiments. The TOE strength of the independent tank regiment is approximately 950 officers and men, 31 light tanks, and 50 medium tanks.

The Japanese also have independent tank companies with a strength of approximately 150 officers and men, 10 medium tanks, and 2 light tanks. Originally, 11 of these tank companies were known to exist; two of these were rendered ineffective on Saipan.

Four independent tankette companies are known to be in existence at present. These companies have a TOE strength of 130 officers and men, and 17 tankettes.

In 1942, several infantry divisions had either tank units (strength 750) or infantry group tankette companies (strength 100), and sometimes both types of organization. Most of these units were demobilised by early 1944. At the present time, only four infantry

Some 2,300 Type 95 Ha-Go light tanks were produced. Designed by Mitsubishi, it had a one-man turret and a crew of three. It weighed 7.5 tons and had a 37mm main armament.

Around 800 of the Type 94 tankette were produced 1935–37. They were given to infantry units and while good for support and reconnaissance were no match for US antitank weapons.

Above: The Type 89 I-Go medium tank was the first mass-produced diesel tank. It had a 57mm main gun and 6–17mm of armour. Designed in the 1920s, it may have performed well against unequal opposition in China, but it was obsolete by the start of World War II.

Below: One of the disputed Kuril islands, Shumshi is the closest to Russia and was heavily defended by the Japanese. Around 25,000 men and 60 tanks defended the island from deep underground positions. The Russians invaded on 18 August 1945 and it surrendered on the 23rd. These damaged Japanese tanks – nearest the camera two Type 95 Ha-Gos – were photographed after the battle.

divisions are known to have tank units. A recently observed trend, however, has been to have two armoured-car or light-tank companies in the division reconnaissance regiments. Such a disposition would make 8–12 light tanks available to the infantry division.

Japanese armoured tactical principles: basic doctrine

Japanese battle principles and concepts presented here are based upon present doctrine and teaching, and on the very limited use of armour encountered up to the present time. It cannot be emphasised too strongly that Japanese tank operations to date have consisted of piecemeal tank counterattacks and defensive siting of tanks as pillboxes in direct contradiction to promulgated doctrine.

Missions
Japanese Field Service Regulations definitely stress the point that all arms must be used to enable the infantry to close with the enemy and annihilate him. This indicates that the basic mission of tanks is still believed to be direct cooperation with infantry.

Present Japanese teachings describe the *principal* function of the tank to be to pave the way for a victory for the entire army by bringing into full play their great mobility and striking force; by containing and destroying the enemy fighting power in detail after making penetrations into the hostile lines; and by expediting prompt exploitation through the coordinated efforts of the participating units. Similarly, the mission of tanks is prescribed to be 'closely to support infantry (cavalry) combat. Depending on the situation, they will infiltrate into the hostile area in order to seize the initiative or to seal the enemy's fate. In the mechanised unit, of which the tank is the main element, they become the very core of a tremendous striking force.'

Formations
According to the *Japanese Field Service Regulations* the platoon deploys normally in a diamond formation and the company in a diamond of diamonds. The normal combat formation is a 'T'. The company is disposed with three platoons abreast and one trailing. Each platoon is in a diamond formation.

Although no large formations of Japanese tanks have been encountered, the Japanese army tank school gives precise instructions for the employment of such formations. For an attack on a lightly held enemy position, Japanese doctrine specifies a minimum of 30 to 40 tanks. If the enemy is in a strongly defended position, at least 60 tanks are required. If hostile artillery shelling and aerial bombing are unusually heavy, 100 tanks are necessary.

Japanese tactical doctrine stresses the use of tanks in what is called a mobile mass. When committed in this manner, tanks constitute the main fire element in what is essentially an attempt to attain a decisive victory by one stroke, preferably by attacking a weak spot in the hostile line. Since the nature of the terrain is considered to be the chief limitation on the employment of large tank formations, such tactics are to be resorted to only in suitable terrain. In any case, tanks are committed as a mobile mass only at 'a momentous time and place, when a decision of the entire army is in balance.' Japanese tanks, when employed as a mobile mass, are allocated into two echelons, in keeping with combat principles for the company and regiment. Dispositions of tanks within the company and regiment are made by the company and regimental commander, respectively.

Tanks in infantry support
Despite the doctrine of mass employment no large Japanese tank forces have been encountered, and the infantry support role has been exclusively emphasized. It general there are two Japanese methods of infantry-tank cooperation. One requires the tank commander to designate the infantry forces with which the tanks are to cooperate, in response to requests for support received from the infantry commanders. The other method is predicated upon advance specification of the objectives for the tanks' attacks.

Exploitation operations
In these operations, Japanese tanks are committed to seize tactically important areas, confuse hostile attack deployments, and strike at enemy artillery or other vital rear installations. If tanks are to give impetus and momentum to the infantry assault, they advance in close coordination with the infantry. It is always possible, according to Japanese doctrine, to employ both methods simultaneously, especially if an ample number of tanks is available. Some can be used in direct support missions, while the remainder are held in reserve to exploit successes achieved by the assault wave. If more tanks are available than the estimated requirements for close infantry support, some may be committed as leading tanks, usually under division control.

Principles of infantry-tank attacks

A number of fundamental principles are emphasized in Japanese infantry-tank attack doctrine. Close liaison is maintained at all times. Liaison means include radio, joint command posts, liaison officers, visual signalling and tank runners. Until recently, available information indicated that only the platoon commander's tank was equipped with a radio. In the 2nd Armoured Division on Luzon, however, it was found that all medium tanks and practically all light tanks encountered were equipped with well-built, two-way radios.

If Japanese tanks encounter an antitank installation within the enemy position, Japanese doctrine prescribes that an immediate decision must be made whether to bypass the installation or to liquidate it by frontal assault. Incipient enemy counterattacks are

Another old design (c1933) that saw service through the war, with some improvement to both gun and engine in later versions, this Type 95 Ha-Go is seen on Makin Atoll. Note the 37mm main gun. The Type 4 Ke-Nu variant was armed with a 57mm in a Type 97 medium tank turret. Both versions were seriously underarmoured at the start of hostilities.

frustrated by striking at the counterattack base, the infantry deployed for the counterattack, or the hostile tanks which may be spearheading the manoeuvre, depending upon the situation. Areas are designated for rallying of the tanks after the accomplishment of their mission and preparing for the next phase. Tanks also assemble at rally points when the assault is suspended at night or broken off because of the tenacity of enemy resistance. Restoration of combat strength is the principal object of rallying. With this in mind, the Japanese choose sites to afford the maximum efficiency in regroupment, replacement, and repair. Special care is taken to collect all damaged vehicles and to initiate repair when feasible.

Example of tank division tactics

The 2nd Armoured Division on Luzon was the first unit encountered by US forces. It was anticipated that the commitment of this Japanese armoured force would provide valuable material for a study of Japanese methods in the employment, of massed armour and coordinated infantry-armour-artillery tactics. Actual operations, however, revealed that the Japanese commanders either did not understand the modern concept of armour employment or simply were unable to employ the armoured division in accordance with promulgated principles of operation. Instead, they frittered away the division in piecemeal counterattacks and immobile defences. They never mounted an attack with more than 16 tanks at one time. The principle of mass was never employed. The inherent mobility of the tanks was not utilised, but was negated by committing the tanks to fixed defensive emplacements. The greatest concentrations of Japanese tanks were in San Manuel and Munoz. Here, the armour, committed to a death stand, was dug in so that only the turrets were exposed. Emplacements had heavy adobe revetments, were under heavy foliage, and were a nucleus for all other defensive measures. Tanks were sited to cover the highways and cross-country approaches with mutually supporting fires. Close-in security of the armoured pillboxes was provided by automatic weapons and infantry dug in around each tank. Artillery, emplaced in covered positions, supplemented the tanks to complete an integrated fire plan. Last-resort counterattacks were launched at night once the local defences were doomed.

Tanks in defence

Japanese defence doctrine emphasises the offensive almost exclusively. The defence is considered to be a temporary phase of combat which the Japanese must accept because of overwhelming enemy superiority. The object of the defence is to deplete the enemy's strength until a counterattack can be initiated. The Japanese views on defensive combat, coupled with the predominantly offensive character of the tank, cause a lack of attention to defensive tactics. Japanese doctrine prescribes the use of tanks in counterattacks. They are expected to deliver short, speedy assaults upon the objectives in close cooperation with artillery. The engagement is to be broken off upon completion of the mission. If enemy tanks are present in superior numbers, counterattacking Japanese tanks try to coordinate their action with their own antitank-weapons fire.

Type 2 Ka-Mi amphibious tank on Babelthuap Island, Palau. With a significant garrison of over 30,000 men of the Imperial Japanese Army and Navy, the island fortress was bypassed in the island-hopping campaign. The Type 2 Ka-Mi was modification of the Ha-Go. Around 200 were built 1942–43. To 'swim' buoyancy pontoons were added to front and back.

In recent operations, the Japanese dug in their tanks and used them defensively as artillery and antitank weapons.

A comparison of Japanese doctrine with actual operations to date definitely reveals a complete failure on the part of Japanese commanders to employ armoured forces as prescribed by *Japanese Field Service Regulations*. Massed armour has never been used in offensive action. Defensive combat has been confined to a static defence with a final uncoordinated banzai counterattack. A truly coordinated attack has never materialized. The use of piecemeal, uncoordinated attacks may be due to physical impossibilities, lack of the proper means, a failure to understand the methods, or lack of training. In any event, one fact is paramount; to date the Japanese have not employed armour according to modern concepts.

When the demonstrated potency of Allied armour compelled the Japanese to seek more effective countermeasures, the strain on their industrial potential was already so great as to preclude satisfaction of field requirements on a scale comparable with the Germans. The result has been the appearance of a great number of improvisations of both standardized and field expedient types. Field improvisations often have sought to provide very powerful antitank mines by converting Navy depth charges, artillery projectiles and aerial bombs to antitank use. The Japanese are continuing to display typical ingenuity, persistence and bravery in this type of antitank warfare. Nonetheless they are handicapped by inferior material, although the crudeness of the various types of hollow charges and demolition charges is offset, to a degree, by the cunning and suicidal fanaticism with which the Japanese soldier handles them.

The Japanese, unable to cope successfully with Allied armour by conventional methods of antitank defence, have put unusual stress on close-quarter attacks. Individuals or small groups making these attacks are known as tank hunters, and their desperate, often suicidal, measures have received increased emphasis in recent operations.

Tank-hunter teams are organized and trained to attack tanks in battle at their vulnerable points, or to infiltrate into tank parks as small raiding parties to destroy the vehicles there. Each Japanese infantry platoon may have one of these units armed with demolition equipment, incendiaries, armour-piercing mines, mines tied to grenades, clusters of grenades, Molotov cocktails, or pole mines. Frequently, a group will operate with a combination of these weapons.

Individual suicide attacks

Japanese antitank methods include considerable individual action by Japanese soldiers in suicidal missions.

Another weapon is the shoulder-pack mine. With the mine strapped to his back, the Japanese conceals himself as close as possible to the path of the approaching tank. When the tank arrives at a point about 15ft from the concealed soldier, he dashes out and throws himself under it, between the tracks. He pulls a detonating cord when the tank is directly over him. The mine explodes 1 to 3 seconds after the cord is pulled.

In recent operations in Burma much reliance was placed on one-man suicide tank-hunting tactics. Types of suicide activities varied. Soldiers sat in fox holes with aerial bombs between their knees, prepared to detonate them by hand when an Allied tank pass over.

The Japanese did not begin to use mines effectively until after the Saipan campaign. Prior to that time, minefields were generally poorly sited and camouflaged, and often appeared to have been laid merely to get them into the ground. In recent operations, however, minefields have been much more soundly employed.

Japanese action against American tanks

Tanks must be supported by other arms, and a series of incidents involving destruction or loss of American tanks in the Solomons is reported by a member of our armed forces. This report shows the importance, at least in close-country, of closely supporting tanks with infantry.

On Guadalcanal a platoon of six light M3 tanks was sent to aid the infantry forces fighting to the west of the Lunga River. Headquarters tank and tanks Nos. 1, 4, and 5 were moved forward in column to attack enemy machine guns on the edge of the jungle across a clearing from the infantry. Tank No. 4 went into the jungle and has not been found since. Tank No. 5, after entering a short way, backed out of the jungle without having found any targets. The driver of Tank No. 5 said that near the edge of the jungle, the Japanese threw grenades under the tracks. The explosion of the grenades would cause the tank to jump somewhat but did not cause any noticeable damage. This tank was stationary when it was hit on the right forward side of the turret. The shell penetrated the tank and hit the opposite turret wall where it exploded. The driver estimated that the antitank gun which hit his tanks was about 100 yards away. Filling from shell ran down and began to burn with a yellow flame and bluish smoke. The driver stated that the fumes were sharp and stifling and caused the mouth to dry and pucker. Almost immediately after the first hit, a second hit was received in the right side of the turret. The shell penetrated and spattered filling around, which likewise began to burn on the floor and on the top of the ammunition lockers. Efforts to put out the fire were unavailing and the survivors jumped out of the tank and started for the rear. Japanese troops were moving toward the tank and shortly after it was abandoned, the driver saw it burning fiercely, but did not know whether the Japanese had thrown gasoline on it or not.

The Headquarters tank was disabled by a hit on the right sprocket wheel while about 40ft into the jungle.

Tank No. 1 was circling in the open field in rear of Tank No. 5 when it was hit in the

Potentially the best of the Japanese tanks, the Type 3 Chi-Nu medium tank had a 75mm main gun – the closest the Japanese came to matching Allied weapons – but saw no action because the complete build (around 150) was kept to defend the mainland.

turret. The lieutenant and radioman were killed but the tank was recovered. Fire in Tank No. 1 was extinguished without great difficulty. The diameter of the hole in Tank No. 1 was slightly larger than that of our 37mm shell.

The company commander estimated that from the number of hits received by his tanks, and the location of the tanks when hit, the enemy had five antitank guns. The calibre of the enemy guns was believed to be 47mm.

This is the first (at time reported) encounter with the Japanese 47mm antitank gun. It easily penetrated turret armour of light M3 tanks. The action of the shell after entering the tank seems to indicate an explosive filler made from a pierate derivative. The enemy apparently waited for a close range shot before opening fire.

There was no evidence of the use of the magnetic tank grenade although some had been captured previously on Guadalcanal.

Above: The impressive Tiger is often seen as the epitome of the World War II tank: strong armour, a powerful main armament – the Tigers earned a reputation that has continued long after the war. There's no doubt that their kill ratios are dramatic but as Lt Col Albin F. Irzyk asked, 'Could 53 Tiger tanks, for instance, move from the vicinity of Fenetrange, France, in the Saar, to an area near Bastogne, Belgium, a distance of 151 miles, in less than twenty-four hours to answer a fire call, as did tanks of the Fourth Armored Division?'   The answer is, almost certainly, no!

Right: On the Burma Road – Chinese and American crews bring M4 Shermans to China.

Appendices

1 Tank Guns, Gunnery and Ammunition

While armour and mobility are important, the gun is what defines the tank. Images of Tigers and Shermans dominate our impression of World War II but it's worth remembering that most of those images are of the second half of the war, from late 1942. Those countries that entered the war in 1939 used much smaller vehicles with lesser armaments. A great progression during the war years saw the tank's main armament increase in size from 37–45mm (the British 2pdr = 40mm) to 3-inch or higher: the Firefly's 17pdr = 3-inch = 76.2mm; the T34/85 had an 85mm main gun; the Tiger I and II had 88mm; the M36 TD and M26 Pershing had a 90mm; the Su-100 TD a 100mm; there was a Sherman variant with a 105mm; the IS-2 and IS-3 fielded a 122mm; the Maus and Jagdtiger a 128mm; and the Red Army's KV-2 a whopping 152mm.

However, size doesn't mean penetration and not all these weapons were antitank guns: the early Infantry or Close Support tanks had 95mm howitzers to fire HE or canister; the same is true of the early PzKpfw IVs, whose short 75mm was for infantry support (the muzzle velocity was too low for it to be a tank killer) while the PzKpfw III's 37mm was for antitank use. However, as the war progressed, the Germans developed a long-barrelled 75mm which reached its peak with the Panther's L/70 gun. The PzKpfw III/IV's longer-barrelled 75mms could still fire HE or smoke, but the Panther's couldn't. The same is true of the Sherman, whose 75mm was a good all-round gun, but the Sherman needed upgunning to 76mm (or to 17pdr by the British) to become an effective antitank gun and in doing so lost its effective HE and smoke shell. The Americans also upgunned the Sherman to 105mm for infantry support or assault.

Smoke was important on the battlefield and most tanks had some method of creating smoke. German and British tanks had smoke dischargers (which had the down side of having to be filled externally; the US Army had an internal 2-inch mortar. Tank smoke shells could be white phosphorous (producing a cloud of white smoke which not only obscured the battlefield but also had an incendiary effect) or chemical smoke (this could be dyed for marking or signalling). The Russians used a different system for making smoke, pumping diesel fuel directly into their exhaust system. This led to a white cloud of smoke behind the tank.

A 1946 memorandum from the US Army Staff College at Fort Leavenworth looked at one of the problems of American tank guns in World War II vis-à-vis the Germans'. The arguments are revealing and show some of the considerations of tank designers and ordnance boards that may not be apparent to the layman. It is a very negative assessment of the US Army's tank force and shows a brutal honesty to identify the issues with US tank guns.

This tank graveyard near Isigny is filled with tanks knocked out in the Normandy campaign. Some of them would have been abandoned – many of the Tigers lost in France were destroyed by their crew after automotive issues. The destruction of tanks and other war matériel – particularly bridges – often required a command decision but the exigencies of war meant that often the decision was taken by a man on the spot. As outlined in the US Army's *FM 17-76* it 'will be undertaken only on authority delegated by division or higher commanders. Destruction is ordered only after every possible measure for the preservation or salvage of the matériel has been taken, and when in the judgment of the person exercising the authority such action is necessary to prevent: (1) Its abandonment in the combat zone; (2) Its capture intact by the enemy; (3) Its use by the enemy, if captured, against our own or allied troops.' How was it done? Two methods are outlined: 'Remove and empty the portable fire extinguishers. Smash the radio. Puncture fuel tanks. Use fire of calibre .50 machine gun, or a cannon, or use a fragmentation grenade for this purpose. Place TNT charges as follows: 3lb between engine oil cooler and right fuel tank; 2lb under left side of transmission as far forward as possible. Insert tetryl nonelectric caps with at least 5ft of safety fuse in each charge. Ignite the fuses and take cover. Elapsed time: 1 to 2 minutes, if charges are prepared beforehand and carried in the vehicle.' Also suggested, if there's time, is destruction of tracks by use of 2lb TNT charges. The manual, however, adds the proviso 'If charges are prepared beforehand and carried in the vehicle, keep the caps and fuses separated from the charges until used.'

The second method is to fire on the vehicle 'using adjacent tanks, antitank or other artillery, or antitank rockets or grenades. Aim at engine, suspension, and armament in the order named. If a good fire is started, the vehicle may be considered destroyed. Elapsed time: About 5 minutes per vehicle. Destroy the last remaining vehicle by the best means available.'

Fire Orders

[from *Armored Force Field Manual FM 17–12 Tank Gunnery*, 22 April 1943]

Enunciate orders clearly. Much time is lost when a crew member has to ask for a repetition of part of the data… Develop the voice of command. This is a businesslike, confident tone of voice which conveys assurance to the crew. A screaming voice marks the amateur, as do overloud commands intended for a single crew.

A Before giving fire orders, alert the gunner. Say 'Gunner' (turret gunner) or 'Bog' (bow gunner). Give the orders in the following sequence:

Sequence	Example
1 Target description	ANTITANK
2 Type of ammunition to fire	HE
3 Direction to traverse turret	TRAVERSE RIGHT
4 Stopping traverse	STEADY … ON
5 Range	ONE, TWO HUNDRED
6 Lead	ONE ZERO
7 Command to open fire	FIRE

B Use the following words to describe the usual targets:

Sequence	Example
1 Any tank	TANK
2 Armored car	ARMORED CAR
3 Any unarmored vehicle	TRUCK
4 Men	DOUGHS
5 Machine gun	MACHINE GUN
6 antitank gun or artillery piece	ANTITANK

C Describe the ammunition as follows:

Sequence	Example
1 Armor-piercing	SHOT
2 High-explosive	HE
3 Smoke	SMOKE
4 Canister	CANISTER
5 Caliber .30 machine gun	CALIBER .30

EXAMPLES OF FIRE ORDERS

1 Tank gun, stationary target.
GUNNER
ANTITANK
HE
TRAVERSE RIGHT
STEADY … ON
ONE TWO HUNDRED
FIRE

2 Tank gun, moving target.
GUNNER
TANK
SHOT
TRAVERSE LEFT
STEADY … ON
EIGHT HUNDRED
LEAD ONE ZERO FIRE

3 Coaxial machine gun, stationary target.
GUNNER
TRUCK
CALIBER THIRTY
TRAVERSE RIGHT
STEADY … ON
FIVE HUNDRED
FIRE

4 Bow machine gun, stationary target.
BOG
DOUGHS
RIGHT FRONT
FIRE

5a Platoon commander concentrating fire of section on stationary target.
FIRST SECTION
ANTITANK
WATCH MY BURST

5b The platoon commander's tank then fires until the target is plainly indicated to the others, after which he commands:
FIRST SECTION
ONE EIGHT HUNDRED
FIRE

Characteristics for tank guns
[Col H. L. Hillyard (edited excerpts)]

The trend in development of tank guns throughout the war was to increase the caliber and improve the mechanical features, also to increase the armour-piercing or explosive power of the ammunition with but little emphasis on the high-velocity flat-trajectory characteristic.

Experience has shown that the ability to get a hit with the first round is often the decisive factor and that flat trajectory is necessary if this is to be accomplished. In tank against tank combat the one getting the hit usually wins. German tank and SP guns were able to get a hit first round because of their flat trajectory. Our tanks had to fire several rounds to get a hit and were subject to being destroyed or having the target obscured during the process. The arguments for and against the adoption of this principle:

Reasons For
• The probability of hitting an enemy tank with the first round could be changed from improbable to almost certain.
• The increased velocity would increase the range and penetration of AP and APC type projectiles.
• Direct hits, even if they do not penetrate, usually get one of three results, i.e., the crew abandons tank, the tank is disabled, or the tank withdraws,
• With the adequate artillery support we have had, the use of tanks for high angle indirect fire is not necessary.
• High velocity direct fire has a great adverse morale effect on the enemy.
• Confidence and morale of tank crews would increase immensely if they/ could expect to get a hit on an enemy tank with the first round.

Reasons Against
• Tank guns with the velocity and trajectory desired wouldn't be suitable for indirect fire.
• The life of the tube per number of rounds fired would be reduced.
• Increasing the size of the shell case would decrease the number of rounds that could be carried.
• Increasing the length of the tube would decrease the maneuverability of the tank in close quarters.
• The problems of design of recoil mechanisms, elevating and transversing mechanisms, etc., would be increased.

Appendix A of the report examined the general characteristics are desired in tank guns and ammunition:

A Tank guns and ammunition: general characteristics

Guns should be specifically designed with reference to the space limitations in tanks, and with emphasis in obtaining:

(1) The shortest practicable chamber.

(2) The shortest distance from trunnion to breech block that is consistent with a balanced turret.

(3) The shortest recoil with a compact recoil mechanism.

(4) A semi-automatic breech.

(5) Automatic loading with selective dual feeding of ammunition and capable of both electrical and mechanical firing.

(6) Automatic gun fume scavenging.

B Tank guns and ammunition: development

Appendix B provides examples of the development of tank guns and ammunition during the war. They show the tendency to increase the size of the weapon and the armour-piercing quality of the ammunition, with little or no increase in the possibility of hitting the target.

Examples

(1) The light tank gun was increased in size from 37mm to 75mm late in the war. The tank as a whole was a great improvement but while the effects against personnel, area targets, etc., are increased, the ability to get direct hits on enemy tanks, vehicles, etc., is actually decreased

(2) The medium tank gun was first increased in size from 75mm to 76mm. This higher velocity did not insure a hit with the first round at ranges where the Germans could expect hits.

Also, the muzzle blast from the 76mm was increased so that it was practically impossible to observe fire from the tank. The net result was that when the 76mm fired at an enemy tank the crew was temporarily blinded.

(3) The 105mm gun was mounted in the medium tank and recommended for use against enemy tanks. This weapon had many uses as direct and indirect artillery fire but was not suitable for tank fighting because of its high trajectory.

(4) The 90mm gun tank was the last wartime development – a definite improvement and was quite successfully mounted in tank destroyers. Its velocity is sufficiently high so that it has a good chance of getting hits but the gun is big and. The same or better results could be obtained in tank combat with a smaller higher velocity gun.

(5) HEAT ammunition was developed and had good penetrating ability. This was a low velocity ammunition and because of its high trajectory, direct hits on enemy tanks were seldom made.

C Tank guns and ammunition: examples of combat

Appendix C of the report provided examples of tank combat in the 2nd Armoured Division which indicate the effectiveness of hits on armoured vehicles. The point to be considered is that direct hits must be made, near misses have little or no effect and that to compensate for errors in range estimation and to reduce dispersion a high-velocity flat-trajectory weapon is necessary:

(1) December 1942 in Tunisia. The first 5 tanks of Co G 67th AR to go on the battlefield received a hail of hits from 88mm guns at about 2,000 yards. All tanks were disabled or destroyed.

(2) July 1943 near Gela, Sicily. Five tanks of Co G 67th AR returning over a previously traveled road met a [German] MkVI tank at a road bend. Four of the tanks were destroyed and the fifth was hit, in a matter of seconds, by five rounds from the Tiger tank.

(3) July 1944 near Notre-Dame le Cenilly, France. The command tank of Co C 67th AR came into the line of fire of a German tank. The first round fired penetrated the turret, killing the company commander and the radio operator.

(4) July 1944 near Notre-Dame le Cenilly, France. The first round fired from a German antitank gun went through the turret of the command tank of the 1st Bn 67th AR, killing Lt-Col Nelson.

(5) August 1944 near St-Sever-Calvados, France. Five tanks of Co G 66th AR were deployed in the open when a German tank 1,500 yards on the flank fired 7 rounds, got 7 hits and destroyed 5 tanks. The fourth and fifth tanks had been able to start traversing their guns before they were destroyed.

(6) August 1944 near le-Neuberg, France. Two scout cars of the 67th AR got close to two Panther tanks. The hits from the 37mm guns caused the two Panthers to make a run for safety. A lucky hit through an open hatch caused one Panther to explode.

(7) October 1944 near Ubach, Germany. C Co 67th AR light tanks mounting 37mm guns broke through into an enemy rear area. Hits and surprise caused five Tiger tanks to withdraw in confusion.

(8) January 1944 near Freynaux, Belgium. During the tank attack on the town, the tanks of the Bn Ex officer and Company Commander (the two command tanks) were singled out of the formation by a German gun and destroyed. Both rounds were through the turrets and the officers were killed.

Ambush

First-time accuracy was an important thing in tank action, but equally if not more important was positioning. The reason that the Allies were able to defeat the top German tanks is because they were adept at setting up ambushes.

Ambushed Tiger pack

SS-pinup boy and killer of 138 tanks and 132 antitank guns on the Eastern and Normandy fronts, SS-Hauptsturmführer Michael Wittmann died on 8 August 1944 in a forlorn counterattack against British and Canadian forces south of Caen. He was one of four tanks knocked out by Joe Ekins of A Squadron, 1st Northamptonshire Yeomanry (although the Canadian Sherbrooke Fusiliers also claim the kill).

Wittmann and three other Tigers were moving north when they walked into a classic tank ambush. Concealed in an orchard, Joe Ekins' tank was in A Squadron's 3 Troop, commanded by Sgt Gordon. At 12:39, when the range was down to 800m and the Tigers were sideways-on exposing thinner armour, Gordon engaged them.

First, Joe Ekins fired two rounds at the rearmost tank. Both rounds hit the Tiger and it quickly burst into flames. Pulling back and heading for a new position, Gordon dodged a return shot by another tank, but was rendered unconscious as the commander's hatch crashed down on his head.

Troop commander Lt James left his vehicle and took over, climbing into the hatch. Shortly after, at 12:47, Ekins fired on Tiger number 007 – Wittmann's tank – and knocked it out before hitting a third with two more 17pdr rounds. In less than 15 minutes with five rounds of ammunition, he'd knocked out three Tigers. Shortly after he knocked out a PzKpfw IV before his vehicle was hit. It was his last shot in anger. Shortly after he was given the job of wireless operator. Wittmann and his crew were buried, at La Cambe cemetery.

Stalking the Panther

Like Ekins, American tank gunner Clarence Smoyer became famous thanks to one engagement. On 6 March 1945, during the Battle of Cologne in March 1945, his duel with a German Panther was filmed. The Panther had already knocked out two Shermans, but it was stalked on foot by M26 Pershing tank commander Sgt Bob Earley. 'In the time between when he saw it and when he got back to us, that Panther turned its gun and was ready for us,' Smoyer said, 'I snapped off a quick shot and hit him first. I kept yelling for AP rounds and hit him again and again until he caught fire. I could hardly breathe as we backed out of there. People always ask why I fired three times, not giving the German crew a chance to flee. Well, that was the rule. Any crewman still alive in that Panther could have pulled the trigger and with that powerful gun pointing at us, we would all be dead and not here to tell the tale.'

Above The Panther knocked out by Clarence Smoyer in Cologne. Even the top tank crews could be caught during urban fighting. Wittmann's famous mauling of 7th Armoured Division's advance guard at Villers Bocage (**Below**) on the morning of June 1944 is the stuff of legend – but sPzAbt 101 and Panzer Lehr lost six Tigers and a PzKpfw IV in the village streets that afternoon thanks to carefully sited antitank guns and the Firefly of Sgt Bobby Bramhall.

Tank ammunition

AP (armour-piecing) These rounds use kinetic energy to penetrate the armour. Key to their success are the mass of the round and the muzzle velocity of the weapon. If it penetrates armour it will damage whatever it hits but if it doesn't cause fire or an explosion the tank may well be recoverable.

APBC (armour-piercing, ballistic cap) The cap acts as a windshield to improve the aerodynamics of an AP round.

APC (armour-piercing, capped) Tank armour was increasingly face-hardened during the war to reduce penetration. A cap with a hard tip was designed to break this. Bad point: against non-hardened plates it reduces KE.

APCBC (armour-piercing, capped, ballistic cap) An APBC round with a piercing cap.

APCR/APCNR (armour-piercing, composite, rigid/non-rigid) Increasing muzzle velocity requires more energy (powder) and shells become unwieldy. This alternative sees a decrease in the calibre of the penetrator and use of a high-density material, in World War II often Tungsten, housed in a lightweight (eg Aluminium) shell. In US parlance this is HVAP. NB the increased muzzle velocity doesn't lead to higher KE because of the reduced mass. Improved penetration is down to the concentration of the KE into a smaller area. This system was used effectively to improve older weapons. The non-rigid type uses the same principle as APCR, but the gun barrel tapers and the shell is squeezed preventing gasses from escaping the barrel. The Germans favoured the APCNR system eg with the 7.5cm Pak 41, which fired a 75mm shell that was reduced to 55mm. Other than the availability of Tungsten, the biggest problem with this was barrel wear. The Pak 41 had a barrel life of 1,000 rounds, compared to 5–7,000 for the Pak 39.

APDS (armour-piercing discarding sabot) Introduced by the British in 1944 for use in the 6pdr/17pdr ATk gun, this was another version of APCR using a smaller hard-rod projectile to attack tanks with high KE rounds. The outer shell – the sabot – was discarded as it left the muzzle.

Canister Shotgun round used against infantry.

HE (high explosive) While mainly used against B vehicles, personnel and buildings, a sufficiently large HE blast (usually by artillery) could seriously damage a tank. Indeed, so could lighter rounds (including mortars) hitting the thinner armour of the roof of a turret. HE also could do damage to tracks and suspension.

-HE (HE filler) Some AP shells were modified to take an explosive filler (AP-HE) but this made the shell more likely to break up on impact, rather than penetrating. If it did penetrate before exploding it did more damage.

HEAT (high explosive, antitank) Shaped-charge round which uses the Munroe effect by focusing the blast energy by means of a conical void at the front of the blasting charge lined with copper to produce a concentrated beam of molten particles which can penetrate armour steel to a depth of 7 times the diameter of the charge. As KE isn't a factor, MV isn't important and this means most infantry-launched weapons (Bazooka, Panzerfaust, Panzerschreck, PIAT) are HEAT rounds. The range is shorter, however, making them less useful for long-range defence favoured by the Germans. NB Stand-off armour – the German Schürzen – was introduced to stop spalling by antitank rifle fire: it had some effect on HEAT rounds but it would take proper spaced armour to be effective against this type of round.

HESH (high-explosive squash-head) Shaped-charge round causing inside spalling that kills crew and destroys internal equipment.

HIGr (*Hohlgranate*) = HEAT.

HVAP (high-velocity, armour-piercing). See APCR.

KE (kinetic energy) What you need to penetrate armour.

Kwk (*Kampfwagenkanone*) = AFV gun (tank or PzSp)

MV (muzzle velocity) Speed increases KE, and increased KE increases penetration.

PzGr (*Panzergranate*) = Tank shell

SpGr (*Sprenggranate*) = HE shell

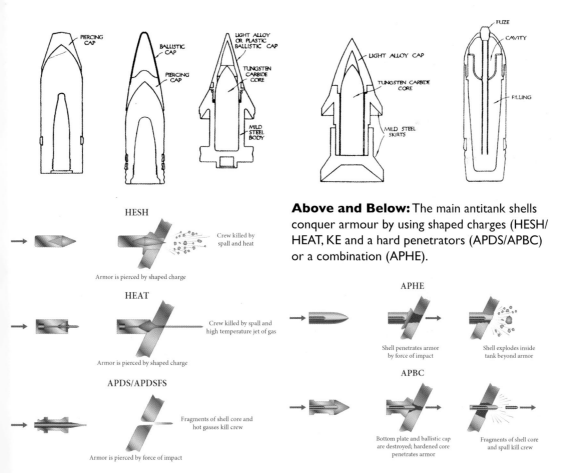

Above and Below: The main antitank shells conquer armour by using shaped charges (HESH/HEAT, KE and a hard penetrators (APDS/APBC) or a combination (APHE).

HESH
Crew killed by spall and heat
Armor is pierced by shaped charge

HEAT
Crew killed by spall and high temperature jet of gas
Armor is pierced by shaped charge

APDS/APDSFS
Fragments of shell core and hot gasses kill crew
Armor is pierced by force of impact

APHE
Shell penetrates armor by force of impact
Shell explodes inside tank beyond armor

APBC
Bottom plate and ballistic cap are destroyed; hardened core penetrates armor
Fragments of shell core and spall kill crew

Ammunition stowage capacity

Tank	Main gun	Rounds	Tank	Main gun	Rounds
Tiger I	88mm	92	M4 Sherman	75mm	95
Tiger II	88mm	86	M4 Sherman	76mm	71
Panther	75mm	79	Sherman Firefly	17pdr	77
PzKpfw IV	75mm	122	Cromwell	75mm	64
PzKpfw III	50mm	90	M10 TD	3-inch	54
T-34 Model 1941	76.2mm	77	M18 TD	76mm	45
T-34/85	85mm	60	M36 TD	90mm	47

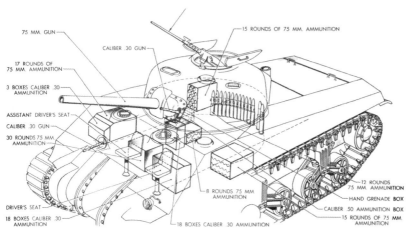

Every tank had different ammunition stowage. Here the diagram for an M4A4 (**Left**) and an M4A2 (**Below and Below Right**). When M4 wet stowage (**Right**) came in, all other than ready rounds were stored below the turret basket and surrounded in liquid to reduce the likelihood of fire if hit.

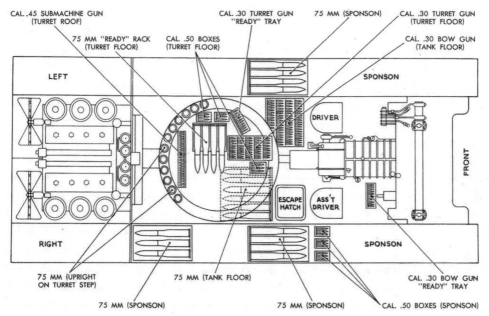

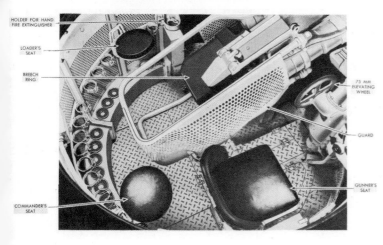

HOLDER FOR HAND
FIRE EXTINGUISHER

LOADER'S
SEAT

BREECH
RING

75 MM
ELEVATING
WHEEL

GUARD

GUNNER'S
SEAT

COMMANDER'S
SEAT

Left The ready rounds are visible in this view of a M10 TD. The *Armored Force Field Manual Tank Gunnery (FM 17-12)* looks closely at ammunition stowage:

'(a) The order of withdrawing ammunition from its stowage space in the tank is based on the principle that some readily accessible rounds always will be saved for emergency use. Other crew members will pass ammunition to the cannoneer if necessary to prevent his having to use these rounds. During combat, the position of the turret will affect the accessibility of the ammunition in various parts of the tank. In drill, however, establish a sound method from which commanders may deviate as the need arise.

(b) Ammunition is taken from its stowage space in the tank in the order:
(1) Three front rows left of power tunnel;
(2) racks beside bow gunner in right sponson; (3) top racks behind bow gunner. The two rear rows left of the power tunnel will be saved as a reserve for action where speed of loading is of the utmost importance. As time permits, or on the command RESTOW AMMUNITION, rounds are moved from the racks beside the gunner in the right sponson and from the bottom racks behind the bow gunner to those which have been emptied in firing.

(c) Upon completion of restowing, reports are given on the number of rounds remaining. For example the bow gunner reports, "Three smoke, six HE in forward racks right sponson; one-two HE remaining right of power tunnel." The gunner reports, "Rear racks right sponson empty." The cannoneer reports, "Three smoke, three HEAT, one-nine HE remaining left of power tunnel." '

Examples of markings on ammunition

[From *Handbuch die Munition der deutschen Geschütze und Werfer*, 1943]

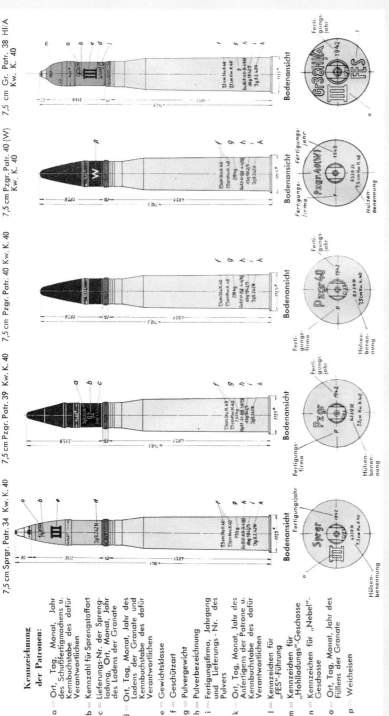

Kennzeichnung der Patronen:

a = Ort, Tag, Monat, Jahr des Schußfertigmachens u. Kennbuchstabe des dafür Verantwortlichen

b = Kennzahl für Sprengstoffart

c = Lieferungs-Nr. der Sprengladung, Ort, Monat, Jahr des Ladens der Granate

d = Ort, Tag, Monat, Jahr des Ladens der Granate und Kennbuchstabe des dafür Verantwortlichen

e = Gewichtsklasse

f = Geschützart

g = Pulvergewicht

h = Pulverbezeichnung

i = Fertigungsfirma, Jahrgang und Lieferungs-Nr. des Pulvers

k = Ort, Tag, Monat, Jahr des Anfertigens der Patrone u. Kennbuchstabe des dafür Verantwortlichen

l = Kennzeichen für "FES"-Führung

m = Kennzeichen für "Hohlladungs"-Geschosse

n = Kennzeichen für "Nebel"-Geschosse

o = Ort, Tag, Monat, Jahr des Füllens der Granate

p = Weicheisen

These are for 7.5cm StuK 40 and 7.5cm Kwk 40. 7.5cm *Sprenggranate* (HE) *Patrone* (shell) 34 Kwk 40, 7.5cm *Panzergranate* (AP) Patrone 39 Kwk 40, 7.5cm PzGr (AP) Patrone 40 Kwk 40, 7.5cm PzGr (AP) Patrone 40 (W = *Weicheisen* = soft iron) Kwk 40, 7.5cm *Granate* Patrone 40 (W) Kwk 40 Hl (*Hohlladung* = shaped charge) A

Identification marks on shells (a) Place, day, month, year that the round was prepared and code letter identifying company responsible; (b) Indicator of type of explosive; (c) Delivery number of the explosive charge and place, month, year of loading of the shell; (d) Place, day, month, year of filling of the shell and code letter for company responsible; (e) Weight class; (f) Type of gun; (g) Powder weight; (h) Powder identification; (i) Company who prepared, year and delivery number of the powder; (k) Place, day, month, year of assembly of the projectile and code letter for company responsible; (l) Mark for FES guide (FES is found on many Pzgr. 39 rounds and indicates iron driving bands); (m) Identification mark indicating hollow charge shot; (n) Identification mark indicating smoke shot; (o) Place, day, month, year of filling of the shell; (p) soft iron.

Bodenansicht = View of baseplate; *Fertigungsjahr* = Year prepared; *Fertigungsfirma* = Firm prepared; *Hülsenbenennung* = Case designation

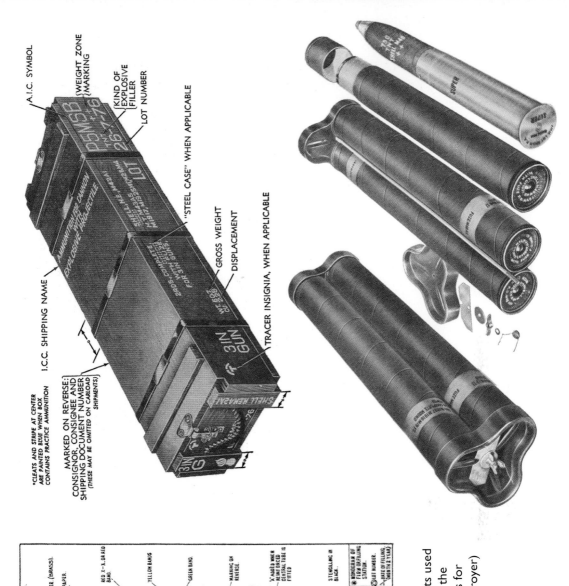

Above Right and Right: All combatants used ammunition packaging. These are typical of the US versions – the box carrying two rounds for a 3-inch gun (as used in the M10 tank destroyer) and a pack of three M48 75mm shells with M48A2 fuses.

Above: PIAT HEAT projectile markings.

Tank Gunnery

[edited excerpts from *FM17–12 Armoured Force Field Manual
Tank Gunnery*, April, 22, 1943]

Gunnery training is divided into 17 steps. Insist on a satisfactory standard for each step.
Give simple tests to determine proficiency in each step.

a. Basic training period (first fifteen weeks).

(1) Operation and handling of equipment.

(2) Care and maintenance. – The continued functioning of weapons in battle is dependent on their receiving proper care and maintenance. Make the crews realize that their lives depend on it.

(3) Crew drill.

(4) Simulated firing, direct laying.

(5) Range and speed estimation – Practice under conditions illustrating the following:

  (1) Targets appear nearer and the range is underestimated when

    a The object is in bright light.

    b The color of the object contrasts sharply with the color of the background.

    c Looking over water, snow, or a uniform surface such as a wheat field or in the desert.

    d Looking down a straight road or along a railroad track.

    e Looking downward from a height.

    f Looking over a depression, most of which is hidden.

  (2) Targets seem more distant and range is overestimated when

    a Looking over a depression, most of which is visible.

    b There is poor light or fog, or in the rain.

    c Only a small part of the target is visible.

    d Looking from low ground toward higher ground.

(6) Ammunition – Selection of weapon and ammunition

    a *General.* Conserve the 75mm and 37mm ammunition. Do not use the tank gun against a target when the machine guns can handle it. When necessary, do not hesitate to use both machine guns and tank against a target.

    b *Machine gun.* Use machine guns against exposed personnel targets, as infantry, crews of weapons who are not protected by armour or emplacements, and personnel in unarmoured vehicles.

    c *Canister (37mm).* Canister is very effective against exposed personnel at ranges less than 200 yards. It is useless at greater ranges.

    d *Armour-piercing ammunition.* Use armour- or armour-piercing HE ammunition against medium and heavy tanks. Do not use it at ranges over 500 yards for 37mm and over 2,000 yards for 75mm.

e *High-explosive shell.* Use high-explosive shell with delay fuse against unarmoured and lightly armoured vehicles, antitank guns, and artillery pieces. If HE shell is lacking, use combination AP-HE against these targets. At ranges over 2,000 yards, use 75mm HE shell against tanks; a hit on the track will disable the tank; fragmentation from near misses harasses the crew.

Armour-piercing ammunition

a *Armour-piercing (AP).* This ammunition is a solid projectile with a tracer element. 75mm shot, AP, M72, and 37mm shot, AP, M74, are in this class. The projectile is painted black.

b *Armour-piercing, capped (APC).* This ammunition is a solid projectile with an armour-piercing cap, a windshield, and a tracer element. The cap is of alloy steel, hardened to insure a very hard face with a tough and relatively soft core in contact with the projectile. 75mm projectile, APC, M61, and 37mm shot, APC, M51, are of this type. The projectile is painted black.

c *Armour-piercing, high explosive (AP-HE).* This ammunition is an armour-piercing projectile containing an explosive charge and a base-detonating fuse. This is the most effective armour-piercing ammunition because the projectile bursts after penetration. 75-mm projectile, APC, M61 with BD (base-detonating) fuse M66 contains a high explosive charge, and is painted yellow.

Gunnery practice on the ranges for these M5 light (Stuart) tanks. Their main armament was a 37mm M6, a peashooter that was only effective against light enemy units.

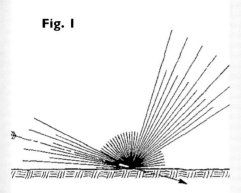

Fig. I

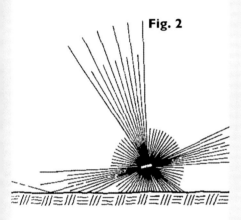

Fig. 2

Fig. 1. Impact burst.

Fig. 2. Ricochet burst.

Fig. 3. Firing 75mm shell, HE. With the fuze set at DELAY, a short bursts on ricochet. Ricochet bursts are deadly against personnel.

High-explosive shell.
The PD fuze M48 used with 75mm shell, HE, M48, is a combination superquick or delay point-detonating fuze. The shell comes set at 'superquick.' It may be set to burst .05 second after impact by turning the slotted key on the side of the fuze so that the slot points to the word DELAY stamped on the body of the fuze. Always set the fuse at DELAY before stowing the ammunition.

(1) Superquick action
The superquick action is so sensitive that the shell detonates immediately on impact. There- fore, when striking armor plate, a gun shield, or a building, the shell will burst before it can penetrate. The superquick burst is effective against personnel in the open (Fig. I).

(2) Delay action
The .05-second delay action results in the shell penetrating before bursting when it strikes light armor, gun shields, or buildings. If the shell strikes the ground, it ricochets, travels 20–25 yards beyond the point of impact, and then bursts about 10ft in the air (Fig. 2). Because of the downspray from the burst in the air, a ricochet burst has devastating effect on personnel without overhead cover. It is much more effective than the impact burst obtained from a superquick fuze setting. When the fuze is set at DELAY a hit will destroy or damage the target and kill or injure nearby personnel; a 'short' will give a ricochet which is deadly against personnel (Fig. 3), Thus with the delay fuze, dispersion is in your favor as long as the range error is not excessive.

Fig. 3

(7) Subcalibre firing, direct laying.
(8) Proficiency test.
(9) Basic firing, direct laying.

b. Unit training period (second twelve weeks).

(10) Platoon drill, direct laying. Platoon drill combines crew drill and simulated firing by the platoon as a whole. This develops the ability to coordinate and concentrate the fire of the platoon.
(11) Platoon firing, direct laying.
(12) Drill, indirect laying, single tank.
(13) Firing, indirect laying, single tank.
(14) Drill, indirect laying, two or more tanks.
(15) Firing, indirect laying, two or more tanks.
(16) Combat firing of small units – Tank versus tank firing with M4 medium or MS light tanks, using caliber .30 ammunition, is appropriate for this step. It is excellent training. Have the tanks completely buttoned up. Remove vulnerable accessories such as lights and sirens. The machine guns are not loaded until the tanks are buttoned up. Exercise strict control over the firing by radio. Use single shots with the coaxial machine guns to simulate the fire of tank cannon.
(17) Combat firing of large units.

Summary

a. Coordinate gunnery training with the progress of training as a whole. Conduct the first nine steps, to include basic firing, during the basic training period. The remaining steps are appropriate for the unit training period.
b. Conduct crew drill and simulated firing constantly. Review previous steps frequently. Have firing as often as ammunition allowances permit. Even though in an advanced state of training, always work on improving the marksmanship of each crew. After maneuvers, changes of station, and like periods, go back and review all steps of gunnery, emphasizing fundamentals. Practice range and speed estimation constantly—it is the key to accurate firing.
c. The most important subject, because it is most easily neglected, is care and maintenance of weapons. This must receive constant thought and supervision, not only by gunnery officers, but by all commanders.
d. Officers' training follows the same phases as enlisted men, but they should receive instruction in indirect laying and discuss its possible uses relatively early in troop school courses.
e. Insist on extreme accuracy at all times.

2 Antitank Warfare

The development of the tank in the early war years, as PzKpfw I and II, Matilda I and lighter tanks gave way to bigger gunned, uparmoured behemoths, led to a similar development in antitank weaponry. Most countries did not see tanks' main function as killing other tanks: they were designed to break through enemy lines and play havoc in the relatively unguarded rear areas. The antitank gun was the main infantry antitank weapon and as tanks' armour improved, so did the antitank guns as 37mm, 2pdr and 50mm gave way to the 6pdr, 75mm and then the heavyweights: the 17pdr and 88mm weapons. From the start the Germans had made use of the flexibility of their Flak 18 antiaircraft gun as a tank killer. However, as well as fixed antitank guns – although they would continue to be an important infantry weapon – other armoured vehicles, dubbed tank destroyers, were designed to kill the tanks. In American doctrine this idea was taken to the extreme and tank destroyers were supposed to be held in reserve awaiting their chance en masse to counter an armoured breakthrough. The Germans had a range of them, Marder I–III, Hornisse/Nashorn, Ferdinand/Elefant and various Jagdpanzers, and even the infantry support Sturm-geschütz series proved an excellent tank destroyer, particularly in the defence. The Italians used their SP artillery Semovente 75/18 as a tank destroyer and the Allies had the US M10/M18/M36. The British produced the Archer (a 17pdr on a Valentine chassis). They upgunned the M10 Achilles with a 17pdr. The Challenger (on a Cromwell chassis) was delayed and saw the Firefly take its role. The Russians followed the Germans' lead and produced a range of tank destroyers – the SU-76 on the T-70 light tank chassis; the SU-85 and -100 on the T-34; the SU-152 on the KV-1; and the ISU-122 and -152 on the IS-2.

During World War I and after, most armies had antitank rifles on their inventory: the Germans' 13mm T-Gewehr was the first and led to a range of Panzerbüchse. The British had the .55in Boys (nicknamed the Elephant Gun). These proved less and less effective against tanks and hand-held infantry antitank weapons seemed dead and buried until the arrival of hand-held, one-shot infantry weapons – Panzerfaust, Panzerschreck, Bazooka, PIAT. These gave the infantry a deadly close-combat weapon that accounted for many Allied vehicles in the final months of fighting in Germany, often wielded by children or old men. Longer range versions – the Raketenwurfer 43 Püppchen – were mounted on wheels. An interesting sideline was the development of the recoilless rifle which would become so popular postwar. The German Leicht-geschütz series was used by German paras and copied by the Americans who developed the 75mm M20 recoilless rifle used in the Korean War.

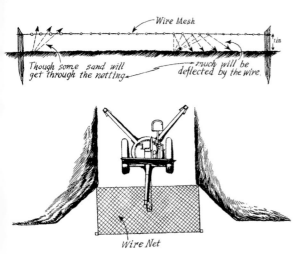

Wire Mesh

1in

Though some sand will get through the netting.

much will be deflected by the wire.

Wire Net

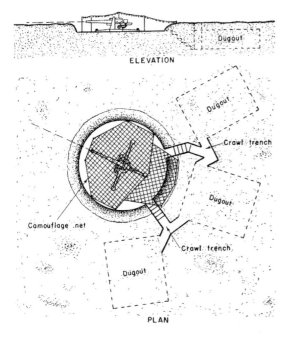

Dugout

ELEVATION

Dugout

Crawl trench

Camouflage net

Dugout

Crawl trench

Dugout

PLAN

The Germans made brilliant use of carefully sited antitank guns, and regularly lured the British tanks onto them in the desert war where long sightlines and little cover played to the strengths of the famous '88'. However, as the war went on and Allied air cover improved, the ability to fire and move became more important militating against towed antitank guns and leading to the increase of mobile SP artillery.

Above Left: Cutting down on dust raised by firing (and thus giving away the gun position) in the desert.

Above: A well-sited Pak dominates these valley roads.

Left and Below: The only defect of the 88 was its height. Where possible, a dug-in emplacement and camouflage helped.

Emplacement of antitank guns

[Pages 148–154 are edited excerpts from 'German Antitank Units and Tactics' from *Tactical and Technical Trends 10*, 22 October 1942]

Antitank guns must be carefully emplaced and effectively camouflaged. Some have a very strong muzzle blast and in desert terrain the force of this blast throws up a cloud of dust and sand that quickly reveals the gun position to enemy observers and often completely obscures the field of fire. Provisions for eliminating the dust include:
- rigging up a blast screen. This one consists of a net of fine wire mesh, supported on pegs extending about one inch above the surface of the ground. The wire mesh should be so painted as to blend into the surrounding terrain.
- covering the critical areas with concrete or cement.
- paving the areas with stone.
- treating the areas with oil.
- The areas should be camouflaged whenever the guns are not firing.

Ensure the inside of the emplacement is as dustproof as possible so that dust will not be sucked up in the rush of air following the discharge.

It is essential to provide alternative gun positions, and to construct all emplacements to permit easy removal of the gun.

When the terrain permits, the gun should be defiladed from the enemy by emplacement on a reverse slope, or if the country is flat, behind a natural or artificial mound. If an artificial mound is constructed, it should be as low as possible.

The arc of fire should be large; 180° is normal.

The gun should have overhead camouflage, but covering should be constructed so that it can be easily removed when there is need to close the station rapidly.

In general conception the emplacement should be a small open pit.

German antitank unit training

All soldiers take an initial basic six-week training course (six weeks prior to being assigned to permanent units. For the men of antitank units, this period consists of:
- intensive training in basic infantry subjects
- recognition of enemy and friendly armoured vehicles
- laying and firing antitank weapons and small arms
- handling antitank vehicles and guns

Along with their technical training, they learn something of the theory of the employment of antitank forces and get a course of physical toughening.

In addition to these basic training courses, there are courses designed to make soldiers antitank specialists.

As the war progressed and the Allies turned to the offensive, they began to make great use of 'tank-busting' ground-support aircraft such as the British Typhoon and Tempest and the US P-47 Thunderbolts and P-51 Mustang. In the Pacific Theatre the TBF/TBM Avenger and F4U Corsair (as here) saw service in the same role. This one is firing HVARs (high velocity aircraft rockets).

The course lasted 8–10 weeks. During the mornings of the first two weeks, we learned the principles of gun laying and aiming, with considerable practice in aiming at a target, which is 10ft high and placed at a distance of 35ft. The gun must be brought into position and correct aim taken in 60 seconds.

Afternoons were spent in manhandling the gun at double time. The 37mm gun was drawn by two men with ropes, with two men pushing behind. The distance to be covered was about 5 miles, the last two of which rose about 330ft and included several hollows. This distance was cross-country and had to be covered in an hour. Arrival was followed by training in judging distances to farmhouses, trees, etc. The distances were checked and corrected with a rangefinder. Aiming and firing with dummy cartridges were then practised on moving targets at ranges of 450–1,350 yards. During this practice the gun positions were moved as much as 100 yards. The return journey, mostly downhill, had to be covered in 70 minutes. For the last 10 minutes before arrival at barracks, the crews marched along, ropes over their shoulders, singing lustily. The whole exercise was carried out in full kit – steel helmet, rifle, gas mask, pack canteen, and cartridge belts filled with old iron.

The third, fourth and fifth weeks were spent mainly in theoretical instruction and firing practice with a detachable sub-calibre barrel liner.

The remainder of the course included further gun drill – laying, sighting and loading with dummy cartridges. All of the exercises were aimed at inculcating speed. The first gun set the pace and the other three guns had to keep up with it. Toward the end of the course there was some field firing. For snap shooting, each gunner was allowed five rounds.

Instruction both practical and theoretical, was also given in fighting British incendiary bombs and land mines. There were occasionally exercises with rubber boats, in which the antitank guns were to be transported across rivers. At the end of the period of training there were manoeuvres for three days.

Next is unit training – the primary objective being teamwork. Since soldiers come to antitank companies and battalions with a good knowledge of their weapons, the first lesson that they learn is the employment of these weapons in a closely coordinated team. Most of this instruction is by platoons, as the platoon is the antitank unit most frequently used in actual combat.

A great deal of the instruction is in the movement and emplacement of the guns, and gun crews are taught rapid and effective means of selecting and camouflaging positions. Gunnery is not neglected, for there is frequent practice in laying and firing.

Officers of antitank units are trained to exercise a great amount of initiative in the disposition of their guns and in coping with unexpected conditions. Speed in making decisions is emphasized … the offensive attitude has been equally important in the evolution of the present German system … guns need no longer lie in wait for the armoured attack, but can seek combat with enemy armoured vehicles. Every soldier was impressed with the ability of new weapons and methods to destroy tanks, and the names of units were changed from *Panzerabwehr* (antitank defence) to *Panzerjäger* (tank hunter).

A captured German training manual emphasizes the offensive role of the division antitank battalion:

'The antitank battalion's object is to engage and destroy enemy tanks by surprise attacks from unexpected directions with concentrated fire. In addition to engaging enemy tanks, the antitank unit has the task of neutralizing antitank defences, supporting its own tanks.

The British produced two excellent antitank guns, the Ordnance Quick-Firing 6pdr 7cwt (**Below**) also used by the US Army and built under licence as the 57mm Gun M1, and the 17pdr (**Above Right**) – a 76.2mm (3-inch) gun that was probably the best Allied antitank gun of the war. The latter fired APC, APCBC and APDS ammunition. It was known for its muzzle flash (hence the name Firefly when it was used in the M4) and muzzle blast.

In battle, emphasis is placed on antitank units moving rapidly in and out of position. All of the personnel and installations of antitank units are required to be prepared for tank attack at all times. Careful and continuous reconnaissance is deemed a necessity, as each unit must be familiar with the most likely routes of tank approach and be prepared to defend these routes.

The antitank battalion of an armoured division goes into the attack with the tanks, following them from objective to objective, and engages all tanks threatening them from the flanks and rear.

If infantry is attacking without tanks, the antitank battalion accompanies it in the same manner as when accompanying the tank attack, except that the main body of the battalion is kept behind the infantry flanks to repulse enemy counterattacks or overcome unexpectedly strong enemy resistance.

In a pursuit, antitank units are attached to the most advanced elements, usually by platoons. They have the mission of giving protection to the flanks of the most advanced elements and of destroying armoured elements in the enemy rearguard, thus breaking the backbone of the enemy delaying action.

In a withdrawal, regimental antitank units normally defend their regimental units along the line of advance of enemy tanks. Part of the division antitank battalion may be used to strengthen this defence.

The remainder of the division antitank battalion is divided into two parts. One reconnoitres and prepares positions for the next delaying action, while the other acts as a mobile reserve for the immediate use of the division commander.

In spite of the offensive emphasis the antitank units' primary mission remains defensive. Terrain plays an important part: after thorough reconnaissance of the assigned defensive sector, the plan for antitank defence is perfected. The principles of this plan are to deny the best avenues of tank approach to the enemy by covering them with liberal anti-tank fire, while the less likely avenues of approach are denied to the enemy by obstacles.'

One of the major forms of antitank warfare, and an important part of in-depth defence lines, mines and minefields played a significant role in the desert – where both sides used them – and in Russia. In the west, where the Allies were more obviously on the offensive, they laid fewer mines. The Germans, however, used them along with antipersonnel mines and booby traps.

Typical German procedure for the preparation of antitank defence in a defensive situation is as follows:

(a) Assume that the division is defending a sector 9,000 yards wide, regiments abreast. The terrain is diversified, offering some tank obstacles, such as canals, thick woods, and a stream, and also offering open, rolling corridors which are excellent avenues of approach for tanks.

(b) Reconnaissance and map study are made to determine two important locations along the front: one, the engineer centre of resistance (*Pionier Schwerpunkt*) and the other, the antitank-gun centre of resistance (*Panzerabwehrgeschütz Schwerpunkt*).

(c) The engineer centre of resistance is located in that section of the front where natural obstacles contribute defensive strength. Engineer troops improve and expand the natural defensive features found in this section.

(d) The antitank gun centre of resistance is located in that section of the front where the ground is open and rolling, ideal terrain for tank operations. The regimental antitank company's guns are emplaced in concealed positions 200–400 yards in rear of the main line of resistance, while the antitank battalion is farther to the rear, with gun positions echeloned in depth. The battalion gun positions are selected, and positions leading thereto carefully reconnoitred, but they are not usually occupied until the warning of a hostile attack is received. The guns remain under cover in positions of readiness, conveniently located to permit rapid movement to any threatened area.

Antitank defence on the march follows the same general principles – that is, the regimental antitank companies provide defence for their units, and the division antitank battalion acts as a general reserve to be used against a concentrated tank attack.

Within the regimental march column, the antitank company is employed in units of full platoons. The four platoons are usually disposed as follows: one platoon has one gun with the point and the remaining two guns at the rear of the advance party; one platoon is placed at the head and one at the rear of the reserve; and the last platoon marches with the combat trains. If the regiment is marching in the division's main body, one platoon marches at the head of the regiment, one at the rear of the foot elements, and the other two platoons with the combat trains.

The location of the division on the march determines the disposition of the division antitank battalion. When the division has both flanks covered, the battalion marches with the combat trains; when there is an exposed flank and a tank attack is possible, the battalion protects the exposed flank, moving from position to position by bounds, the companies leap-frogging each other so that two companies are always in position to fire.

Obstacles and mines

German engineers cooperate closely with antimechanised units in defence against tanks. Engineers reinforce by obstacles and mines the terrain less favour-able for tank attack, whereas the antitank guns are massed in those areas not easily defended by artificial barriers. Both obstacles and minefields are always covered by the fire of antitank weapons and small arms. As a matter of fact, the Germans often use these antimechanised obstacles to slow or halt tanks and make them good targets. The Germans make every effort to slow or halt pursuing hostile forces by mining roads and bridges. Mines are buried under the earth or in snow. The Germans employ antitank minefields extensively, finding them particularly valuable in the desert, where flat terrain and hard soil makes the construction of artificial obstacles quite difficult. Minefields are employed with great care, as the Germans appreciate that it is possible for them to be turned to the disadvantage of the unit that lays them. The object is to construct an obstacle that will block enemy vehicles without hampering the manoeuvre of German forces.

Antitank warfare is not all about guns and rockets. Obstacles – whether they be concrete dragon's teeth, reinforced-concrete antitank walls or ditches – when allied to minefields and barbed wire can seriously impede tanks and motorised infantry. The Germans had ample time in Normandy and along the Westwall to prepare in-depth defence lines.

Infantry tank hunting

German training and operations emphasise the importance of aggressive action against tanks by dismounted infantry. All tanks, they teach, have certain vulnerable points which make them easy prey for close-combat weapons employed by aggressive, trained soldiers. The chief weaknesses of tanks are their relatively poor visibility, their inability to defend themselves within a close radius of the vehicle (dead space), and the time lag in shifting guns from target to target. They also need certain times, usually at night or in rear areas, to carry out maintenance and repairs. This is always a favourable time for the dismounted tank hunter. A German training instruction, issued to an infantry unit shortly after it had successfully repelled a British attack, sets out the technique of infantry tank hunting (as reported in *Tactical and Technical Trends 10*, 22 October 1942).

'The construction of our defensive areas has proved extremely effective, particularly the provision of antitank trenches. No casualties were sustained when British AFVs penetrated our position. The troops were protected by the trenches and could fire on the infantry with the tanks, while the AFVs were engaged by antitank weapons.

The lesson to be drawn is that the infantryman should allow the tank to pass overhead while he is in his antitank trench. If he attempts to jump clear, he draws fire on himself from the tank, whose field of fire is extremely limited. The infantryman's main task remains the repulsing of the assaulting infantry. In addition to this, however, enemy tanks can be knocked out by courageous-action with close-combat weapons.

The most important weapons for this purpose are the Molotov cocktail and the pole charge. The most convenient charge is the prepared charge (*Pionier Sprengbuchse*), which contains 2.2lb of explosive. Its strength is such that it can knock out a British infantry tank without unduly endangering its user by the explosion. The drag-mine is also highly successful. Molotov cocktails are most effective if they burst on the ribs of the engine cover. The flaming contents envelop the motor, which is usually set afire.

To employ close-combat weapons, the infantryman must at least be within throwing range of the tank. He must, therefore, wait in his cover for the tank to approach. But this cover is useful only when it has been specifically constructed as an antitank ditch — that is, it must be level with the ground, well camouflaged, and not more than 40 inches wide, so that the tank can pass overhead without endangering the infantryman.

The danger to the infantryman who finds himself close to a tank is slight. An infantryman in his antitank trench is always superior to an enemy tank that is within throwing range if he is properly equipped. The periscope of the British tanks is inadequate, allowing the driver to see straight ahead only, and the gunner can only see in the line of his gun. Because of the limited play of the weapons mountings, they cannot be depressed sufficiently to cover the immediate vicinity of the tank. An infantryman in this dead area must inevitably use his close-combat weapons effectively.'

A range of antitank weapons. The US Bazooka (**Above Left**) started off as the M1 and improved M1A1 firing 2.36-inch rockets. The M9 began production in 1944 and the M20, firing a larger 3.5-inch warhead entered service later in the war. The Germans' reverse-engineered the Bazooka and created the 88mm Panzerschreck (**Below Right**) which proved a successful weapon that worked well for the Germans, Finns, Italians and other Axis troops. It and the Panzerfaust (**Below Left**) – a disposable weapon – led to the development of other forms of armour protection, such as spaced armour and Schürzen – bazooka plates. Col W.L. Roberts, who commanded a combat command in US 4th Armored Division, said on 21 April 1945, 'Panzerfaust is the worst weapon we have encountered in this exploitation type of war. It will go through any US tank, and can be handled by even man inexperienced individual. It is the only weapon that is getting our tanks today.'

First used in anger by Canadians during the Allied invasion of Sicily, the PIAT (**Above Right**) looks like one of Heath Robinson's inventions. The cocking and firing of the weapon was difficult and they were bulky, but they were cheap and effective: 7% of German tanks destroyed by the British forces during the Normandy campaign were destroyed by PIATs. On 16 May 1944, during an attack on the Gustav Line Fusilier Francis Arthur Jefferson, 2nd Battalion, The Lancashire Fusiliers won a VC for destroying the leading tank of an enemy counter-attack that was only twenty yards away. It burst into flames and all the crew were killed.

US Army Tank Destroyers*

In late 1941, the US War Department inaugurated its tank destroyer concept. The Germans had their tank hunters, the *Panzerjäger*, and US Army would have its version. It was an answer to Blitzkrieg: the pooling of antitank weapons into battalions at divisional level and the massing of those battalions, when needed, into regimental-sized groups or even brigades.

The new arm's motto was 'Seek, Strike, and Destroy' and its shoulder patch shows a black panther crushing a tank in its jaws – indicative that they were to seize the initiative and take the battle to the enemy. And, while the concept proved flawed, no one can doubt that the men of the tank destroyer battalions performed bravely and well during World War II.

As with most countries, the US armed forces initially assigned all tanks to the infantry. Tanks were there 'to facilitate the uninterrupted advance of the rifleman in the attack' just as the British had intended in World War I, and nothing in the interwar years changed that view. Indeed, the US Army's reading of tank warfare in the Spanish Civil War was that the tank could be halted quite easily by artillery. This complacent attitude degenerated arguments about which arm should control the antitank assets – artillery or infantry – rather than watching closely events in France in 1940. There, German Panzer divisions in conjunction with close-air support were blowing away professional French and British armies.

To the Americans, their reading of the debacle was that the Allies had too few antitank weapons to contend with the huge number of massive German tanks. So, on 27 November 1941 the US Army activated 53 tank destroyer battalions under the direct control of GHQ, not of the line units. A further directive of 3 December removed all existing antitank battalions from their parent arms, redesignated them tank destroyer battalions, and placed them under GHQ as well. The battalions withdrawn from infantry divisions received numbers in the 600s, those from armoured divisions in the 700s, and those from field artillery units in the 800s.

Their mission was outlined in FM 18–5: 'There is but one battle objective of tank destroyer units, this being plainly inferred by their designation. It is the destruction of hostile tanks.' The trouble was that the strategists hadn't been watching Europe carefully. The manual portrayed tanks as operating in large masses that entered battle at top speed. It suggested that armoured formations consisted of distinct tank, infantry, and artillery echelons, rather than the combined-arms battle groups the Germans employed. Above all, it assumed the Germans would be on the attack: in North Africa after Alamein it was the Allies who held the initiative and German Panzer doctrine bore little relationship to the headstrong tank tactics described in FM 18–5.

* This section makes heavy use of material from Gabel, *Leavenworth Papers No 12*.

Top: The original M3 GMC married a 75mm gun to an M3 halftrack body. Some 2,200 of the M3 and subsequent M3A1 saw service until superseded by the M10 whereupon a number were returned to M3A1 halftrack status.

Above: Another early tank destroyer combined an M3 37mm antitank gun and a Dodge WC52 light truck chassis. Many of them ended up being used by the FFI (French Forces of the Interior) in 1944–45 following the invasion of southern France.

The most outstanding characteristic of German armoured doctrine was the close integration of tanks, antitank guns, infantry, artillery and aircraft into a combined-arms team. German tanks almost invariably operated under the protective fire of an antitank screen – typically, 88mm guns flanked by lighter pieces and protected by infantry – which covered all German tank movements from concealed overwatch positions. Even when on the offensive, the Germans made every effort to support their tank with anti-tank weapons and artillery. The British veterans knew well what the Americans were

M10 TDs are passed by towed 37mm antitank guns pulled by jeeps. By 1943 the 37mm was ineffective against most German tanks and was replaced by the 57mm and others in Europe. In the Pacific they stayed in service until the end of the war.

to learn: any attempt by armour to attack German mechanised elements, even those that appeared to be isolated and vulnerable, was likely to bring down a murderous converging fire from concealed antitank guns. Any Allied attack that did not provide for the neutralisation of this antitank defence risked defeat.

The tank destroyers would even find it difficult to ambush attacking German armour, for German tanks rarely attacked blindly or recklessly. One American officer reported that 'when the German tanks come out, they stay out of range and sit and watch. Then they move a little, stop, and watch some more. They have excellent glasses [binoculars] and they use them carefully. They always seem to make sure of what they are going to do and where they are going before they move …'

The tank destroyers found themselves at an immediate disadvantage. Their doctrine, force structuring and weaponry prepared them to deal exclusively with tanks. In North Africa, the battle was not tank destroyer against tank, but tank destroyer against an integrated combined-arms force conducting a skilful defence.

The qualitative superiority of German weaponry made it even harder. FM 18–5 implied that tank destroyers would enjoy a significant superiority in firepower over enemy armour. By 1943, however, the German arsenal included the PzKpfw IV mounting a long-barrelled, high-velocity 75mm and the Tiger, with its thick armour and 88mm main gun. By comparison, the M3 tank destroyer was a halftrack with a 75mm gun designed in 1897 that was not really an antitank gun at all. The M6 towed TD was much worse. Its only armor was a .25-inch gun shield. The gun itself was the 37mm antitank piece that FM 18–5 said was effective to a range of 500 yards. In practice, it was effective only against the sides and rears of most tanks, and that at under 400 yards. One 37mm gun of the 601st Tank Destroyer Battalion scored five hits on a PzKpfw IV at 1,000 yards with no observed effect.

The advent of the M10 TD helped and the similarly armed M18, which first saw combat in Italy, was also welcome. Events would prove, however, that even when armed with adequate weapons, the tank destroyers could do little to alter the tactical and strategic circumstances that militated against their employment in accordance with doctrine. Division commanders could hardly be expected to allow the 36 guns of each TD battalion to lie idle simply because battlefield realities did not conform with FM 18–5 and so there was widespread 'misuse' of tank destroyers.

Like most US units in Tunisia, the TD battalions involved at Kasserine were fragmented and dispersed. The 601st and 701st TD Battalions, scattered in companies and understrength due to attrition, were thrashed by Rommel's veterans. The initial 14 February assault of the 10th and 21st Panzer Divisions at Sidi-bou-Zid swept away A/701st TD Battalion, along with CCA/1st Armored Division. Next day, C/701st joined CCC/1st Armored Division's ill-conceived counterattack aimed at recapturing the Sidi-bou-Zid position was badly battered in the ensuing German ambush.

One month after Kasserine, enemy tanks challenged an intact TD battalion for the first time. The action took place against the 601st at El Guettar. Except for friendly artillery, the tank destroyers were unsupported. On 23 March, about 50 tanks of the 10th Panzer Division attacked the 601st, which was still using the M3 halftrack. A company of the 899th TD Battalion, equipped with M10s, advanced to reinforce the 601st but was slow in arriving due to traffic and minefields. The tank destroyers, employing the fire-and-movement tactics prescribed by doctrine, turned back the Axis attack and accounted for a reported 30 enemy tanks. But the victory was dearly bought—about 20 of the 28 M3s engaged, plus seven of the new M10s, were lost.

The costly victory at El Guettar was the only engagement of the North African and Italian campaigns in which a united tank destroyer battalion met and stopped a concerted tank attack. In fact, it was increasingly rare for TD battalions to be held back in antitank reserve. Experience showed that if they were not on hand when the enemy tank attack started, they were unlikely to arrive in time to influence the outcome.

Portrait of an M10. The problem with the tank destroyers wasn't the vehicles or the men, it was the doctrine. Note the bosses on the sides and turret – there for appliqué armour panels.

Dispersal, however, proved to be an administrative nightmare. One TD unit is reported to have requested fuel and ammunition from the division it was attached to and to have received gasoline and 75mm shells in return: the M10 tank destroyer used diesel fuel and three-inch ammunition. In spite of this, TD battalions contributed significantly to frontline antitank firepower and developed new missions that were not to be found in FM 18–5 – such as indirect fire complementing 105mm howitzers which worked well as they could reach out to 14,000 yards, 4,000 yards farther than the 105mm.

The towed TD battalion demonstrated significant drawbacks almost immediately. The towed gun was easier to conceal than the M10 but it was harder to man and fire and was a less versatile weapon. Indeed, everywhere armies were turning to SP anti-tank guns in increasing numbers, even as the US Army adopted towed tank destroyers.

Ordnance tests had indicated that TD guns would be able to penetrate the frontal armour of the Tiger tank at a comfortable 2,000 yards. Unfortunately, they were in error, and the confidence residing in tank and tank destroyer armament was mis-placed. American troops in Normandy found themselves unexpectedly vulnerable to the German Panzers – and lucky that the heaviest armour, Tigers and Jagdpanthers, were ranged exclusively against the British and Canadians. Subsequent events would prove that no tank destroyer could reliably stop a Tiger at any more than close range and the Panther was not much easier. US firing tests conducted in Normandy on actual Panther hulks, demonstrated that only the 90mm antiaircraft gun and the 105mm howitzer, firing shaped charges, could penetrate the Panther's frontal armor. On the other hand, the Tiger's 88mm and the Panther's high-velocity 75mm could destroy any American armoured vehicle with ease. The lapse in technological planning that sent American tanks and tank destroyers into Europe with inadequate armament occurred despite the fact that American troops in the Mediterranean theatre had been fighting both the Tiger and the Panther since 1943.

Almost by accident, a remedy was at hand. In 1942, the Ordnance Department on its own initiative (and against the wishes of the Tank Destroyer Center, which disapproved of expedients) experimentally mounted a 90mm antiaircraft gun in the modified turret of an M10 tank destroyer. The design was standardized as the M36 in June 1944.

The M36 would not arrive in Europe until September 1944, but once it reached the front, it proved to be the only American armoured vehicle that could match the heavier German tanks in firepower. One M36 destroyed a Panther with one round at a range of 3,200 yards. The M36 was equally impressive in the secondary missions. In the direct-fire role, a 90mm armour-piercing shell could penetrate 4.5ft of non-reinforced concrete, while in the indirect-fire mission, the M36 could throw a projectile 19,000 yards.

Notwithstanding the praise of tank destroyer crews, the fact remained that once landed in Normandy, the tank destroyers found it highly inadvisable to react aggressively

The upgunned M36 married a 90mm gun to the M10 chassis. Over 2,300 were made, a number conversions from M10s. To the left are the discs of a T1E1 'Earthworm' mine roller which was linked to an M32 ARV.

to enemy armour, even though every German tank encountered was by no means a Panther or a Tiger. Fortunately, the full-blooded Panzer counterattack against the beachhead never materialised, thanks to their being used piecemeal as they arrived in theatre to block the armoured thrusts of the British and Canadians around Caen. Thus, the major problem confronting American troops in Normandy was not the staving off massed tanks but rather the rooting out a stubborn, entrenched enemy.

The primary task of the tank destroyer became infantry support. When the infantry attacked, tank destroyers would roll with the advance some 500–800 yards behind the assault elements, shooting up all potential enemy positions in the path of the infantry. The infantry, in turn, neutralized antitank positions that threatened the tank destroyer. The armour on the M10 and M18 tank destroyers was adequate to protect their crews from small-arms fire, and the high velocity and flat trajectory of their guns made them very effective against enemy strongpoints. The presence of rapid-firing tank destroyers noticeably eroded enemy morale and bolstered that of the assaulting infantry.

When the German tank attack came – on 7 August 1944 at Mortain – it only contained elements of three understrength Panzer divisions and one Panzergrenadier division. The brunt of the attack fell upon the 30th Infantry Division, with the 823rd TD Battalion (towed) attached. The guns of the 823rd had been hastily sited and were not in mutually supporting positions. Some platoons were without infantry support. But first the defenders fought off an infantry attack and then an assault mounted by Panzers accompanied by infantry. The tank destroyers fought stubbornly but without coordination, for all of the 823rd's fighting elements had been parcelled out to the regiments, and tactical control was in the hands of the infantry commanders. Those tank destroyers supported by other arms did well; those not supported were quickly overrun. Companies A and B,

823rd Tank Destroyer Battalion, received the Presidential Unit Citation for the part they played in stopping the Mortain counterattack, but the cost had come high, prompting the 823rd to train its gun crews to fire the three-inch weapon with two or three men, freeing the remainder of the crew to fight off enemy infantry.

Perhaps the best example of TD capabilities came in September 1944 as the Germans tried to stem the American advance in Lorraine. The Germans scraped together a force they nominated Fifth Panzer Army, commanded by General Hasso von Manteuffel, an armour expert from the Russian Front. From 19 to 25 September, two Panzer brigades of the LVIII Panzer Corps – mainly green troops, but equipped with Panthers – hammered at 4th Armored Division's CCA, around Arracourt.

Although outgunned by the German tanks, the American Shermans and, more importantly, tank destroyers enjoyed superior mobility and received overwhelming, air support when the weather permitted. And when the fogs interfered with American air strikes they also neutralized the superior range of German tank armament. The *History of the 704th TD Battalion*, takes up the story:

'C Company moved into Arracourt thinking of a rest, but was sent out on a routine mission near Réchicourt-la-Petite. The 3rd Platoon, under command of Lt Leiper, came face to face with what seemed to be all the armor of the German army. Guns instantly flamed into action and Cpl Stewart, gunner for Sgt Stasis, knocked out two Kraut tanks before his tank was hit and put out of action. Cpl Eidenschink of Sgt Ferraro's crew accounted for three more before his tank was hit. Cpl Eaton of Sgt Krewsky's section destroyed four more German tanks in fast, furious firing before he, too, was knocked out of action.

'Sgt Mcgurk, with Cpt Sorrentino firing, "liberated" the crews of two other enemy tanks with neat AP hits. At the same time more enemy tanks moving to assist their apparently , "outnumbered" cohorts lumbered across the front of the gun positions of the 1st Platoon. That was their last mistake, for Pfc Amodio, gunner for Sgt Hartman, nailed five of them before they could even swing their turrets to bear on him. Cpl Ewamtako of Sgt Donovan's crew clouted three into oblivion. When the smoke cleared, the count showed that eight gun crews had knocked out 19 German tanks with the loss of three destroyers, only one man killed and five wounded. Truly a record to be proud of. B Company had accounted for six while the 2nd Platoon of B Company, working with the 25th Cavalry, destroyed five more near Marsal

'A Company was also involved in the dismemberment of the 11th Panzer for four enemy tanks came out through a drizzling rain looking for trouble and found it waiting for them near Arracourt. Sgt Hicklin's gunner, Cpl Hosey, through a dank fog, calmly laid his sights and squeezed off his shots. And called them, too, in spite of return fire, for the four tanks were "finis". ...

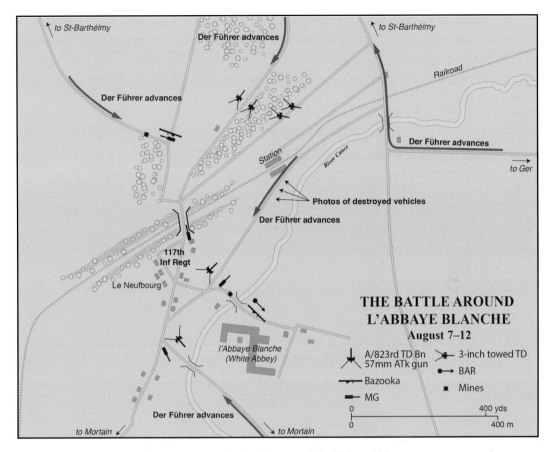

THE BATTLE AROUND
L'ABBAYE BLANCHE
August 7–12

A/823rd TD Bn
57mm ATk gun

Bazooka

MG

3-inch towed TD

BAR

Mines

0		400 yds
0		400 m

Above A classic wargaming scenario, the battle around the White Abbey, a nunnery near Le Neufbourg/Mortain railroad station, pitted F Coy, 2nd Bn, 120th Inf Regt and the 3in towed antitank guns of 1st Pl, A Coy, 823rd TD Bn against 9./SS-PzGr-Regt 4 Der Führer and elements of 2nd SS-Pz Division (Das Reich). Six German SdKfz 251 APCs were KO'd as well as Schwimmwagen (amphibious jeeps) and Kübelwagen. The diagram shows the US defensive position; the photo (**Below**) is one of a set of images that shows the results.

'Finally, on 27 October, the battalion moved back into a rest area near Lenoncourt and was attached to CCR of the 4th Armored. Here a tally was made, and the count of enemy tanks destroyed was 29 Mark Vs, 4 Tigers and 2 SPs against a loss of 5 M18s. The CO of CCA of the 4th said that except for the 704th the 11th Panzer could have wiped out his command.'

During the race to the German frontier, tank destroyers replayed their success in direct-support missions, but this time American troops confronted the interlocking fortifications of the Westwall (known to the Allies as the Siegfried Line), rather than hedgerows. From a range of 1,000 yards, ten rounds from a tank destroyer gun would penetrate a small pillbox or jam the shutters of a larger work and would often cause the pillbox crew to surrender.

During the Battle of the Bulge, on the northern shoulder of the German break-through, the 99th and 2nd Infantry Divisions, with the aid of a number of tank destroyer elements, defended the vital Elsenborn Ridge against repeated heavy assaults. The Germans attacked in company-size task forces consisting of both Panzers and infantry. The defenders responded by first breaking up the enemy formations with artillery fire and then striking them from the flanks with tank and tank destroyer fire. The fighting surged back and forth through villages and rough terrain, a circumstance that provided ample opportunities for tank destroyer ambushes and cut ranges down to as little as 25 yards. One company of the 644th TD Battalion (with M10s) destroyed 17 tanks with the loss of two tank destroyers. Towed tank destroyers, unable to manoeuvre for flank shots or evade enemy thrusts, fared less well: the 801st TD Battalion (towed) lost 17 guns and 16 halftrack prime movers in two days because the guns bogged down in the mud and fell easy prey to German artillery and infantry.

The M18 was agile and armed with a 76mm main gun. It performed well against all German tanks other than the massive Tiger II. Just over 2,500 were built. It had a crew of five (commander, gunner, loader, driver and assistant driver).

TDs in the Pacific theatre

Tank employment and tank destroyer employment in the Pacific were essentially the same. The minimal threat posed by Japanese tanks, saw the three TDs battalions operating almost exclusively as assault guns and supporting artillery. Later, in preparation for the invasion of Japan, the Tank Destroyer Center at Camp Hood turned away from the problems of killing tanks and devoted its experimental efforts instead to the use of tank destroyers in reducing Japanese-style fortifications.

Assessment

After the cessation of hostilities in Europe, a board of senior field artillery officers convened to evaluate the contributions of the tank destroyer. They based their study in part upon the after-action reports of 49 TD battalions that had fought in Europe. It noted that the tank destroyer was 'a most versatile weapon on the battlefield' and admitted that there existed a need for self-propelled, high-velocity guns within the infantry division, a function that the tank destroyers had fulfilled admirably.

The battalions sampled had destroyed, on average, 34 German tanks and SP guns, 17 artillery and antitank guns, and 16 pillboxes apiece, with one battalion claiming 105 tanks destroyed.

However, the board recognized that tank destroyers had never validated the TD doctrine and, in fact, had not adhered to it on the battlefield. The report finished by recommending that high-velocity self-propelled guns be made organic to the infantry division, that Field Artillery assume responsibility for antitank defence-in-depth, that the Armored Force modify and adopt certain aspects of tank destroyer doctrine, and that 'the tank destroyers as a separate force be discontinued.'

M10s saw significant action in Philippines – but tank destroyers weren't very popular because of their open turret tops. They also had little chance to fulfil their primary mission as there were few Japanese tanks. this meant that the M10s were mainly used for artillery support. These M10s of 632nd TD Battalion, 32nd Infantry are in a night bivouac on New Guinea, 1 August 1944.

3 Tank Maintenance and Recovery

Maintenance is an obvious requirement for mechanised forces and at every level it was controlled carefully. In the US armored division it was regarded as a function of command. Division, combat command, battalion and company commanders were held personally responsible for the maintenance of the vehicles and weapons assigned to their units. Each vehicle had a toolkit so that the crew could perform basic maintenance: lubrication, inspection, and minor adjustments such as the replacement of spark-plugs. Companies had a maintenance section and battalions a maintenance platoon. A service company was able to perform minor repairs, recovery of disabled vehicles by use of ARVs, and the replacement of certain unit assemblies. The maintenance platoon operated under the battalion motor officer. Each division had an ordnance maintenance battalion consisting of an HQ, HQ company and three maintenance companies. The maintenance battalion performed third echelon maintenance on all ordnance and engineer equipment, including the replacement of major unit assemblies. In combat, maintenance companies might be attached to or placed in direct support of combat commands. The maintenance battalion was equipped for the evacuation of disabled vehicles and equipment.

Recovery of bogged or damaged tanks was essential. Indeed, many knocked out tanks – specifically those that did not burn – could be returned to combat within hours of recovery. Belton Cooper in his book *Death Traps: The Survival of an American Armored Division in World War II,* said: 'The 3rd Armored Division entered combat in Normandy with 232 M4 Sherman tanks. During the European Campaign, the Division had some 648 Shermans completely destroyed in combat and we had another 700 knocked out, repaired, and put back into operation.'

The following information on German tank recovery platoons was obtained by British interrogation of POWs.

Battlefield recovery ensured that many knocked-out vehicles returned to service. There are many mechanical problems that can put a tank out of action – often involving tracks, as here – that can be fixed easily. Here an M31 ARV – based on the body of an M3 medium – works on an M10 tank destroyer. (The M32 was based on the M4 medium.)

German tank recovery platoons

[From 'German Tank Maintenance and Recovery'
from *Tactical and Technical Trends 10*, 22 October 1942]

The principle is to have two or three recovery vehicles forward with the fighting units. These vehicles advance in the line of attack and cruise across the width of the battle front. The Germans believe that hostile forces will be preoccupied with the German tanks and will not bother with the recovery vehicles, no matter how close they are.

If a member of a tank crew orders the driver of a recovery vehicle to tow his tank to the rear, the former assumes responsibility in case it later proves that the damage is negligible and could have been fixed on the spot by the repair sections – but asking that a damaged vehicle be towed away is always permissible if it is in danger of being shot up.

The towing vehicle usually goes forward alone and tows a disabled tank away by tow ropes. Towing is used in preference to loading on the trailer, as this latter operation may take 20 minutes (regarded by a prisoner as too much time under battle conditions).

The recovered tanks are towed to an assembly point behind the combat area, where they are lined up to protect themselves as far as possible. Trailers may be used to take back the disabled tanks from this point to the workshop company, but trailers are being used less and less, and their use is confined mainly to roads. On roads, they enable a higher speed to be maintained, do not weave as much as a towed tank, and do not cut up the road surface. In the desert, trailers would be used on bad ground rather than where there is good going.

Drivers of recovery vehicles did front-line duty for about eight days at a time; then they worked at the rear, between assembly point and workshop.

German unit organisation

(1) Tank Company Repair Section
Men: 1 NCO (tank mechanic), section leader; 3 NCOs, tank mechanics; 13 privates, tank mechanics; 2 privates, tank radio electricians; 1 private, armourer's assistant; 4 privates, drivers. Total: 4 NCOs and 20 EM.
Vehicles: 1 × small repair car (Kfz 2/40); 1 × medium cross-country repair truck, for spare parts and tools; 2 × halftrack vehicles (SdKfz 10) for personnel, capable of towing 1 ton; 3 × motorcycles with sidecars.

(2) Battalion and Regimental Repair Sections
Men: 1 NCO (tank mechanic), section leader; 3 privates, tank mechanics (for a tank RHQ) or 5 privates, tank mechanics (for a tank Bn HQ); 1 private, motorcyclist, tank radio electrician; 1 private, driver, tank radio electrician; 1 driver. Total: 1 NCO and 6 men (RHQ); 1 NCO and 8 men (Bn HQ).

Vehicles: 1 × small repair car (Kfz 2/40); 1 × medium cross-country repair truck, for spare parts and tools; 1 × motorcycle with sidecar.

(3) Workshop Company

This information comes from a captured German document and gives this organisation of a Panzer workshop company, as at 15 September 1941 in a Panzer regiment with six companies (as in Libya). Additional information (in square brackets) is from *German Tank Maintenance in WW2* (Department of Army June 1954).

[The principal function of the maintenance/workshop company of a tank regiment was to perform those repairs which could not be carried out by the detachments in the tank companies. The company's mission was to eliminate technical defects, repair electrical equipment, radio sets, tank weapons, optical instruments, damage resulting from direct hits, recover and remove disabled tanks from the battlefield, and maintain stocks of spare parts.]

(a) Headquarters Platoon

1 × cross-country truck (Kfz 1): 1 driver, 1 company commander (engineer), 1 officer for special duties (engineer), 1 clerk (draftsman). One of the two officers may be other than an engineer officer.

1 × motorcycle: 1 motorcyclist (orderly).

1 × medium truck: 1 driver, 2 men for salvaging spare parts.

1 × light personnel car: 1 driver, 1 official (K-motor transport), 1 NCO for spare parts, 1 clerk (asst. driver).

1 × motorcycle with sidecar: 1 motorcyclist (orderly), 1 foreman for motor transport equipment (Maybach Specialist).

(b) 1st and 2nd Maintenance Platoons

1 × motor bus (*Kraftomnibus*): 1 driver, 4 NCOs for workshop service, 1 tank electrician and mechanic, 1 tank electric welder, 1 saddler, 1 tinsmith, 1 carpenter, 1 painter, 7 tank motor mechanics, 3 tank transmission mechanics, 1 automobile mechanic, 1 clerk.

5 × medium trucks, for spare parts and assemblies: (each) 1 driver, 1 tank transmission mechanic (asst. driver), 1 automobile mechanic.

1 × medium truck for spare parts and assemblies: 1 driver, 1 NCO in charge of spare parts, 1 depot chief.

1 × truck with special workshop and trailer for arc-welding apparatus: 1 driver, 1 NCO for workshop service, 1 tank electric welder (asst. driver).

1 × heavy truck, tools and equipment: 1 driver, 1 tank motor mechanic, 1 blacksmith.

1 × workshop truck (Kfz 19), with trailer for heavy machine apparatus, Set A: 1 driver, 1 foreman (leader), 1 turner.

(c) 3rd (Recovery) Platoon

[Tank recovery implied the removal of disabled vehicles from the battlefield, their collection at a point where they were protected from enemy observation and fire, and their evacuation from the collecting point to the field repair shop or the nearest railhead for shipment to a rear area installation. It also included pulling immobilised tanks out of mud, snow, swamps, and ditches as well as righting overturned vehicles. If the organic recovery elements were unable to accomplish their mission alone, the assistance of one of the nonorganic recovery units attached to army or army group headquarters could be requested.]

1 × light cross-country automobile (Kfz 1): 1 driver, 1 officer (Pl leader), NCO (*Panzerwart*, tank mechanic)

1 × medium cross-country truck (Kfz 100) for towing apparatus, with rotating crane (3 tons): 1 driver, 1 asst. driver (automobile mechanic).

1 × medium halftrack prime mover (8 tons):

Tiger workshop companies had two platoons, one of which was set up as a maintenance base with heavy lifting gear; the other nearer the front. The armoured maintenance team takes care of breakdowns; for heavy duty repairs the tanks are either towed back or, if available, put onto a transporter (Kässbohrer developed six-axle trailers for a payload of 60 and 75 tons –Tigers I and II). The Strabokram gantry crane could lift 15 tons; the smaller Faun 10 tons. Tigers were notably unreliable and averaged around 10 hours of maintenance for just one hour of driving.

1 driver, 1 assistant driver (automobile mechanic).

2 x medium halftrack prime movers (8 tons) with underslung trailers (10 tons): (each) 1 driver, 1 asst. driver (mechanic), and (for one only of these trucks) 1 NCO (tank mechanic).

2 x vehicles (6 tons, SdKfz 41): (each) 1 driver, 1 assistant driver (automobile mechanic).

5 x heavy halftrack prime movers (18 tons), with underslung trailers (20 tons): (each) 1 driver, 1 assistant driver (automobile mechanic), 1 steerer for trailer; one prime mover has, in addition, an NCO (tank mechanic).

2 x motorcycles with sidecars: (each) 1 driver (tank mechanic), 1 NCO (tank mechanic). One of the NCOs is 2IC.

(d) Armoury [Weapons] Section

1 x medium cross-country automobile (Kfz 15mG): 1 driver, 2 armourers (one is section leader), 1 armourer's helper.

1 x motorcycle with sidecar: 1 NCO armourer, 1 helper.

3 x vehicles for armourer's tools: One with 1 driver, 1 NCO, armourer, 1 tank electrician and mechanic (asst. driver); one with 1 driver, 1 tank electrician (asst. driver), 1 armourer's helper; one with 1 driver, 2 armourer's helpers (one is asst. driver).

1 x light cross-country car for supply of tools: 1 driver, 1 armourer's helper.

(e) Workshops for Communications Equipment [Radio Repair Section]

1 x battery-charging truck (Kfz 42): 1 driver, 1 NCO mechanic (leader), 1 mechanic.

1 x communications workshop truck (Kfz 42): 1 driver, 1 mechanic (asst. driver).

1 x light cross-country truck: 1 driver, 1 mechanic (asst. driver).

(f) Company Supply

1 x medium truck for rations and baggage: 1 driver, 1 NCO in charge of equipment (leader).

1 x motorcycle with sidecar: 1 supply sergeant, 1 clerk (asst. motorcyclist).

1 x anti-aircraft truck (Kfz 4): 1 driver, 1 NCO (in charge), 1 machine gunner.

Tanks always need attention, from loose nuts or bolts to track bashing. The first people to do the checking and repairing were the tank crews. It is a physically demanding job and everyone in the crew takes part.

2 x medium trucks for fuel: One with 1 driver and 1 tailor (asst. driver); one with 1 driver and 1 shoemaker (asst. driver).

2 x medium trucks for large field-kitchen stoves: One with 1 driver, 1 NCO in charge of rations (asst. driver), 1 cook, 1 asst. cook; one with 1 driver, 1 NCO (accountant), 1 NCO (cook), 1 asst. cook (asst. driver).

1 x light automobile: 1 driver (clerk), 1 master sergeant, 1 medical officer.

Total strength of Workshop Company: 3 officers, 5 officials (inc foreman and depot chief 1st and 2nd Pls), 29 NCOs, 158 EM (total, 195 men) and 1 shop foreman for motor transport equipment (group leader).

For tank Regts with three Bns, add one workshop Pl (same organization as 1st Pl above). Add to the Recovery Pl two heavy halftrack prime movers (18 tons) with 22-ton trailers, each to have 1 driver, 1 asst. driver (automobile mechanic), 1 trailer steerer. This involves additional personnel of 1 official, 6 NCOs, 49 EM – total, 56 men. The workshop company then has a total strength of 251 men.

For tank Regts with 4 companies in a Bn (i.e., two Bns to the Regt), add:
• To each of the 1st and 2nd Pls – 2 medium trucks for spare parts, each with 1 driver and 1 motor mechanic (asst. driver).
• To the Recovery Pl – 1 halftrack prime mover (18 tons) with trailer (22 tons), and personnel of 1 driver, 1 asst. driver (automobile mechanic), and 1 trailer steerer.

The strength of the company depended upon the type of armoured vehicles issued to the tank regiment and varied between 120 and 200 men.

(4) Light Workshop Platoon
According to prewar organization, a tank regiment of three battalions had (in addition to the workshop company) a regimental workshop platoon. This unit comprised 1 officer, 2 officials, 3 NCOs, and 48 EM; the vehicles consisted of 1 x automobile, 13 x trucks (5–7 with trailers), and 3 x motorcycles with sidecars.

A captured document from Africa (1941) gives detailed instructions for organizing a workshop platoon in a two-battalion tank regiment of the Afrika Korps (which normally would not have this unit). In this case, an example of the flexibility of German organization, the personnel assigned to the platoon was obtained by breaking up the battalion HQ repair sections of the two battalions. This workshop platoon was smaller than normal and was to operate, in place of the battalion HQ repair sections, under command of the regiment. The platoon was composed of: 1 sergeant mechanic (platoon leader), 1 Maybach specialist (for engines and Variorex gears), 2 NCOs, tank mechanics (one an engine mechanic and electrician, the other to be also a welder), 2 tank mechanics, 1 car driver, 2 motorcyclists (mechanics), 3 truck drivers.

The platoon had the following equipment in vehicles:
1 × light cross-country automobile (for platoon leader and Maybach specialist), 2 × motorcycles with side cars (for the two NCOs), 1 × truck with repair equipment (for 1 mechanic, 1 tank fitter), 2 × trucks with materials and spare parts (each for 1 mechanic, 1 tank fitter), 1 × light two-wheeled trailer, 1 × trailer with reserve of oxygen and acetylene containers.

(5) Divisional Workshop Companies
According to prewar organization, each armoured division had, as part of divisional services, three divisional workshop companies. These companies would, on occasion, presumably aid the workshop units of the tank regiments, but information on this function is not available.

Functions of tank repair and workshop units
(1) The repair sections (the available information apparently applies to both types of repair section mentioned above) are responsible for the general maintenance of the tanks, and of their armament and radio apparatus.

In camp and rest areas, they keep a check upon the serviceability of vehicles in the unit to which they are attached, mechanics are given advanced training through attachment to the workshop company or under master-mechanics transferred to the unit.

On the march, repair sections travel with the tank units and deal with any breakdowns in vehicles or equipment, in so far as these repairs can be effected in less than four hours and with field equipment. If a tank breaks down, the repair section leader inspects it and determines the nature of the damage. If the damage warrants it, the tank is handed over to the recovery platoon to be towed away; otherwise, a motorcycle with mechanics stays with the tank to effect repairs, while the other elements of the repair section go on with the column. In this way, one vehicle after another of the repair section stays behind; ordinarily the motorcycles, but, if damage is serious, a halftrack. The repair automobile always goes on with the column, while the repair truck always stays with the repair vehicle left farthest to the rear.

In the assembly area, the repair sections thoroughly test all tanks and equipment for fitness for battle. Any breakdowns are reported at once to the unit motor-transport sergeant.

In battle, the company repair sections are under the order of the battalion commander and are directed by a battalion motor-transport officer. As a rule they follow closely behind the fighting units and range over the battle area looking for broken-down tanks. If the tank cannot be repaired on the spot it is made towable and its position reported to the recovery platoon (of the workshop company).

In one tank battalion in Libya, an armour-repair section was added to the normal repair sections. The personnel was made up of armourer mechanics detached from other repair units, and included an armourer sergeant, an armourer corporal, and seven armourer's assistants. The equipment included an automobile, a motorcycle, and two trucks. This section was to follow the tanks in battle and to work with repair sections on weapons and turrets.

Repair sections are not allowed to undertake the welding of armour gashes longer than four inches. In battle, the RHQ repair section is attached to a battalion.

(2) *The armoured workshop company* operates as far as 15–20 miles behind the fighting tanks of its regiment, except that the recovery platoon works in the battle area, mainly to tow out disabled tanks. The workshop company handles heavier repair jobs, up to those requiring 12 hours. Repair jobs requiring up to 24 hours are sent back to rear repair bases. The workshop company has its own power tools, a crane, and apparatus for

Field maintenance and minor repairs took place behind the fighting, where possible, and under camouflage. Here an M20 command car (called the Greyhound by the British) receives a new or repaired front axle.

electric welding and vulcanizing. Its platoons may be separated, and may operate independently. According to one captured document, a workshop company dealt with 18 tanks in 17 days, under conditions where there was no shortage of spare parts.

(3) The light workshop platoon in the Afrika Korps tank regiment, replaced the battalion HQ repair sections and operated under command of the regiment as a connecting link between the workshop company and the company repair sections. Like the latter, it would handle work requiring less than four hours. In attack, this platoon would follow along the central axis of advance, in close touch with the recovery platoon of the workshop company.

The platoon was to carry out work as follows: on brakes, gears, and clutches of PzKpfw II (light) tanks; on damaged gear-mechanism of PzKpfw III tanks; and on valve defects of all types of truck and tank engines except PzKpfw III and IV tanks. They were to remove electrical and fuel-system faults; salvage and tow wheeled vehicles; make repairs on wheeled vehicles; perform autogene welding and soldering work; and charge and test batteries and electrical apparatus.

Tank recovery methods

All observers stress the efficiency of the German recovery and maintenance units. The following points have been noted:

(1) The Germans will use combat tanks to tow disabled tanks in case of retirement; even during a battle, instances are reported, both from France and Africa, where combat tanks were employed both to protect towing operations and to assist in the towing. The recovery platoon, with its trailers, is not given the whole burden of this main job of salvage.

(2) The same principle of cooperation prevails on repair jobs in the field. Tanks carry many tools, spare parts, and equipment for repair work, and observers believe that the tank crews are trained to assist the repair crews as well as to service and maintain their own vehicles.

(3) Not only is the recovery of German vehicles very efficient, but units will often send out detachments to recover those of the enemy. For instance, a tank battalion may send out a detachment consisting of an officer, one or two NCOs, and six or eight men, transported in one or two cross-country vehicles and protected by one or two light tanks, to search for and recover disabled hostile vehicles.

Russia

The rigours of the Russian campaign led to increased need for tank maintenance closer to the battlefield and to a heavy demand for spare parts. German losses in Russia – particularly of tanks and armoured vehicles – were far heavier than during the preceding campaigns. The extremes of heat and dust in summer, the mud of spring and autumn – the seasons of *rasputitsa* – and subzero temperatures in winter, led to a huge rate of

Russian lakes and rivers took their toll of the invading German tanks, and many were recovered by their companions – as here – rather than by specialised equipment. Additionally, the wheeled and halftrack vehicles in an armoured division far outnumbered the tracked. One of the drawbacks of the Germans' use of vehicles looted from subjugated territories was the sheer number of types on inventory – a similar problem to that of supplying so many different ammunition calibres.

mechanical attrition that added to the heavy combat losses. Maintenance had to happen closer to the front as the rail system was a target for air and partisan attack. To effect this a number of changes took place.

- The strength of the field units was increased and replacements were given better technical training.
- Improved equipment and more efficient recovery vehicles were made available.
- New depot installations were established to take over those functions formerly performed in Germany.
- The manufacture of spare parts was increased and the supply organisation was changed to improve speed and efficiency – although the Allied bombing campaign quickly rendered this problematic. 'The failure of the armament industry to provide sufficient spare parts forced the tank maintenance personnel to improvise. One of the most widespread expedients was the practice of cannibalising disabled tanks, especially those destined for return to the zone of interior. The Germans experienced very few instances in which it was not considered worthwhile to recover a disabled tank. The guiding principle was that no tank would be abandoned unless it was blown to bits or completely burnt out. In every other case recovery was mandatory, even though cannibalisation was often the only possible use to which the recovered vehicle could be put. The cannibalisation crews were so thorough that the manufacturer would rarely receive more than the empty hull by the time the tank reached his plant. Disabled tanks awaiting engine replacements at field repair shops were also subject to being stripped, and by the time the new engine arrived there usually was little left of the tank for which it had been intended.' *German Tank Maintenance in WW2.*
- Officer training was improved with specific maintenance training.

4 Tank radios

Communications are crucial for armoured warfare: inside the tank to enable the commander to instruct the crew; external links with other tanks and commands; liaison with infantry, artillery and air assets. World War II saw considerable use of radios and units that did not have them suffered accordingly. However, it is worth remembering that radios in the 1930s and 1940s were, of course, much less sophisticated than they are today. They were much bigger, contained many more fragile parts that broke regularly (this was well before the days of solid state) and had to be replaced – particularly so in vehicles negotiating bad terrain and exposure to a range of temperatures. They ate batteries and were hungry for power and required a well-trained operator. This made it a difficult role to double up – especially if the tank commander was the man to be doubled up.

In the early war years, most countries started with command networks and many of German and Allied vehicles were equipped from the start – although not all. The Russians tried to catch up. By early 1944 most new Russian tanks had radios and those that didn't – mainly early T-34/76, T-70 and T-80 models – were retro-fitted with, at least, *malyutka* receivers (part of the 9-R radio). Many tank units used runners and flags – a good example being the Italians a number of whose tanks were, it is said, captured by a man with a pistol knocking on the outside and pretending to be a messenger.

The Germans had understood the need for good communications and had ensured that many of their tanks were well equipped, although as elsewhere most of the early tanks only had receivers linked to a command net. The commanders used specialist vehicles such as – between 1935 and 1940 – the SdKfz 265 kleiner Panzerbefehlswagen. These command vehicles may well have included Enigma machines (such as that shown in the photo of Guderian in France in 1940). Other German command vehicles included:

SdKfz 250/3 leichter Funkpanzer in various versions.
SdKfz 251/3 mittlerer Kommandopanzerwagen (Funkpanzer) in various versions, with differing radio fits depending on use (eg for ground to air coordination)
SdKfz 260 leichter Funkpanzer
SdKfz 261 kleiner Funkpanzer
SdKfz 263 mittlerer Funkpanzer (6- and 8-wheel vehicles)

SdKfz 265 kleine PzBefw (PzKpfw I)
SdKfz 266 PzBefw III (early form of the PzKpfw III), 38(t)
SdKfz 267/268 PzBefw: this came in a range of 38(t), III, IV, V (Panther) and Tiger I and II versions, depending on role and radios used (eg the Panther *Flivo* used for air to ground coordination)
There was also a range of observation vehicles linked into the artillery net.

German radios

The 1945 US Army's *Handbook on German Military Forces* lists sets likely to be installed in various types of armoured and self-propelled artillery vehicles. Most were identified with a *Fu* prefix (*Fünkgerät* = radio). The other prefix, *FuSpr* (*Funksprecher* = radio/telephone) was mainly used for types mounted on artillery, Panzerjäger and SPW (light armoured cars). The most usual versions were *FuSpr a, d* and, latterly, *f*.

Vehicle	Radio
Commander's tank	Fu8 and Fu5; or Fu7 and Fu5
Fighting tanks, all types	Fu5 and Fu2; or Fu5
Assault guns (in armoured formations)	Fu5 and Fu2; or Fu5
Armoured OP vehicles (artillery)	Fu8 and Fu4; or Fu8, Fu4, and FuSpr f
Assault guns (artillery)	Fu8, Fu16, and Fu15; or Fu16 and Fu15; or Fu16
SP antitank guns (light and medium chassis)	Fu8 and Fu5; or Fu5
SP antitank guns (heavy chassis)	Fu8 and Fu5; or Fu7 and Fu5; or Fu5 and Fu2
Antitank–assault guns	Fu8 and Fu5; or Fu5
Lynx (reconnaissance)	Fu12 and FuSpr f or FuSpr f
AA tanks (Flakpanzer)	FuS or Fw2
SP heavy infantry gun	Fu16
Wespe and Hummel SP guns	FuSpr f
Armoured cars (except 8-wheeled vehicles)	Fu12 and/or FuSpr f
Semi-tracked vehicles with armament	FuSpr f
8-wheeled armoured car	Fu12 and FuSpr f or FuSpr f

Commanders in the field: Gen Maj Georg von Bismarck, commander 21st Panzer Division, in front of a Panzer III Ausf H Befehlspanzer from Panzer-Regiment 5 (**Left**). Heinz Guderian in a SdKfz 251/3 command vehicle, France, May 1940; note the early three-rotor Enigma machine.

Communications in a German PzKpfw IV tank

[*Tactical and Technical Trends 12*, November 19, 1942.]

For the radio, the voice range between two moving vehicles is about 3.75 miles and CW about 6.25 miles. The radio set, in conjunction with the intercom, provides the tank commander, radio operator and driver with a means for external and internal voice communication, the same throat microphones and telephone receiver headsets being used for both radio and telephone.

When the control switch on the radio is set at *Empfang* (receive) and that on the junction box of the intercom at *Bord und Funk* (internal and radio), the commander, radio operator, and driver hear all incoming radio signals. Any one of them can also speak to the other two, after switching his microphone into circuit by means of the switch on his chest.

For radio transmission, the switch on the set is adjusted to *Telephonie*. The telephone switch may be left at *Bord und Funk*. Either the tank commander or the radio operator can then transmit, and they and the driver will all hear the messages transmitted. Internal communication is also possible at the same time, but such conversation will also be transmitted by the radio.

If the radio set is disconnected or out of order, the telephone switch may be adjusted to *Bord* (internal). The tank commander and driver can then speak to one another, and the radio operator can speak to them, but cannot hear what they say. The same applies when a radio receiver is available but no transmitter, with the difference that incoming radio signals can then be heard by the radio operator.

The signal flags are normally carried in holders on the left of the driver's seat. When the cupola is open, flag signals are given by the tank commander, and when it is closed, the loader raises the circular flap in the left of the turret roof and signals with the appropriate flag through the port thus opened. The flag is used for short-range communications only.

The signal pistol is fired either through the signal port in the turret roof, through the cupola, or through one of the vision openings in the turret wall. The signal pistol must not be cocked until the barrel is already projecting outside the tank. It is only used normally when the vehicle is stationary. Its main use is giving prearranged signals to the infantry or other troops.

When travelling by night with lights dimmed or switched off altogether, driving signals are given with the aid of a dimmed flashlight. The same method is also employed when tanks are in a position of readiness and when in bivouac.

Orders are transmitted from the tank commander to the gunner by speaking tube and by touch signals. The latter are also used for messages from the commander to the loader, and between the gunner and loader.

Japanese radios

The main Japanese radio was the Type TM Model 305 Mobile Radio Set, which had a range of 25. It was well-designed and built, as would be expected of Japanese manufacturers, and was comparable Allied designs.

Allied radios

In America, the arguments between armour and cavalry were played out in the field of communications as elsewhere, the Signal Corps wasting its efforts on delivering a brilliant radio for use on horseback rather than for tanks. The discovery of FM radio was a big step forward in clarity of communications. (FM eliminates much of the engine interference and is easier to tune automatically and precisely.) However, the Signal Corps was loth to divert from AM – influenced in part by the vested interests of the manufacturers. The result was the SCR-245 AM radio, standardized on 10 June 1937 replacing the earlier SCR-189. This was used by armoured forces for command and control of tank units and saw use in the M2 and M3 light tanks as well as the early M3 mediums. These were big radios and had to be mounted in the sponsons.

In 1940 the FM party won the battle of the airwaves and the SCR-293 and -294 were produced: compact, short-range sets which went into the tanks of the 1st and 2nd Armoured Divisions in North Africa, the first FM radios used in combat. It was swiftly overtaken by the excellent SCR-508, based on Link Radio Corporation designs, with development performed by Bell Laboratories and Western Electric. It was introduced in late 1941. It was immediately incorporated in the M5 light and M4 medium. The US Army had a tank radio as good as or better than any on the market and the

Below Left: Checking the radios on a Ninth Army M20 command car. Nearly 3,000 were built by Ford's Chicago plant.

Below Right: Infantry talk to the tank crew through a telephone in a box attached to the rear of the vehicle.

SCR-508, 528 or 538 would be used throughout the war, each being slightly different: the -508 – in platoon and company commanders' tanks, had a BC-604 transmitter and two BC-603 receivers, as well as BC-606 intercom boxes at each crew station; the -528 had only one BC-603 and was the version found in most vehicles; the -538 had no transmitter. Command tanks had an extra radio, an SCR-506 mounted in the front right sponson to communicate with battalion HQs or other commands. M8 and M20 armoured cars assigned to the reconnaissance companies received the SCR-608, almost identical to the -508, but on different frequencies and used also by the field artillery.

As well as these radio, to get over the problem of talking to infantry outside the tank, Shermans mounted an EE-8 field telephone linked into the crew intercom in a .30-calibre ammunition box on the back of the tank.

In late 1944 a tank-mounted version of the SCR-300, the AN/VRC-3, was provided to tank platoon leaders.

Interphone Language [From *FM 17-76*]

a. Terms

Tank commander	LIEUTENANT or SERGEANT
Driver	DRIVER
Gunner	GUNNER
Cannoneer	LOADER
Bow gunner	BOG
Any tank	TANK
Armored car	ARMORED CAR
Any unarmored vehicle	TRUCK
Any antitank gun	ANTITANK
Infantry	DOUGHS
Machine gun	MACHINE GUN
Airplane	PLANE

b. Commands for movement of tank

To move forward	DRIVER MOVE OUT
To halt	DRIVER STOP
To reverse	DRIVER REVERSE
To decrease speed	DRIVER SLOW DOWN
To turn right 90	DRIVER CLOCK 3 - STEADY ... ON
To turn left 60	DRIVER CLOCK 10 - STEADY ... ON
To turn right (left) 180	DRIVER CLOCK 6 RIGHT (LEFT) - STEADY ... ON
To have driver move	DRIVER MARCH ON
toward a terrain feature or reference point	WHITE HOUSE, HILL, DEAD TREE, the tank being headed ETC in proper direction
To follow in column	DRIVER FOLLOW THAT TANK (DRIVER FOLLOW TANK NO. B-9)
To follow on road or trail	DRIVER RIGHT ON ROAD (DRIVER RIGHT ON TRAIL)
To start engine	DRIVER CRANK UP
To stop engine	DRIVER CUT ENGINE
To proceed in a specific gear	DRIVER THIRD GEAR (FIRST GEAR) (FOURTH GEAR)
To proceed at same speed	DRIVER STEADY

c. Commands for control of turret

To traverse turret	GUNNER TRAVERSE LEFT (RIGHT)
To stop turret traverse	GUNNER STEADY ... ON

Wireless Set No. 19

The British and Canadian mainstay was the No 19 Set, designed up to 1940 by the Royal Signals Experimental Establishment and Pye Radio to give armoured troops reliable communications. A Mk II version was quickly produced to bring it up to required specifications in 1941 and that was superseded by even better version, the Mk III, in 1942. Tested in the Western Desert, they provided (to quote www.radiomuseumuk.com) 'HF inter-tank and tank-to-HQ R/T, CW and MCW communications, VHF inter-tank communications and an intercom facility for a tank's crew. The HF part, the A set, is tuned to receive and transmit with a single dial and has a 'flick' switch for rapidly changing between two previously set frequencies, a device still used in aircraft today.'

The Royal Signals Museum (Blandford, Dorset) summed up the set in its *History of Signalling in 100 Objects*: 'It was soon realised that the frequency coverage of the Mk I was too limited and a Mk II with a better frequency range was introduced into service in 1942. Further modifications were made to improve efficiency especially of CW (continuous wave) and to reduce the drain on power and the Mk III set was introduced in 1943. Despite initial difficulties the No 19 Wireless Set gave good service and revolutionised armoured formation communications in World War II.'

The sets were built in Australia (AWA), Canada (Northern Electric, Canadian Marconi and RCA Victor) and the United States (Zenith, RCA and Philco) as well as the UK (Pye, Ekco, Philips and AGI). There were many Lend-Lease versions, some with Cyrillic text labelling intended for supply to the Russian front (see photo opposite).

Anthony C. Davies explained the technicalities (in 'WW2 British Army Battlefield Wireless Communications Equipment'): 'The frequency range of the main A set is 2.5–6.25MHz for the first version, made by Pye Radio, the Mk II extended this to 2.0–8.0MHz . . . Nine indirectly-heated valves are used, with an ATS25 beam tetrode (similar to the 807 and CV124) for the main transmitter power-amplifier valve, operated in Class C. The range of ~15km from the 5W output can be boosted by RF Amplifier No2 (in a metal box similar in size and shape to the WS19) to 35W giving a range of ~70km. The amplifier uses four ATS25 valves (the later Mk III uses two, but achieves the same power output)

The WS 19 also contains a VHF B set for inter-tank communications, operating at 240MHz, and an intercom amplifier for communications within a tank. The B set has a super-regenerative receiver, using a CV6 triode valve, which is distinctive in having both anode and grid brought out to top caps.

For infantry to talk to tanks, there was a WS38 AFV pouch transceiver, weighing 10kg, range 7.3–9.0 MHz, 200mW Transmitter output, Receiver i.f. 285KHz. Five valves, of which two are shared between transmitter and receiver. Well over 100,000 had been manufactured by the end of World War II.'

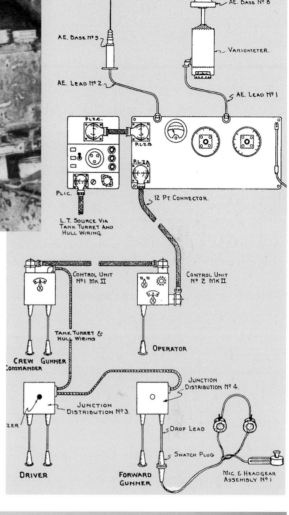

A set: tuneable 2–8MHz HF radio transmitter-receiver operating on R/T, CW or MCW with a range of 10 miles on R/T or 20 miles on CW (Morse code) between vehicles, using a simple 8ft vertical antenna located on the top of the vehicle. It was intended for communication from troop to troop, troop to base. One of the tanks in a squadron HQ would extend the net to the regiment.

B set: 230–240MHz VHF R/T (so, speech only) transmitter-receiver with a range of up to 1,000 yards over unobstructed level ground using a half-wave aerial. Its purpose was communication between vehicles within a troop.

C set: the in-tank intercom – all crew members having headsets and microphones (**Right**).

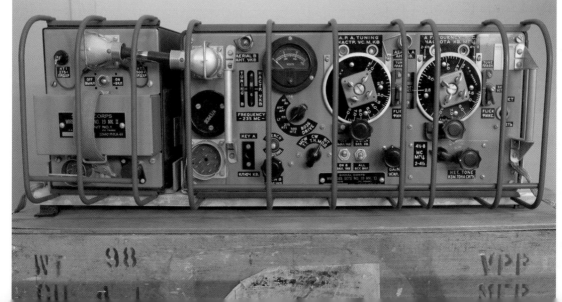

5 Bridging and Bridgelayers

River crossing is difficult enough for infantry, for armour it's even more complicated. If a bridge can be seized, such as happened at Nijmegen in 1944 or Remagen over the Rhine in 1945, then the rule is: get the armour across to help hold and expand the bridgehead. If there's no bridge and fording is impossible, then you need to make one – and to carry tanks it needs to be substantial and quick to erect. Blitzkrieg can't be sustained without speedy bridge crossings. The Germans were good at improvisation, but most crossings required specialist equipment carried by engineer battalions. Every army made provision for bridging – no army fighting in Europe could do otherwise – and it was a key feature of the Allied drive across northwest Europe.

Many of the crossings were contested and required assault crossings. These, almost always, start out with infantry storm boats, usually small, unarmoured, wooden and in the case of the British and Russians, often collapsible. These were supplemented by pneumatic boats which subsequently filled an important role ferrying personnel and stores, and in the construction of rafts and light treadway bridges. Early in the war, many divisional bridging columns held more substantial bridging equipment but later this tended to be concentrated at corps or army level.

The main German bridging equipment were the Brückengerät B, which could build 8 ton bridges to a length of 83 meters and 16 ton bridges to a length of 54 meters. Fine for infantry/Panzergrenadiers and B vehicles, tanks needed something stronger – Brückengerät J, which was need to carry PzKpfw V Panthers and could build bridges to carry tanks up to 80 tons. The German heavies – particularly Tiger I and II – proved too heavy for many bridges, even when captured intact. Leibstandarte's meandering during the Battle of the Bulge ended with bridges blown by US engineers, others too weak to carry their tanks and bridging columns caught up in a traffic jam. As well as these pontoon bridges, larger ones could be erected from the Brückengerät K small box girder bridge or the ex-Czech Herbert Bridge.

Otherwise, the Panzer division standards were the Brückengerät J42 and J43 (a strengthened version of the J42). The J42 comprised steel box-girder sections, of which any number up to four could be bolted together to form a maximum span of 64 feet.

The Allies

In the American Blitzkrieg of 1944, as Patton's Third Army brushed through the scattered German defences as they retreated from Normandy, one spearhead was 6th Armoured Division – the Super Sixth – commanded by Maj Gen Robert W. Grow. Postwar he wrote a paper ('Armour and Mobility in Maintaining the Momentum

Bridging is an essential requirement for armoured formations – the holdups occasioned by the slow replacement bridge over the railway lines at Scheid (**Above**) held up the bulk of Peiper's Kampfgruppe for over two hours. On the other hand, the Allies had the Bailey bridge (**Below**) – the first one built in contact with the enemy being that across the River Medjerda at Madjez el Bab in Tunisia. Erected in November 1942 by the Canadian 237 Field Company, RE of 78th Division, it was the first of many. Some tanks – such as the Tiger I – were capable of snorkelling.

of a River Crossing Examples from the Lorraine Campaign') that sums up well the difficulties of river crossings:

'The tactical principles of a river crossing have been thoroughly developed and tested for centuries. There is little dispute among students on such questions as the selection of crossing sites, use of supporting fires, main and secondary crossings, surprise, and build-up of bridgeheads. A well planned and skillfully executed attack of a river line seldom fails to secure a crossing. The defender relies primarily on use of his reserves

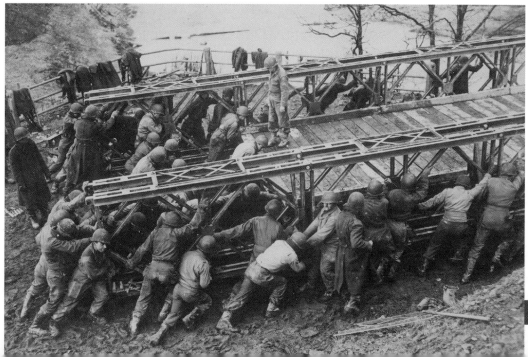

in counterattack while the attacker is still confined to a defile. In other words, it is not the crossing operation that proves most difficult for the attacker but the exploitation. It is rare that the capture of a river line itself is the object of a campaign. The river is normally only an obstacle. However, if the river be a formidable obstacle it sometimes acquires such high importance as temporarily, at least, to transcend the true objective, drawing to it the forces necessary to effect a crossing and obtain a secure bridgehead and relegating the exploitation to an entirely new and later operation.

If the enemy can contain the bridgehead initially he at once gains a tremendous advantage. He has confined the attacker to a defile and is able to throw his reserves at a definite and fixed target which in most cases will be relatively inferior. Therefore, to the attacker, the expansion of his bridgehead at the earliest is vital. The physical difficulties of a river crossing restrict the attacker's ability to cross the number of troops he needs to establish a bridgehead and, to an even greater extent; exploit it. This fact points to the necessity of careful determination of the order of crossing.

When bridges exist and can be seized we have a simple case in which to exploit mobility. Armoured units load, rapidly deploy, and enable the commander to retain a high degree of maneuver ability. When, however, the crossing must be forced and a bridgehead secured to cover the building of a bridge before mobile troops can cross, the problem is not simple.'

Grow discusses a number of examples, including this by XX Corps:

'The plan called for a wide double envelopment. The 5th Infantry Division on the south, with only the Seille River to cross and greatly assisted by the XII Corps attack which jumped off one day earlier and by the 6th Armoured Division, which led the way along the corps boundary and seized a crossing of the Nied River, turning it over to the 5th Infantry Division, closed the circle on this flank. The 95th Infantry Division made a diversionary close-in crossing south of Thionville during the night of 8 November.

The following night the 90th Infantry Division forced the main crossing north of Thionville and gradually expanded its bridgehead during the following five days. Not until 13 November were bridges in shape to bring heavy support vehicles across, although some ferrying had been done. When the 10th Armoured Division crossed on the newly constructed bridges at Thionville and to the north on 14-15 November the attack of the two divisions broke out rapidly and completed the encirclement of the Metz garrison.

In the November operation there was no question about leading with armour because XX Corps was confronted by an established defence along the Seille and Moselle rivers, with the fortress of Metz in the center of the line. Although the Seille was the less formidable obstacle and a crossing there would probably permit his

Above and Below: Pontoon treadway bridges were used by all armie – as here a ISU-122S in April 1945 (**Above**) and M4A3 (**Below**). The British classification system – which went on to be used by NATO – gave each vehicle a bridge rating which was displayed in a yellow circle with black writing. The number wasn't the same as the weight – other factors such as axle loading – were taken into consideration. A Sherman was classified 33; a Jeep 2 and a DUKW 9. But to build a treadway bridge required a bridgehead and that usually came about following an amphibious assault. During such manoeuvres, tank support was essential – as the 760th Tank Battalion report for January 1944 makes clear: 'During the attack of the 36th Division across the Rapido, effective tank support was not possible due to fog and the great quantity of smoke employed. From later experiences during periods of good visibility, it is believed that with clear visibility tank fires from the positions occupied would have been invaluable to the infantry in this operation.' The Rapido crossing was a debacle that hung over Mark Clarke's head for the rest of his life and occasioned a career-threatening congressional hearing postwar. The 'T-Patchers' lost 2,000 men killed, wounded and taken prisoner. The 760th could only stand and watch: 'Throughout the day of the 21st Companies "B" and "C" remained in position but were unable to fire because of poor visibility. The entire area being smoked to aid the infantry crossing.'

armour to exploit at an earlier date, more compelling reasons caused the corps commander to choose the northern bridgehead for his 10th Armoured Division. The wide envelopment by the 90th Division would leave a long open flank and in addition the opportunity for a quick dash to the Saar dictated employing his most mobile unit on the left flank.'

That's the bare bones of what happened. The detail shows the difficulty of the operation:

'Eight battalions of the Division with some AT guns were ferried across by the end of the first day, 9 November, and the bridgehead was up to three miles in depth and six miles at the base, although not all cleared or solid. The first counterattack came in the early hours of 10 November, a reinforced company supported by three assault guns. It made a deep penetration but was eventually wiped out. By the end of the second day (10 November) the troops were tired and soaked. They had made some advance but still had no tank support and they anxiously awaited an expected strong counterattack. On the third day (11 November) supplies and AT guns were still being ferried across but the three regiments continued to enlarge their bridgehead perimeter and withstand small but repeated counterattacks. The first major counterattack struck at 0300 on 12 November, supported by ten tanks and assault guns. The German force made a deep penetration but was finally stopped and destroyed by the infantry, artillery support from across the Moselle, and two tank destroyers which had managed to get across the first completed bridge just before it was broken by artillery fire. This counterattack cost the enemy 4 tanks, 5 assault guns, and 400 killed. Finally by midnight 12 November, with the river receding, two bridges were completed and the weary troops were reinforced by tanks and tank destroyers. They had gained a bridgehead about five miles deep and nine miles across the base. By dawn on 14 November, the 90th Division had all of its organic equipment in the bridgehead and the combat regiments were in position to break out.'

The British and Canadian Armies also had to contend with the same problems. Thanks to Donald Bailey, a British civil servant, they had an answer that would quickly become the standard for the Allies. The first Bailey bridge built in earnest was in Tunisia on 26 November 1942 by 237 Field Company, RE. The Allies built over 2,500 in the Italian campaign. The Americans licenced the Bailey Bridge and built it themselves in large quantities. An example of an opposed crossing took place at Vernon as is remembered on a memorial stone: 'On the 25th August 1944, the 43rd (Wessex) Division liberated Vernon and crossed the River Seine under the fire of the German units dug in on the prominent hills of the eastern bank. The infantry supported by 4 armoured regiments fought during 3 days to repulse the enemy. The crossing was achieved by the use of 3 floating bridges built by the Royal Engineers. From this initial bridgehead the 30th Corps led the advance towards Belgium. The British troops suffered 550 casualties in this operation.'

In 1938 the RE Board produced a scale, or classification, of all bridge types based not just on weight but taking into account other factors. Each vehicle was given a load class number from 3 to 24, as were the bridges, and if the numbers matched or the vehicle's was less than the bridge's, it could cross.

Bridgelayers

In World War I it became quickly apparent that tanks needed to be able to cross trenches or they wouldn't get very far. They used fascines, bundles of wood, which did the trick, and were taken up in World War II, but it was obvious that something more was needed. The answer came in the form of the AVLB – armoured vehicle launched bridge – which was developed by both sides. Krupp was contracted in February 1939 and by April 1940 the German army had 20 Brückenleger IVs built on the PzKpfw IV body. They never worked well and most were reconverted into tanks. The British, however, developed a scissors bridge for the Covenanter tank. It ended up being paired first with the Valentine II (as **Below**) and then the Churchill and saw extensive service during the war.

Underwater bridges

Finally, it's worth mentioning the prodigious efforts made by the Germans in Italy where intensive Allied air attack rendered the majority of bridges unusable. To counter this, the Germans used a technique they copied from the Russians: underwater bridging – anything up to 6in below water level, their use strictly limited to hours of darkness and their approaches well-camouflaged so as not to betray the site.

6 Amphibious Tanks

The Allies had a need for amphibious tanks: the DD drive enabled Shermans to 'swim' ashore on D-Day and cross the Rhine; the LVT(A)s allowed immediate support of amphibious landings. Six LVT(A) squadrons were activated by the US during World War II: the USMC's 1st, 2nd and 3rd Armored Amphibian Battalions; the US Army's 708th, 776th and 780th Amphibian Tank Battalions. The Marines came mainly from the reserves. The army turned three land battalions into amphibians.

776th Amtank Battalion Operation Report Ryukyu Campaign
[Action Report, 9 August 1945]

This report describes the first large-scale deployment of amphibian tanks as supporting artillery. During the Ryukyus campaign the 776th Amphibian Tank Battalion fired a total of 41,297 rounds of 75mm ammunition in support of infantry operations.

Landing on Okinawa unopposed obscures the importance of the secondary mission: supporting fire. Placed ashore in the first wave the 776th was the equivalent of four well trained battalions of artillery hours before the landing of Div Arty.

Six vehicles were struck by enemy shell fire only one – which hit a mine – was damaged beyond repair. The battalion embarked as follows:

Bn HQ, HQ & Serv Co:		Line Companies:	
CO and half Bn staff	LVT(A)4	Co CO & FDC*	LVT(A)1
Bn ExO and half Bn staff	LVT(A)4	Con & Rcn Sec	LVT(A)1
Bn Maint Sect & shops in	3 x LVT4	Each platoon in	LVT(A)4
Med Det, initially in	2 x LVT4	Co Maint Sect	LVT4
Bn Com Sec & Msg Cen	LVT(A)4		

*FDC personnel were distributed among the platoons' 4 amtanks. [LVT(A)4s]. Each platoon amtank carried 8 men or 1 in excess of normal crew

20 LVT(A)1s thus made surplus were left on Leyte with the rear echelon.

The combat elements of the battalion were transported to the target in eight LSTs, with other impedimenta and wheeled vehicles in a ninth. Launching 5,000 yards offshore. Howitzers in first wave fired c16 rounds per gun. No damage from enemy fire. Sufficient seawall holes allowed battalion to reach objective 200 yards inland and

While they aren't amphibious tanks per se, the DD – Duplex Drive – tanks had a floatation screen erected around their superstructure. This allowed them to use a propeller driven by power take off from the engine to 'swim' through the sea and cross rivers, which they did to great effect. Save for the disaster off Omaha Beach, when the 741st Tank Battalion was released too far out in too rough a sea (6ft waves) and lost 27 of 32 tanks, the DD usage on D-Day and elsewhere in Europe – for example the Scheldt, Rhine and Elbe – proved effective. The concept was first tried using the Tetrarch light tank and, proving successful, then moved to the Valentine, and finally the Sherman became the most successful version.

delivered supporting fire for the infantry within 30 minutes of landing. By the end of 1 April (D-Day) infantry had advanced 4,700 yards inland. [The 776th had expended 691 rounds of ammunition.]

Casualties suffered were 2 officers and 36 men including 6 dead.

Amtanks [LVT(A)4s] possess enough mobility to be employed with field artillery, and they provide stable gun platforms for accurate firing. However, the high silhouette of these vehicles and their relatively light armor render them very vulnerable to enemy counterbattery fire unless they are dug in to the tops of their tracks. This was done on this operation by bulldozers borrowed from artillery battalions. Plans should provide for one bulldozer per company to be made available for this work and for digging trenches for the protection of the large ammunition supplies necessary.

Prior to the first use of LVTs in combat by this battalion, extensive modifications and improvements were made on them by the battalion maintenance section. Mention is

Left and Opposite: Basic data for the LVTs. They used cup-shaped cleats on their tracks to propel themselves through the water.

Above: The LVT (landing vehicles tracked) series first came into use for ship-to-shore haulage using the unarmoured LVT1 and 2s in 1941–43. After Tarawa an armoured version – the LVT(A)1 with a turret-mounted 37mm – was hurried into service in 1944. Here they land on Eniwetok. On top of the six armored battalions raised by the US Army and Marine Corps, the US Army also integrated some into cavalry units (such as 6th Cavalry Recon Troop and 31st Cavalry Recon Squadron. These units mainly used LVT(A)1s assaulting New Guinea, Morotai Island and Luzon.

Below: The 37mm of the LVT(A)1 proved too small and so the 75mm howitzer that had armed the M8 GMC was used to create the LVT(A)4. These carried 100 rounds of 75mm ammo and had an open top clearly seen here. A32, an LVT(A)4, is seen on Iwo Jima with the distinctive bump of Mt Suribachi in the background. In total 1,890 of these were built, seeing action first at Saipan. Behind A32 are two (marked **1** and **2**) LVT4s with rear ramps and (**3**) an LVT2 which had no ramp and from which the passengers had to exit over the side. Note the gunshields (not always employed) on the machine guns.

Above and Below: LVT(A)4 D35 is lifted from US Navy attack transport USS *Hansford* preparatory to lowering into the sea off Iwo Jima, 19 February 1945. The turreted version were known as Amtanks, the unturreted as Amtrac/Amtracks or Alligators. The LVT(A)4 was heavily used in the battle for Iwo Jima: it was the only vehicle that could negotiate the volcanic sand easily. The 3rd, 5th, 10th and 11th Amtrac and 2nd Armored Amphibious Battalions landed with the 4th and 5th Marines on Iwo Jima and fought on the island until it was taken. The 2nd Armored had led the way at Saipan (15 June 1944), and Tinian (24 July).

made of these improvements because of the fact that they have helped make it possible to maintain the vehicles in fighting condition after the intensive use to which they were put in the Philippines and on Okinawa. In addition, those modifications had to be performed on some of the vehicles of Co D prior to the Ryukyu Campaign. (This Company had been detached from the battalion during the Leyte Operation.) New ammunition stowage racks and brackets for fuel and water cans, turret equipment, and personal gear were installed. Rust preventives were used extensively to counteract the effects of corrosion.

7 A Survey of Allied Tank Casualties in WW2

Alvin D. Coox & L. Van Loan Naisawald

This analysis is based on the causes of casualties of a sample of 12,140 Allied tanks: British, Canadian, French and, above all, US records. The statistics are skewed in places by lack of information and lack of consistent reporting, but the assessors have compensated for this.

Main causes of casualties in all theatres

1. Gunfire: 54%

A study of average range indicates a figure of 785 yards; site of hits: turret 31%, hull 52%, suspension 17%. 75mm guns account for 36% of kills and 88mm for 50% – that's 86% of the total gunfire kills. These are both tank and antitank gun kills. See also Gunfire casualties by theatre on page 196. A British analysis of 139 tanks immobilised by gunfire after the Rhine crossing gave: 37% hit from front; 60% (half and half left and right) side; and 3% rear.

2. Land mines: 20%

German land mine production was around 72 million and battle use was around 25 million. The Allies used fewer mines (other than in the desert war) because they were on the attack. German usage rose from 150,000 annually in 1939–41 to 14 million in 1944. The US total production of land mines was less than 25 million. Theatre played an important factor in mine warfare and the Italian terrain channelised armour's movement and room for manoeuvre. This and the slow retreat up Italy explains the larger number of mine casualties – 23% of US vehicles from a known sample of 588; British 25% from 728; Canadians 16% from 567. If a proportion of unknown causes and multiple weapons is factored in, the overall percentage could be around 25–30%. Analysis of US First Army mined tank casualties showed that less than 10% burned and only 3% had their ammo

IMMOBILIZED BY GUNFIRE

IMMOBILIZED BY HOLLOW CHARGE

hit. Less than 15% had been penetrated (and 3% of these included artillery penetration). The largest percentage of mine casualties was in the Pacific where 30% were mined and a large proportion of the 20% casualties to miscellaneous/multiple weapons were attacks on mined tanks. The report analyses separately the cost of mining against its target and shows how successful it was, not just in terms of cost, lives and destroyed equipment, but – more important strategically – in terms of time. Each time a tank strikes a mine there's a morale issue and a tactical delay. Looking at 97 British tank regiments in Africa, Italy and Europe there were 22 instances where delays amount to more than 15 hours and a further 20 when an advance was stopped. US research shows 21 incidents 13 of which (mainly in Italy) saw an American advance either abandoned or delays up to 24 hours. The slow pursuit of Rommel by Eighth Army testifies to the amount of mine warfare and, as the report points out, it is no surprise to see Rommel advocating the use of millions of mines in Normandy to halt Allied opportunities. Over 360,000 man-hours were taken up by mine clearing in France.

3. Mechanical and non-enemy weapons: 13%
However, this is low because US and British data are only concerned with battle damage. Incomplete US data shows 15% minimum but probably higher. Canadian and USMC data suggest a more accurate figure of 25–40%. As an example the report cites a US Third Army study of 107 M4 casualties that indicated 30 tanks (28%) 'were destroyed by terrain obstacles or mechanical deficiencies'. This factor would be more noticeable in the exploitation and pursuit periods when it could rise to a ratio of four to one over tank casualties due to enemy action. See table on page 196 examining British tank casualties after crossing the Seine.

4. Hollow charge weapons: 7.5%
Not used in North Africa and the Pacific, and more available late in the war, a more accurate figure would be 10% in early 1944 (first recorded use in this analysis Jan/Feb 1944 in Italy) and up to 25–35% in spring 1945. After crossing the Rhine, 25–35% of all Allied tank casualties were inflicted by Panzerfaust-type weapons. So, an adjusted figure to include only Italy and Europe would give a casualty figure of 10% of 7,700 casualties, and this could be higher if multiple weapon/unknown reasons are factored in. A study of average range indicates a figure of 50 yards; site of hits: turret 44%, hull 48%, suspension 8%. See also table on page 197 examining hollow charge hits against AFVs.

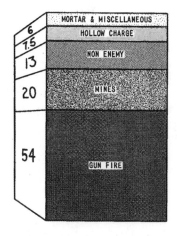

Allied tank casualties showing the percentage of losses by cause.

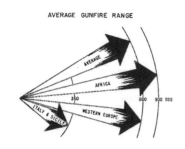

AVERAGE GUNFIRE RANGE

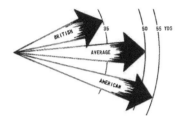

AVERAGE BAZOOKA RANGE
(all theaters)

Top: Average ranges at which tanks were immobilised by gunfire, as derived from data covering Allied experience in Western Europe, Africa, Italy and Sicily.

Above: Average ranges at which tanks were immobilised by hollow-charge weapons, as experienced in all theatres of war

5. Miscellaneous and mortar: 5.5%

This includes air attack, combinations of weapons (may casualties are identified as being hit by multiple weapons and these have been left out of the specific casualty figures), mortars (1% rising to 2% in the Pacific), Japanese improvisations – because the Japanese theatre involved fewer enemy tanks and massed artillery, more casualties came from satchel charges, Molotov cocktails, grenades, improvised mines etc.

Vehicles repairable after being knocked out, by weapon*

Mine	78%
Panzerfaust	71%
Gunfire	51%

*This isn't particularly strong data as the records are incomplete, the terminology loose.

Causes of immobilisation of German tanks

Gunfire	44%
Self-destruction	20.8%
Abandonment	18.4%
Air attack	8%
Hollow charge	4.5%
Mechanical	4.1%
Mines and misc	1%

Tank crew casualties

Outside the vehicle	40%

Of this figure 30% – 11% of the total – became casualties while trying to escape from immobilised vehicles. US figures for this are larger.

Observations by tank crew (taken from *Tank Personnel Casualty Reports*) stated that the 'effect of AT mines on personnel riding in tanks has been very small. It is only in exceptional cases that any member of a tank is injured by a mine … Where tanks have encountered AT mines that were protected by enemy fire, casualties have occurred in crews due to sniper or MG fire when the vehicle had to be evacuated. Whenever possible, the enemy brings fire down on stalled tanks and attempts to

Above: The Sherman wasn't known for its armour – a Canadian study by No 2 Operational Research Section analysed 75mm-armed Sherman casualties suffered 6 June–10 July 1944. The result? 'Sixty per cent of Allied tank losses were the result of a single shot from a 75mm or 88mm gun and two-thirds of all tanks "brewed up" when hit.'

Below Right: Average ranges at which tanks were immobilised by gunfire, as derived from data covering Allied experience in Western Europe, Africa, Italy and Sicily.

Bottom Right: Percentage of tank crew casualties broken down by crew position.

destroy them by burning.' It goes on to discuss artillery casualties: 'Commanders all agree that the effect of artillery fire on tanks is slight. Direct hits are the exception.'

As far as AT fire is concerned, 'Penetrations of the tank by AT projectiles usually result in about two casualties, one killed and one wounded. When tanks have been penetrated by AT fire, members of the crew who have not been killed or wounded or knocked unconscious usually manage to escape even though the tank is set on fire . . . Where complete crews are lost, unit COs attribute casualties to flash ammunition fires.'

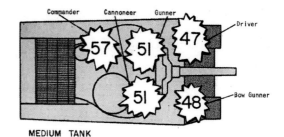

MEDIUM TANK

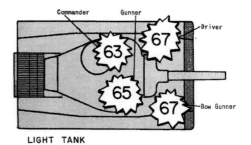

LIGHT TANK

On average between 2 and 2.5 crewmen per tank became casualties but no one crew position was hugely more dangerous, with commanders (particularly when travelling heads-up) in the most dangerous position.

Gunfire (tank and antitank) casualties by theatre (Western Allies)

North Africa	80%
Italy	45%
Western Europe	50%
Pacific	35%
Overall average	55%

This is based on 10,500 known US, British, Canadian, and French casualties. No clear-cut breakdown of the gunfire category was possible because of the divergence of nomenclature and thus the difficulty in evaluating the data. Tactics and available armament played a great role as did terrain – in North Africa gunfire and mines accounted for an overwhelming share. The Italian figure, on a total of 2,300 tank casualties, is skewed by 20% immobilised by unknown cause and 25% down to bogging and other non-enemy causes. Based on the weighted sample of 1,450 tanks, the gunfire percentage would increase from 45% to 60%. The arrival of the Panzerfaust/Panzerschreck also affected gunfire totals in Western Europe. The Pacific percentage is also skewed by non-enemy causes and miscellaneous kills by such methods as satchel charges etc. When weighted down to a sample of 500 tank casualties the gunfire total would be closer to 50%. What all this means is that a truer picture of the overall figure of tanks immobilised by gunfire in all theatres for 8,500 known cases is nearer 65% – so, two out of three tank casualties.

British tank casualties after crossing the Seine

Unit	Number of tank casualties due to:		Total
	Mechanical (% of total)	Enemy action	
Guards Armoured	59 (92.2)	5	64
8th Armoured Brigade	57 (74)	20	77
11th Armoured Division	44 (88)	6	50
7th Armoured Division	38 (76)	12	50
1st Polish Armoured Division	50 (62.5)	30	80
4th Canadian Armoured Division	57 (91.9)	5	62
Total	305 (79.6)	78	383
Average per unit	51 (79.7)	13	64
Average per days in pursuit	5.4 (79.4)	1.4	6.8
Average per 100 miles	16 (79.6)	4.1	20.1

*All units equipped with Shermans save 7th Armoured (Cromwells)

Very little maintenance work can be performed during operational phases, because of the distances involved, the times travelled and the need to be ready for instant action.

Hollow charge hits against AFVs

Range in yards	0–20	21–40	41–60	61–80	81–100	100+
Hits	35	22	13	4	3	3
Misses	15	14	13	5	4	7

Info from *British Operational Report No 33* use of Panzerfaust in the NW European Campaign studying Allied tanks immobilised east of the Rhine, based on 80 hits.

Tank Target Analysis

Type	Average all theatres (%)
Buildings	17.3
Personnel	15.5
Tanks	14.2
AT guns and artillery	12.8
Fortifications and caves	21.2
Wheeled vehicles	8.2
Others	10.8

Tanks have multiple types of target, of which tank on tank action was, on the western front, comparatively, rare. Similar figures for the Eastern Front would have reflected greater tank on tank action. Note, the report was based on the subjective reports of 100 US tank commanders. The theatre had an effect on the figures: highest percentage of fortification and cave targets was the Pacific at 36.4%; highest percentage of buildings as targets was Italy (28%). The highest tank on tank action was in North Africa (24.4%).

Causes of immobilisation of German tanks (Allied figures in brackets for comparison)

Gunfire	44% (52%)
Self-destruction	20.8%
Abandonment	18.4%
Air attack	8%
Hollow charge	4.5% (11%)
Mechanical	4.1%
Mines and misc	1% (20%)

Report quotes Chester Wilmot who felt that the large losses due to mechanical failures was down to (1) manufacturing flaws; (2) bad training; (3) lack of rail transport so more forced travel on tracks and because, 'The Germans tended to handle their armour with a rather brutal stupidity.'

Soviet claims of sample German tank losses

Cause	Claimed	Percentage
AT guns and artillery	2,601	75.3
Tanks	435	12.6
AT rifles and Molotov cocktails	18	0.5
Air (Sturmovik)	400	11.6
Total	3454	

Sample German tank casualties to US Third Army

	100 PzKpfw III and IV examined	36 PzKpfw V and VI examined (%)
Gunfire	59	30 (83%)
Rockets	8	9
90mm AP	4	2
75mm/76mm	47	19
Number burned	20 (34%)	12 (40%)
Mines	1	0
Terrain obstacles/mechanical	40	6 (17%)

A tank graveyard: a Sherman and three Panther Ausf Gs. The German tanks were knocked out by US 4th Armored Division near the German border, as Third Army pushed through France towards the Saar. Some 83% of Panthers and Tigers knocked out by Third Army were through tank fire. However, it's interesting to note that of the 136 tanks examined in the sample above, only one was knocked out by mines while the corresponding Allied figure would be around 20%. The reason for that is straightforward: advancing so quickly across France and into Germany, the Allies were almost continuously on the offensive. Most minefields are laid by defenders.

8 Tank and SP Gun Production in WW2

Tanks in service 1939-1945

Canada

RAM I	50
RAM II	1094
Grizzly	188

France

FCM 21	90
Renault R35	900
Renault D1/D2	260
Renault B1 bis	300
Somua S35	400

Germany

See table on page 201

Italy

L3	2500
M11/39	100
M13/40	800

Japan

97 tankette	58
95 light	1599
98 light	104
2 light	34
97 medium	535
97-kai medium	930
1 medium	170
3 medium	144
3 gun	31
2 amphibious	182
3 amphibious	12

Poland

TKS	300
Vickers Mk E	38
7TPjw	95

United Kingdom

A9 Cruiser I	125
A10 Cruiser II	175
A11 Matilda I	140
A12 Matilda II	2987
A13 Cruiser III	65
A13 Mk II Cruiser IV/IVA	855
A13 Mk III Cruiser IV Covenanter	1771
A15 Cruiser VI Crusader (inc variants)	5300
A24 Cruiser VII Cavalier	500
A27L Cruiser VIII Centaur	950
A27M Cruiser VIII Cromwell	4016
A30 Challenger	200
Valentine (inc variants)*	9700
A22 Churchill VII	5640
Comet (most postwar)	1186

United States

M3 light (Stuart)	13859
M5 light (Stuart)**	2663
M3 medium (Lee/Grant)	6258
M4 medium (75mm) Sherman	33403
M4 medium (76mm) Sherman	10883
M4 medium (105mm) Sherman	4680
Sherman Firefly (British modified)	2100
M24 light (Chaffee)	4415
M26 Pershing	1436

* inc 1420 built in Canada for Russia
** inc 1778 M8 Howitzers

USSR

BT-7	780
T-60	c. 5900
T-70	8231
KV-1	3010
KV-1S	1232
T-34	35488
T-34/85	23213
IS-2	3854
IS-3	350

Lend-Lease played an important role in assisting the Russian war effort as both America and Britain delivered tanks, aircraft and war matériel to the USSR, usually by means of the Arctic convoys to Murmansk. Around 13,000 armoured vehicles came from US Lend-Lease (including 7,000 tanks, of which nearly 2,000 were M3 mediums and 4,000 were Shermans) and over 427,000 trucks out of a Russian total inventory of 665,000 trucks. One top of this clothing and raw materials should not be discounted. Britain's contribution was smaller, but between June 1941 and May 1945, it included around 5,250 tanks (including 1,380 Valentines from Canada) and over 5,000 antitank guns. And they helped! Lend-Lease tanks made up 30–40% of the Russian heavy and medium tank strength in front of Moscow at the crucial moment of Operation Barbarossa at the beginning of December 1941. Here are two examples of Lend-Lease tanks to Russia: a British Valentine (**Top**), suitably named! – and an American M4A2 76(W), late production, with an M1A2 gun (**Above**).

Tank and SP gun production 1939-1945

Date	Canada	Germany	Hungary	Italy	Japan	UK	USA	USSR
1939	?	247	-	40	-	969	-	2950
1940	?	1643	-	250	315	1399	331	2794
1941	?	3790	-	595	1216	4841	4052	6590
1942	?	6180	)	1252	1271	8611	24997	24446
1943	?	12063	) 500	336	891	7476	29497	24089
1944	?	19002	)	-	371	4600	17565	28963
1945	?	3932	-	-	130	?	11968	15419
Total	5678	46857	500	2473	4194	27896	88410	105251

German tank production 1939-1945

	Prewar	1939	1940	1941	1942	1943	1944	1945	39–45	Total
PzKpfw I	1893	-	-	-	-	-	-	-	-	1893
PzKpfw II	1223	15	99	265	848	803	151	-	2,181	3404
PzKpfw 38(t)	78	153	367	678	652	1,008	2356	1335	6549	6627
PzKpfw III	98	157	1054	2213	2958	3379	4752	1136	15649	15747
PzKpfw IV	210	45	368	467	994	3822	6625	1090	13311	13522
PzKpfw V Panther	-	-	-	-	-	1849	4003	705	6557	6557
PzKpfw VI E Tiger I	-	-	-	-	78	649	641	-	1368	1,368
PzKpfw VI B Tiger II	-	-	-	-	-	1	428	140	569	69
Total	3,503	370	1888	3623	5530	11601	18956	4406	46274	49777

Self-propelled guns 1939-1945

	Gun	Chassis		Gun	Chassis
Italy			Jagdtiger	128mm Pak 44	PzKpfw VI (II)
L40	47/32mm 35	L6/40	Grille	150mm sIG 33	PzKpfw 38(t)
M40	75/18mm 35	M13/40	Hummel	150mm sFH 18	PzKpfw IV
M41	75/18mm 35	M14/41	*United States*		
M42	75/18mm 35	M15/42	M3 75mm	75mm M1897A	M3 halftrack
Germany			M8 Scott	75mm M1A1	M5 Stuart
Marder II	75mm Pak 40	PzKpfw II	M18 Hellcat	76mm M1	-
Marder III	75mm Pak 40	PzKpfw 38(t)	M10 Wolverine	3 inch M7	M4
SdKfz 138	75mm Pak 40	PzKpfw 38(t)	M36	90mm M3	M4
Hetzer	75mm Pak 39	PzKpfw 38(t)	M4 (105mm)	105mm M2A1	M4
StuG IIIG	75mm StuK 40	PzKpfw III	M7 Priest	105mm M2A1	M3
SdKfz 167	75mm StuK 40	PzKpfw IV	M7B1	105mm M2A1	M4
PzKpfw IV/70	75mm StuK 43	PzKpfw IV	M12	155mm M1A1	M3
SdKfz 132	76.2mm StuK 36(r)	PzKpfw II	*USSR*		
Marder VII/VIII	76.2mm StuK 36(r)	PzKpfw 38(t)	SU-76M	76.2mm Zis-3	T-70M
Nashorn	88mm Pak 43	PzKpfw IV	SU-85	85mm D5S	T-34
Jagdpanther	88mm Pak 43	PzKpfw V	SU-100	100mm D10S	T-34
Ferdinand	88mm Pak 43	PzKpfw VI (I)	SU-122	122mm M30S	T-34
StuH42	105mm StuH 42	PzKpfw III	SU-152	152mm ML20	KV-1S
Wespe	105mm le FH 18	PzKpfw II	ISU-122	122mm A195	IS-1
			ISU-152	152mm ML20	IS-1

	Gun	Chassis		Gun	Chassis
Japan			*United Kingdom*		
Ho-Ni I	75mm Type 90	Type 97	Bishop	25pdr	Valentine
Ho-Ni II	100mm Type 91	Type 97	Archer	17pdr	Valentine
			Sexton	25pdr	M3 Ram

M4 production by type

Type	Total	Production dates	Manufacturers
Prototype	1	September 1941	Aberdeen Proving Ground
M4 (75) (incl. composites)	6748	July 1942–January 1944	Pressed Steel Car, ALCO, Baldwin LW, Pullman Std, Chrysler
M4A1(75)	6281	February 1942–December 1943	Lima LW, Pressed Steel Car, Pacific Car & Foundry
M4A2(75)	8053	April 1942–May 1944	Pullman Std, ALCO, Baldwin LW, Fisher, Federal Machine
M4A3(75)	1690	June 1942–September 1943	Ford
M4A4	7499	July 1942–November 1943	Chrysler
M4A6	75	October 1943–February 1944	Chrysler
M4(105)	800	February 1944–September 1944	Chrysler
M4(105) HVSS	841	September 1944–March 1945	Chrysler
M4A1(76)W	2171	January 1944–December 1944	Pressed Steel Car
M4A1(76) HVSS	1255	January 1945–July 1945	Pressed Steel Car
M4A2(76)W	1594	May 1944–December 1944	Fisher
M4A2(76) HVSS	1321	January 1945–May 1945	Fisher, Pressed Steel Car
M4A3(75)W	3071	February 1944–March 1945	Fisher
M4A3E2 Jumbo	254	Jun 1944– July 1944	Fisher
M4A3(76)W	1925	March 1944–December 1944	Fisher, Chrysler
M4A3(76) HVSS	2617	August 1944–April 1945	Chrysler
M4A3(105)	500	May 1944–September 1944	Chrysler
M4A3(105) HVSS	2539	September 1944–June 1945	Chrysler
TOTAL	49234	February 1942–July 1945	

T-34 and variants production by type

Type	1939	1940	1941	1942	1943	1944	1945	Total
Tanks								
T-28	131	13						144
T-34		115	3016	12,661	15,710	3,986		35,488
T-34/85						10,662	12,551	23,213
T-44							25	545
SU-76				25	1,908	7,155	2,966	12,054
SU-85				761	1,578	315		2,654
SU-100						500	1,060	1,560
SU-122				26	612			638
TOTAL	131	128	3,016	13,473	19,808	22,618	16,606	76,296

Tiger production

	1942	1943	1944	1945	Total
Tiger I	78	649	623	-	1,350
Sturmtiger	-	-	18	-	18
Tiger II	-	1	377	112	490
Jagdtiger	-	-	51	28	79
TOTAL	78	650	1,069	140	1,937

Tiger losses and kills

Unit	Total losses	In action	Enemy tanks killed
sPzAbt 501	120	24	450
sPzAbt 502	107	88	1400
sPzAbt 503	252	113	1700*
sPzAbt 504	109	29	250
sPzAbt 505	126	47	900
sPzAbt 506	179	61	400
sPzAbt 507	104	43	600
sPzAbt 508	78	15	100
sPzAbt 509	120	76	500
sPzAbt 510	65	35	200
sSS-PzAbt 101	107	72	500
sSS-PzAbt 102	76	38	600
sSS-PzAbt 103	39	10	500
III/PzRegt Grossdeutschland	98	62	500
TOTAL	1580	713 (45%)	8600

It looked impressive and its Kwk 43 L/71 main gun was as good as any tank gun in the war. Nearly 500 Tiger IIs were built. With a range of 75 miles, it was a gas-guzzler, but its reliability improved over its production life and it made a formidable enemy.

German armour strengths

A. Western Campaign May 1940

Vehicle	In west	Total army	Vehicle	In west	Total army
PzKpfw I	523	1062	PzKpfw 35(t)	106	143
PzKpfw II	955	1079	PzKpfw 38(t)	228	238
PzKpfw III	349	329*	PzBefw	135	243
PzKpfw IV	278	280	Total	2574	3379

*The figure for PzKpfw III is explained by the fact that vehicles of this type rolling off production lines in April were delivered to the field forces in time for the campaign

b. Eastern Front 4 May 1943 inclusive of the Waffen-SS

Vehicle	In east	Total army 1 May 1943	Vehicle	In east	Total army 1 May 1943
PzKpfw III	507	1465	PzKpfw VI	72	165
PzKpfw IV	541	1077	In repair installations	501	–
			Total:	1621	2630

c. Eastern Front 10 June 1943 inclusive of the Waffen-SS

PzKpfw II–VI and assault guns

Ready for employment	2569
In repair installations	463
Total	3032 (5416)*

The PzKpfw IV was steadily upgunned through the war, starting off with a 7.5cm Kwk 37 L/24 with a muzzle velocity of 385m/sec in the Ausf A to F, and ending with a long-barrelled 7.5cm Kwk 40 L/48 with an MV of 930m/sec and correspondingly better armour penetration figures. The gun was used on more than 6,000 later PzKpfw IVs, over 8,000 StuG IIIs, all 1,139 StuG IVs and 780 Jagdpanzer IVs.

d. Ready for action totals, 1944

Vehicle	Italy 1 Feb 44	West 29 Feb 44	East 23 Feb 44	ZI Repair 29 Feb 44	Total	Total Strength 1 Mar 44
PzKpfw III	106	99		450	655	888
PzKpfw IV	171	587		405	1163	1824
PzKpfw V		290		128	418	1339
PzKpfw VI	8	63		78	149	504
PzBefw	6				6	466
Assault guns	141	194		171	506	3010
Total	432	1233	1519			
In repair installations	49		1534	1232		
Grand total	481	1233	3053	1232	5999	8031

The difference of 2032 vehicles between total and total strength covers vehicles in use by occupation troops in Norway and in the Balkans, including Crete and Rhodes, newly activated units in the Zone of Interior, ordnance depots and the Replacement Army.

e. Tank forces in the West

Date	Pz III (%)*	Pz IV (%)	Pz V (%)	Pz VI (%)	StuG and JagdPz (%)	Total (%)
31 Dec 43	145 (16)	316 (19)	157 (14)	38 (10)	223 (10)	879 (14)
31 Jan 44	98 (11)	410 (24)	180 (15)	64 (15)	171 (7)	923 (14)
29 Feb 44	99 (11)	587 (32)	290 (22)	63 (12)	194 (6)	1210 (16)
31 Mar 44	99 (12)	527 (25)	323 (20)	45 (9)	211 (7)	1205 (15)
30 Apr 44	114 (14)	674 (32)	514 (31)	101 (18)	219 (7)	1622 (19)
10 Jun 44	39 (5)	748 (32)	663 (35)	102 (16)	310 (8)	1862 (20)

*The percentage of tank strength represented by each month's reinforcement is indicated by figures in brackets.

f. Tanks and StuGs on Eastern Front 5 January 1945

Vehicle	Pz units	StuG brigades*	Pz Jäger companies**	Total Eastern Front	Army Strength
PzKpfw IV	596			596	2259
PzKpfw V	670			670	1982
PzKpfw VI	26			26	428
PzBefw, FlakPz	***				576
StuG, JagdPz	641	902	949	2492	6167
	1933	902	949	3784	11412

* StuG brigades are GHQ, troops for the reinforcement of infantry divisions
** Pz Jäger companies are component parts of infantry divisions
*** Included in the Pz IV/V/VI figures directly above.

Tank and SP gun by bridging weight [From *FM 30-40*]

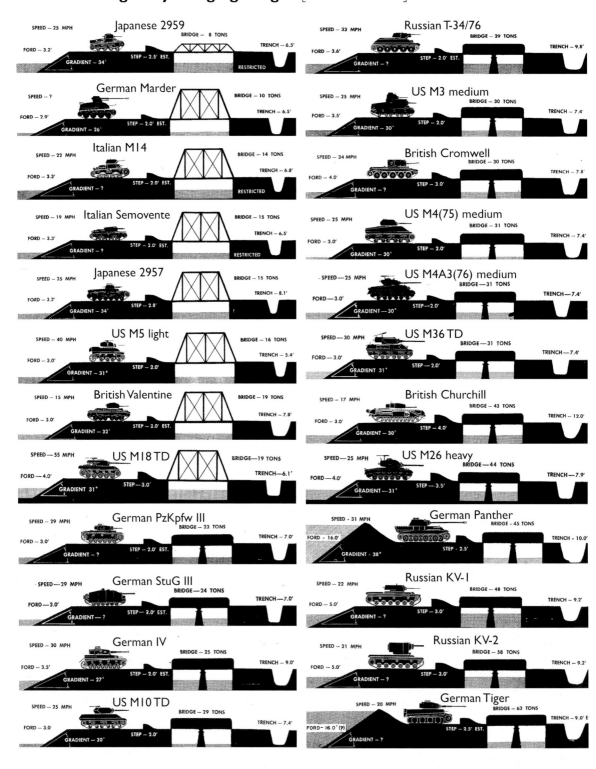

g. Tank strength Western Front 5 February 1945

	Strength	Ready for action	Total German army strength
PzKpfw III and IV	110	68	2810
PzKpfw V	219	96	1964
PzKpfw VI	61	26	404
PzBefw			299
Flak tanks			228
Total number vehicles	390	190	5705
StuG and Jagdpanzer IV	892	533	6054
Assault tank	32	15	188
Jagdpanther	66	43	208
Jagdtiger	28	21	51
Total number of JagdPz and StuG	1018	612	6501
Nashorn (Pak/Sfl) with 88mm	12	8	141
Grand total	1420	810	12,277

h. Panzer Divisions in Normandy June/July 1944

Unit	men	arrival date	Unit	men	date
1.SS Leibstandarte	19691	30 June	2.Pz	16762	31 May
2.SS Das Reich	17283	1 June	21.Pz	16925	1 June
9.SS Hohenstaufen	15898	30 June	116.Pz.	13621	1 June
10.SS Frundsberg	16011	start June	Panzer Lehr Div	14699	1 June
12.SS Hitlerjugend	18102	start June	Total army	62007	
Total SS	69685		(9.Pz		only in August)

The Nazis loved big weapons of war. This is the Sturmtiger or Sturmmörserwagen 606/4 mit 38cm RW61. 18 were built. It had 150mm of armour in the front and a 380mm *Raketen-Werfer* whose rounds could penetrate up to 2.5 of concrete.

Bibliography

Official documents

7th Armd Div: *Battle Lessons from a British Armoured Division,* 1943.

760th Tank Battalion: *Operations in Italy January 1944.*

776 Amtank Bn *Operation Report Ryukyu Campaign,* 1945.

After Action Report, 7th Armored Division, 1–31 October 1944.

Armor in the Invasion of North Africa; The Armored School, 1949–50.

Armored Force Command and Center, The; Army Ground Force Study No. 27, 1946.

Burma Operations Record 15th Army Operations in Imphal Area and Withdrawal to Northern Burma, 1952.

Engineer Technical Bulletin No. 28, 1945.

Finito! The Po Valley Campaign, 1945; HQ 15th Army Group, 1945.

FM 17-12 Field Manual Armored Force Field Manual Tank Gunnery; War Dept, 1943.

FM 17-30 Armored Force Field Manual Tank Platoon; War Dept, 1942.

FM 17-76 Field Manual Crew Drill and Service of the Piece Medium Tank, M4 series (105-mm howitzer); War Dept, 1944.

FM 30-40 Recognition Pictorial Manual on Armored Vehicles War Dept 1943.

German Armored Army; Military Intelligence Service Special Series 2, 1942.

German Motorized Infantry Regiment; Military Intelligence Service Special Series 4, 1942.

German Tactical Doctrine; Military Intelligence Service Special Series 8, 1942.

Handbuch die Munition der deutschen Geschütze und Werfer, 1943.

Historical Study: *German Tank Maintenance in World War II;* Dept of the Army No. 20-202, 1954.

History of the 704th Tank Destroyer Battalion, The, 1945.

Japanese Tank and Antitank Warfare; Military Intelligence Service Special Series 34, 1945.

Maintenance of Armor in World War II; The Armored School, 1950.

Panther-Fibel, 1944.

Peculiarities of Russian Warfare; Dept of the Army Hist Div, 1949.

Tactical and Technical Trends, various issues; Military Intelligence Service, 1942–43.

Tigerfibel, 1943.

TM 9-731B Technical Manual Medium Tank M4A2; War Dept, 1943.

TM 9-748 Technical Manual 90-mm Gun Motor Carriage M36B1; War Dept, 1945.

TM 9-750 Technical Manual Ordnance Maintenance Medium Tanks M3, M3A1, and M3A2; War Dept, 1942.

TM 9-754 Technical Manual Medium Tank M4A4; War Dept, 1943.

TM 9-759 Technical Manual Medium Tank M4A3; War Dept, 1942.

TM-E 30-451 Handbook on German Military Forces, 15 March 1945.

Books and articles

Chamberlain, Peter and Ellis, Chris: *British and American Tanks of World War II;* A&AP, 1977.

Chew, Dr. Allen F.: *Leavenworth Papers No. 5 Fighting the Russians in Winter: Three Case Studies:* U.S. Army Tank Destroyer Doctrine in World War II; Combat Studies Institute, 1981.

Connor, Lt Col William M: 'Analysis of Deep Attack Operations Operation Bagration'; Fort Leavenworth, 1987.

Coox, Alvin D. and Naisawald, L. Van Loan: *Survey of Allied Tank Casualties in World War II;* Operations Research Office, 1951.

Davies, Anthony C.: 'WW2 British Army Battlefield Wireless Communications Equipment;

Fletcher, David and Bryan, Tony: *New Vanguard 110 Universal Carrier 1936-48;* Osprey, 2005.

Fox, Jacob: 'The Wrong Track: Errors in American tank development in World War II'; Masters Thesis, 2013 (via https://commons.lib.jmu.edu/master201019/215).

Futter, Geoffrey W.: *The Funnies;* MAP, 1974.

Glantz, Colonel David M.: *CSI Report No. 11: Soviet Defensive Tactics at Kursk, July 1943;* Combat Studies Institute, 1986.

Gabel, Dr. Christopher R.: *Leavenworth Papers No. 12 Seek, Strike, and Destroy: U.S. Army Tank Destroyer Doctrine in World War II;* Combat Studies Institute, 1985.

Grow, Gen Robert W.: 'Armor and Mobility in Maintaining the Momentum of a River Crossing'; Fort Leavenworth, 1952.

Gullachsen, Arthur: 'Destroying the Panthers: The Effect of Allied Combat Action on I.SS Panzer Regiment 12 in Normandy, 1944'; *Canadian Military History,* 2016.

Gullachsen, Arthur: 'No Shortage of Tanks!: The Canadian Army's System for the Recovery, Repair and Replacement of A and B Vehicles and Major Weapons Systems'; *Canadian Military History,* 2018.

Hart, Dr Stephen A.: *Duel Sherman Firefly vs Tiger;* Osprey, 2007.

Hillyard, Col H.L.: *Characteristics for Tank Guns;* Fort Leavenworth, 1946.

Irzyk, Lt Col Albin F.: 'Tank vs Tank'; *Military Review,* Jan 1946.

Jandrew, William C.: 'Georgi Zhukov and the Resurrection of "Deep Battle"'; American Military University, 2012.

Jeffreys, Alan: *Battle Orders 13 The British Army in the Far East 1941–45;* Osprey, 2005.

Littlepage, Maj Samuel D.: *Armored Operation on Iwo Jima;* 1945.

Müller-Hillebrand, GenMaj Burkhart; *German Tank Losses;* Hist Div European Command, 1950.

Prenatt, Jamie and Morshead, Henry: *New Vanguard 224 Polish Armor of the Blitzkrieg;* Osprey, 2014.

Sasso, Maj Claude R.: *Leavenworth Papers No. 6 Soviet Night Operations in World War II;* Combat Studies Institute, 1982.

Zaloga, Steven J.: *Vanguard 31 US Half-Tracks of World War II;* Osprey, 1983.

Zaloga, Steven J. and Bull, Peter: *New Vanguard 137 Japanese Tanks 1939–45;* Osprey, 2007.

Zaloga, Steven J. and Chasemore, Richard: *New Vanguard 215 Panzer 38(t);* Osprey, 2012.

Zaloga, Steven J. and Morshead, Henry: *New Vanguard 192 US Amphibious Tanks of World War II;* Osprey, 2012.

Zaloga, Steven J. and Palmer, Ian: *New Vanguard 209 French Tanks of World War II (1) and 213 (2);* Osprey, 2014.

Zaloga, Steven J. and Sarson, Peter: *New Vanguard 11 M3 Infantry Half-Track 1940–73;* Osprey, 2014.